Debating Deliberative Democracy

Dedicated to the memory of Peter Laslett, 1915–2001,
who helped us see worlds we have lost – and gained

Philosophy, Politics and Society 7

Debating Deliberative Democracy

Edited by

JAMES S. FISHKIN AND
PETER LASLETT

© 2003 by Blackwell Publishing Ltd

BLACKWELL PUBLISHING
350 Main Street, Malden, MA 02148-5020, USA
9600 Garsington Road, Oxford OX4 2DQ, UK
550 Swanston Street, Carlton, Victoria 3053, Australia

The right of James S. Fishkin and Peter Laslett to be identified as the Authors of the
Editorial Material in this Work has been asserted in accordance with the UK Copyright,
Designs, and Patents Act 1988.

First published 2003 by Blackwell Publishing Ltd

3   2006

Library of Congress Cataloging-in-Publication Data

Debating deliberative democracy / edited by James S. Fishkin and Peter Laslett.
    p. cm.
Includes bibliographical references and index. ISBN 1-4051-0042-7 (hardcover :
alk. paper) — ISBN 1-4051-0043-5 (pbk. : alk. paper)
1. Democracy.   2. Representative government and representation.   I. Fishkin, James S.
II. Laslett, Peter.
JC423 .D375 2003
321.8—dc21

                                                            2002008003

ISBN-13: 978-1-4051-0042-7 (hardcover : alk. paper) — ISBN-13: 978-1-4051-0043-4 (pbk. :
alk. paper)

A catalogue record for this title is available from the British Library.

Set in 10 on 12.5pt Bembo
by Ace Filmsetting Ltd, Frome, Somerset

For further information on
Blackwell Publishing, visit our website:
www.blackwellpublishing.com

Contents

vi   Contents

Contributors

Bruce Ackerman is Sterling Professor of Law and Political Science, Yale University.

James S. Fishkin is Patterson-Banister Chair in Government, Law, and Philosophy, University of Texas at Austin.

Robert E. Goodin is Professor of Social and Political Theory and Philosophy, Research School of Social Sciences, Australian National University.

Amy Gutmann is Laurance S. Rockefeller University Professor of Politics and the University Center for Human Values, Princeton University

Russell Hardin is Professor of Political Science at Stanford University and Professor of Politics at New York University.

Peter Laslett was Reader in Politics and the History of Social Structure, Cambridge University, and Fellow of Trinity College, Cambridge.

David Miller is Official Fellow in Social and Political Theory, Nuffield College, Oxford.

Philip Pettit is William Nelson Cromwell Professor of Politics, Princeton University.

Ian Shapiro is William R. Kenan Jr. Professor and Chairman, Department of Political Science, Yale University.

Cass R. Sunstein is Karl N. Llewellyn Distinguished Service Professor of Jurisprudence, University of Chicago, Law School and Department of Political Science.

Dennis Thompson is Alfred North Whitehead Professor of Political Philosophy, Harvard University.

Jeffrey K. Tulis is Associate Professor, Department of Government, University of Texas at Austin.

Iris Marion Young is Professor of Political Science, University of Chicago.

Acknowledgments

The editor and publisher gratefully acknowledge the following for permission to reproduce the copyright material in this book:

Chapter 1: Blackwell Publishing for Bruce Ackerman and James S. Fishkin, "Deliberation Day" from *Journal of Political Philosophy* (June 2002);

Chapter 2: Blackwell Publishing for Amy Gutmann and Dennis Thompson, "Deliberative Democracy Beyond Process" from *Journal of Political Philosophy* (June 2002);

Chapter 3: Princeton University Press for Robert E. Goodin, "Democratic Deliberation Within" from *Philosophy & Public Affairs* 29:1 (Winter 2000), pp. 79–107. © 2000 by Princeton University Press;

Chapter 4: Blackwell Publishing for Cass R. Sunstein, "The Law of Group Polarization" from *Journal of Political Philosophy* (June 2002);

Chapter 5: Sage Publications, Inc. and the author for Iris Marion Young, "Activist Challenges to Deliberative Democracy" from *Political Theory* (Oct. 2001);

Chapter 6: Blackwell Publishing for Ian Shapiro, "Optimal Deliberation?" from *Journal of Political Philosophy* (June 2002);

Chapter 7: Philip Pettit for "Deliberative Democracy, the Discursive Dilemma and Republican Theory." This chapter was written especially for this volume;

Chapter 8: Blackwell Publishing for Russell Hardin, "Street-level Epistemology and Democratic Participation" from *Journal of Political Philosophy* (June 2002);

Chapter 9: Blackwell Publishing for David Miller, "Deliberative Democracy and Social Choice" from *Political Studies* 40 (1992), pp. 54–67;

Chapter 10: Jeffrey K. Tulis for "Deliberation Between Institutions." This chapter was written especially for this volume.

Chapter 11: Palgrave Macmillan for Peter Laslett, "Environmental Ethics and the Obsolescence of Existing Political Institutions" from Brendan Gleeson and Nicholas Low (eds), *Governing for the Environment*, 2nd ed. (2001).

The publisher apologizes for any errors or omissions in the above list and would be grateful if notified of any corrections that should be incorporated in future reprints or editions of this book.

Introduction

James S. Fishkin and Peter Laslett

In his essay for the first volume of *Philosophy, Politics and Society*, Peter Laslett posed the problem of whether the politics of "face to face society," of small groups of manageable size talking to one another before taking decisions, could be adapted to the "territorial societies" of the large-scale nation-state. In that essay, Laslett probed the gap between face-to-face discussion as a preface to decision-making in small polities and the kinds of opportunities left for citizens in mass societies.

"The Face to Face Society" helped inspire work in political science and political theory that would attempt to bring some of the characteristics of small group face-to-face deliberation to the large-scale nation-state. In particular, it influenced James Fishkin to develop "Deliberative Polling," a process discussed by several of the contributors to this volume. At the time Laslett's essay was written, none of these issues were on the agenda of political theory (or related areas of the social sciences). In fact, it was reasonable for Laslett to ask at the time whether or not political theory would even continue to exist.

As political theory underwent a major revival, a process evident from the succeeding volumes in this series, a great deal of it came to focus not on realistic deliberations of the kind possible in a "face to face society," but rather on the deliberations of agents in purely imaginary thought experiments. The work of John Rawls, in particular, inspired a flowering of work on hypothetical decision procedures, asking us what principles we would choose if we could hypothesize ourselves behind a "veil of ignorance" in which we lacked knowledge of all particulars about ourselves or our society. The Rawlsian "original position" was not meant to be instituted, it was only meant to be imagined. The claim was that if we envision it faithfully, we can work out the appropriate first principles of justice for the whole society.

The very abstractness of the Rawlsian hypothetical allows it largely to avoid a number of questions that more realistic prescriptions of deliberation would have to face. What goes on in a deliberative process? Is it necessarily a good thing? Who participates? Under what social conditions or institutions might it take place? Apart from a few stipulated assumptions, it is not merely the Rawlsian agents who are behind a veil of ignorance. Rawls's proposed conditions also shield us from any particular information that might fill out the picture of deliberation.

But the move from imaginary thought experiments to real (or at least possible) institutions, or the move from deliberators behind a "veil of ignorance" to those in a "face to face society" confronts us with precisely such questions. Instead of deliberations behind a veil, we are to envisage real people under realistic conditions making actual policy choices. But this greater realism prompts the questions already mentioned. First, what goes on in a deliberative process? At the core of any notion of deliberation is the idea that reasons for and against various options are to be weighed on their merits. But what kinds of reasons or arguments need to be weighed? Is deliberation limited to considerations of justice or the public good, or may citizens take account of their self-interest? Is deliberation inherently a social process, requiring shared discussion? Or can it be accomplished in isolation, as Robert Goodin suggests in his contribution, "Deliberation Within"? If it requires or includes discussion, does that include discussion limited to the like-minded, as in Cass Sunstein's notion of "enclave deliberation" (one of the forms of deliberation he discusses in his "Law of Group Polarization")? Or does deliberation require a consideration of diverse and competing viewpoints, as many of the other contributors hold? What counts as making an "argument"? Does deliberation include story telling or perhaps even street demonstrations? Or is it just the rational discussion of "talking heads"? Our contributors cover the spectrum on such issues.

Second, is deliberation necessarily a good thing? Sunstein argues that under most conditions, group discussion will produce "polarization" in which people move to more extreme positions. But he admits that his work on juries and other small group discussions does not apply to "Deliberative Polls" where there may be a number of factors (moderators, balanced briefings, balanced panels and random samples of the public randomly assigned to groups) enforcing a balance in the arguments considered by the participants. So there may be different forms of structured deliberation that are less subject to his critique. Nevertheless, his critique shows that deliberation may not always be a good thing. Iris Marion Young, in her "Activist Challenges to Deliberative Democracy," shows how an activist might have legitimate moral objections to the compromises required for deliberative discussion. There are some issues for which deliberative discussion might assume too much of the status quo and might only amount to complicity with injustice because only small changes from the status quo get on the agenda.

Even if deliberation is a good thing, can there be too much of it? Or too much to justify all the effort and expense or all the "decision costs" as economists would say? This is Ian Shapiro's question in "Optimal Deliberation?" How much deliberation is enough? While he does not finally give us an answer, he proposes some frameworks for considering the question.

In different ways, David Miller and Philip Pettit raise the issue of collective consistency. It would be an important challenge to deliberative democracy if we should expect it to be confused or incoherent. Miller's essay, "Deliberative Democracy and Social Choice," proposes a hypothesis very much to the contrary: that deliberation may induce a shared preference structure, a shared sense of the problem being decided upon, that allows the respondents to locate themselves along a dimension for evaluating the alternatives. This collective structuration of preferences (technically termed "single-peakedness") guarantees protection against the cycles violating transitivity that have fascinated social choice theorists from the Marquis de Condorcet to Kenneth Arrow. Some political scientists, notably the late William Riker, famously argued that democracy was "meaningless" because of the prevalence of cycles.[1] Miller's hypothesis is that, post-deliberation, democracy may become more meaningful. This idea has since been supported by empirical evidence from Deliberative Polls. In a number of separate Deliberative Polling investigations with random samples of the public on realistic public policy questions, levels of single-peakedness that would rule out cycles were found after deliberation.[2] There is thus empirical support for the proposition Miller puts forward that deliberative democracy offers some protection against the conundrums of social choice theory.

Yet as Philip Pettit shows, cycles violating transitivity are not the only kind of collective inconsistency relevant to democracy. The "doctrinal paradox" he explores focuses on inconsistencies between premises and conclusions. It is possible for majorities to approve the premises supporting one alternative but the conclusions supporting another. Which alternative then does a consistent form of democracy require? The doctrinal paradox applies to nondeliberative as much as to deliberative democracy, but Pettit argues that deliberative democracy suggests the appropriate response.

If we are committed to deliberative democracy, does this mean that we are committed to other good things, say, values of justice or the general welfare? With the Rawlsian hypothetical, the imaginary deliberations come out with set priorities for the first principles of justice – priorities, which, if the philosopher's arguments are correct, do not change. But with real deliberations among real people who bring their own values, interests and priorities to bear on the process, the results are far less predictable. But the idea of going from deliberations that have a recommending force to prescriptions for public policy is roughly parallel. Amy Gutmann and Dennis Thompson argue that deliberative democracy cannot be just about process – that it carries with it certain substantive commitments. Perhaps so. But then can we tell what these are? Their position is that we can do so only provisionally, precisely because real deliberative processes may vary. Yet they do argue that certain kinds of bad outcomes can be ruled out. In this, they are consonant with a long tradition in democratic theory that has made substantive prescriptions, such as those against "tyranny of the majority."

Whether or not deliberation is a good thing might also be held to depend on whether it makes any difference. Here, Russell Hardin's "Street-level Epistemology and Democratic Participation" tells us a great deal about how ordinary citizens in mass society are likely to think and behave *without* deliberation. While the behavior of citizens subject to what Anthony Downs called "rational ignorance" can be explained and understood, it falls far short of the levels of information and engagement that democratic theory would ideally demand.

Hence deliberative democracy is likely to be quite different from conventional democracy. And while it may not adequately respond to all the criticisms, it does appear to have some laudable characteristics. If we value it, how can it be achieved? What institutions, if any, might facilitate making democracy more deliberative?

As the readers to this volume will realize, there are many possible sites or institutional settings for deliberation. Goodin wants institutions that will encourage citizens to think for themselves, by themselves. In his "Deliberation Between Institutions," Jeffrey Tulis uses some early history of the American republic to expand our sense of how institutions can deliberate with each other. Gutmann and Thompson apply their criteria to a wide variety of settings, as does Cass Sunstein in his important work on polarization in juries and group discussions of various sorts.

A number of the papers make reference to more structured sites for deliberation, particularly Deliberative Polls. These events are both social science investigations and public consultation exercises, often leading to television broadcasts intended to inform the rest of the public about their conclusions. What is distinctive about Deliberative Polls is that they combine scientific random sampling of the population with two or three days of carefully balanced deliberation, both in small group discussions and then in larger plenary sessions. Data about opinion change in the Deliberative Polls confirm that there are large changes of opinion, that these changes are connected to the participants becoming better informed, and that these changes have a big effect on the voting behavior of the participants. So deliberation makes a difference and it makes a difference both to opinion and behavior. In addition, there is at least some evidence that the participants have more highly structured preferences (in the sense that more of them are single-peaked so that the collectivity can avoid voting cycles) and that they become more public-spirited, in the sense that they become more willing to make at least some sacrifices in the public interest. However, all of these laudable effects of deliberation are, of course, limited to participants in the scientific samples who participate (numbering in each case, a few hundred). What is to be done, if anything, to promote deliberation in the wider public?

In their contribution to this volume, Bruce Ackerman and James Fishkin propose a scheme, called "Deliberation Day," that has the potential to do precisely that. It is, admittedly, quasi-utopian in that it would be a very ambitious (and expensive) contribution to civic education. However, the proposal is meant to expand the debate about how we might bring serious thought and discussion to the wider public in a manner that approximates at least some of the conditions of the Deliberative Poll. It is meant to overcome, for the entire mass public the incentives for rational ignorance described in Russell Hardin's essay.

Imagine if everyone were to participate in a Deliberative Poll before a general election. It seems reasonable to expect all the laudable effects just catalogued above being brought to life for the whole electorate. However, even in the spirit of quasi-utopian theorizing, the idea of everyone actually engaging in a Deliberative Poll seems far-fetched. Nevertheless, Deliberation Day is meant to constitute a practical scenario for an institution that might begin to approximate such an effect for the whole electorate.

It is a kind of decentralized national discussion with every citizen randomly assigned to a nearby site for small group discussions and larger sessions, where key questions can get answered by competing party representatives in innumerable forums around the country, and where the small group discussions use a time management process to make sure that participation is roughly equalized. Recruitment would be facilitated by the payment of a fee to each citizen who participates. If millions of citizens participated in the discussions as planned, then the result would not only inform citizens, it would also alter the strategic calculations of politicians and media decision-makers leading up to the event. Political ads and speeches by politicians would have to anticipate a well-informed audience. On this scenario, it might well be possible to have a deliberating mass democracy. But such a massive change requires new institutions.

This volume closes with Peter Laslett's "Environmental Ethics and the Obsolescence of Current Political Institutions." Laslett's essay dramatizes the fact that even if we were to achieve an advanced and deliberative form of democracy within the boundaries of the modern nation-state, we would still find that many key questions facing mankind are beyond the control of a single nation-state. The environment poses an inextricably global challenge. If dealing with it adequately requires deliberative democracy, then we lack deliberative democratic institutions that cross the boundaries of the nation-state. As a first step towards the international experimentation that would be required, Laslett recommends Deliberative Polling across national boundaries and perhaps, most ambitiously, across the world. Just as it seemed impossibly difficult to bring the "face to face society" to the democracy of the large-scale nation-state, it seems even more difficult to apply it to the resolution of global problems. Posing the problem, however, should offer a useful beginning.

Editorial Note: As the work on this volume was nearing completion, the sad news came that the founding editor of the series, Peter Laslett, passed away at the age of 85. Laslett made profound contributions to many areas of scholarship – the history of political thought, the development of the field of historical demography, the study of aging in historical perspective, to name but a few. He also played a key role in the founding of the Open University and the University of the Third Age. Among his many accomplishments, he had the insight to start this series almost half a century ago, at a time when there was so little political philosophy that he said "editorial policy has been a difficult problem, as might be expected when the task has been to draw a circle around a hole." He was delighted by its revival in the years since, a revival in which he played an important part and one that can be chronicled in the subsequent volumes. I know that he would have been gratified to see this project finally in print. I would like to dedicate this volume to his memory.

Notes

1   See William H. Riker, *Liberalism against Populism: A Confrontation between the Theory of Democracy and the Theory of Social Choice* (San Francisco: W. H. Freeman, 1982).
2   For an overview of these results see Christian List, Iain McLean, James Fishkin, and Robert C. Luskin, "Deliberation, Preference Structuration and Cycles: Evidence from Deliberative Polls," Paper presented at the meetings of the American Political Science Association, Sept. 2000.

1

Deliberation Day

Bruce Ackerman and James S. Fishkin

Deliberation Day – a new national holiday. It will be held one week before major national elections. Registered voters will be called together in neighborhood meeting places, in small groups of 15, and larger groups of 500, to discuss the central issues raised by the campaign. Each deliberator will be paid $150 for the day's work of citizenship, on condition that he or she shows up at the polls the next week. All other work, except the most essential, will be prohibited by law.

Details follow.

I. VOTING

A. Civic privatism

Our present voting ritual is little more than a century old. There was a time when citizens cast their ballots in public, and no less a thinker than John Stuart Mill wanted to keep it that way.[1] The secret ballot, he predicted, would encourage voters to look upon the ballot as if it were just another commodity for private gratification. Rather than standing up in public to declare which candidate was best for the country, the secret balloter would merely choose the politician who most pandered to his private interest. Citizens would choose on the basis of "interest, pleasure or caprice."[2] These escalating appeals to conflicting private interests slowly erode the very idea that citizens should be trying to regulate fractional interests on behalf of the common good.

Mill's insight was that the very process of public discussion would encourage sensitivity to the public interest. The secret ballot, however admirable on other grounds, sacrificed something important – a social context (public voting) that encouraged public discussion on the part of every voter. We propose to consider whether it might be possible to recreate such a social context for most voters while also maintaining the benefits of the secret ballot.

These Millian anxieties were pushed aside in the nineteenth century – but not because they were bogus. They were instead outweighed by a competing aspect of the democratic ideal – the egalitarian demand for a revolutionary expansion of the franchise. Public balloting might be tolerable in a political world which imposed restrictive property requirements. If the only voters were substantial property owners, they might have sufficient economic independence to state their sincere opinions about the public good on election day, without fearing reprisals afterwards. But as the franchise widened, public voting took on a different appearance. It began to look like a trick by which the rich might retain effective electoral power at the same time as they formally conceded the right to vote to the unwashed. If the poor could only vote in public, they could not afford to deviate from the political opinions of their economic masters. It was, in fact, John Stuart Mill's father, the philosopher James Mill, who powerfully articulated the concern that without a secret ballot, the people who vote would only "go through the formalities, the mummery of voting . . . while the whole power of choosing, should be really possessed by other parties."[3] As the debate between father and son dramatized, there was a deep functional connection between the expansion of the franchise and the rise of the secret ballot.

This link remains today, and so the case for the secret ballot remains intact. Nevertheless, the younger Mill has proved a prescient prophet – his anxieties have become our realities. Privatism has eroded central ideals of democratic citizenship, and in ways that are ultimately incompatible with the satisfactory operation of a democratic government. Good government does not require a hyperactive citizenry, but neither can it thrive in a narrowly privatistic world.

Worse yet, the Invisible Hand does not seem to be guiding Western democracies to a promising future. Despite our present infatuation with the internet, the rising forces of technology threaten to make the consequences of civic privatism worse, not better. We have a public dialogue that is ever more efficiently segmented in its audiences and morselized in its sound bites. We have an ever more tabloid news agenda dulling the sensitivities of an increasingly inattentive citizenry. And we have mechanisms of feedback from the public, from viewer call-ins to self-selected internet polls that emphasize intense constituencies, unrepresentative of the public at large. If we are to preserve and deepen our democratic life, we must take the future into our own hands. We must create institutions that sustain citizen engagement in a shared public dialogue.

This is an essay in utopian realism. As to realism: We hope to persuade you that the formidable difficulties involved in organizing Deliberation Day are manageable, and well worth the distinctive contribution the new holiday makes to our democratic life. In making the case, we emphasize the problems, as well as solutions, and refuse to claim too much for our innovation. Even if successful, it would constrain, but not eliminate, the dangers posed by civic privatism.

As to utopianism: We hardly wish to deny the existence of political obstacles to our proposal. As the sorry story of campaign finance reform teaches, these roadblocks will be substantial. Nonetheless, they should not be allowed to deflect us from another, and deeper, problem. Though liberal ideals of democracy are currently ascendant, triumphalism has provoked self-congratulation, not political imagination. Westerners have been content to offer up present practice as if it were an adequate model for the world.

This is a serious mistake. Liberal democracy is a relative newcomer on the world historical stage – very much a work in progress, rather than a stable institutional arrangement, even in those few countries with established traditions. Short-term roadblocks should not prevent vigorous exploration of the horizon of realistic possibilities. If we convince you that Deliberation Day is a good idea, it will be time enough to consider the political challenges involved in its realization.

B. Renewing citizenship

There is a contradiction at the heart of modern democratic practice. On the one hand, we expect our elected governors to take the basic interests of *all* citizens into account, and not only the narrow interests of the majority that voted them into office. On the other hand, we do not expect voters to take the obligations of citizenship seriously. They can be as uninformed and self-interested as they like, and nobody will blame them as they enter the polling booth. To the contrary, political participation has so declined (and not only in America) that voters bask in the faint glow of community approval if they merely take the trouble to go to the polls – regardless of how ignorant or selfish they may be in casting their ballots in the privacy of the ballot box. The problem this raises is obvious enough: Why should the government consider the interests of all citizens if voters are uninformed and selfish?

This is not a new question. Since the days of Madison, we have been struggling with the problem – and there is no reason to think it will ever be solved definitively. Nevertheless, changing conditions change the terms in which the problem is expressed, and the institutional modes through which it may be ameliorated, if not resolved.

Madison famously focused on the capacities of political elites to filter out the most irrational and self-interested aspects of public opinion, and provide more enlightened judgments than the general public. One of the great aims of the *Federalist Papers* was the design of a constitutional framework that would subtly reward political elites for filtering, rather than mirroring, the more egregious forms of ignorant and selfish factionalism. By no means do we wish to dismiss the continuing importance of this enterprise. Nonetheless, several forces have conspired to undermine elite tendencies to resist the temptation to pander to the most ignorant and selfish motivations of their constituents.

The first force is the modern science of public opinion. However much earlier politicians might have wished to exploit the ignorance and selfishness of their constituents, they labored under certain technical disadvantages. To be sure, they might read newspapers, talk to cronies, attend countless community functions, weigh letters from constituents and even canvass opinion informally through local political organizations. But without scientific random sampling and the modern art of survey design, they had a hard time getting an accurate picture of public opinion. They had a hard time penetrating into the hearts and minds of ordinary Americans to learn *precisely* which combinations of myth and greed might work to generate support from key voting groups. In the absence of good data, even the most cynical politicians sometimes were obliged to consider the good of the country.

But over the last decades, this uncertainty has been dissolved by modern public opinion research. The entire point of polling and "focus group" research in campaigns is to discover the popular appeal of different combinations of myth and greed that will effectively motivate voters in an exceedingly fine-grained fashion. Politicians formulate appeals from focus groups and "pre-test" their positions with pollsters, constantly modifying them to increase their appeal to marginal voting groups. Within this high-tech environment, the Madisonian idea that a legislator has a high responsibility to filter out ignorant and selfish impulses seems hopelessly old-fashioned. The aim is to spin a message that will snare a majority.

Especially given a second major transformation – the scientific marketing of candidates by soundbite specialists. Sloganeering and flag-waving have been important in American politics for centuries. Nevertheless, contemporary developments represent a great leap forward into a brave new world. Candidates really are being sold like commodities nowadays. Commercial norms have completely colonized the norms for political "advertisements." Techniques for selling a Lexus or a Marlboro are simply carried over when selling the President. The idea that principles of deliberative democracy might require, for example, that no "advertisement" last for less than five minutes would be dismissed out-of-hand by the highly paid consultants who take their cue from Madison Avenue (of all places). The search is on for eight-second soundbites that hit "hot-button" issues discovered through focus group research.

Matters are made even worse by the failure of campaign finance reform. The new techniques cost lots of money. Given the current financial imbalance, the invisible hand of the political marketplace is leading us to the plutocratic management of democratic forms. But the basic problem would not go away even if we managed to equalize the financial playing field. At best, this would lead to the redistribution of effective soundbites, not the creation of a deliberative democracy.

We do not wish to paint too dark a picture. The Madisonian project is by no means obsolete. In other work, we have both sought to describe how old institutions have adapted themselves to filter out the worst of public opinion, and how new ones might be designed that might subtly reward elite politicians for engaging in an updated version of the Madisonian enterprise.

This essay takes a different tack. Rather than improving the filtering capacities of elite politicians, we propose to improve the character of public opinion itself.

1. Rational ignorance

But does public opinion need improving? Perhaps the public is already well informed. Or, if not, perhaps it would not make much difference if it were.

First things first: if six decades of modern public opinion research establish anything, it is that the public's most basic political knowledge is appalling by any normative standard.[4] One explanation is that the opinions which conventional polls give us are often the product of what Anthony Downs famously termed "rational ignorance."[5] For most complex policy questions, it may be fairly time consuming for me to form an opinion or become well-informed. Yet I can be fairly confident that my individual vote or my individual opinion is unlikely to make much difference. Hence the calculation that it may be "rational" for me to remain ignorant, as there are many more pressing demands on my time for activities in which I can actually make a difference.

We do not mean to endorse the cynical conception of "instrumental rationality" that often motivates the expositors of the theory of "rational ignorance." To the contrary, we think that most residents of Western democracies recognize that they have a responsibility as citizens to take the public good seriously. Nonetheless, the political economists are on the right track in explaining why Westerners do such a terrible job fulfilling these responsibilities. If, as they suggest, ignorance is instrumentally rational, there is only one way of getting at the root of our present predicament – *and that is to change incentives*. In saying this, we do not mean merely to point to the fact that deliberators will be paid $150 for their efforts – though this is not unimportant. If Deliberation Day gets off the ground, it will generate a host of other incentives of even greater importance – or so, at least, we shall argue

2. Deliberative polling

For a number of years, one of us has been engaged in a research program called Deliberative Polling that explores what public opinion would be like if the public were effectively motivated to behave a bit more like ideal citizens. A random sample is first given a survey of the conventional sort. Then, it is invited to come to a single place, at the expense of the project, to engage in a weekend of small group discussions and larger plenary sessions in which it is given extensive opportunities to get good information, exchange competing points of view and come to a considered judgment. At the end of the weekend, it is given the same questionnaire as on first contact. The resulting changes of opinion are often dramatic. They offer a glimpse of democratic possibilities – the views people would have if they were effectively motivated to pay attention and get good information and discuss the issues together. The Deliberative Poll puts scientific random samples in a situation where they have incentives, in effect, to overcome rational ignorance.[6]

Individual respondents in a Deliberative Poll find themselves randomly assigned to small groups where they have one voice in fifteen or so, rather than one voice in millions. They are thrust into a context of mutual discussion where they offer reasons and hear the reasons of others. Instead of anonymous votes lost among millions, they have real voices in a small group. In addition, they vote, in effect by secret ballot so that we can study the changes in opinion at the individual level without worrying about the social pressures of a false consensus. In effect, we have the best of both worlds in the debate between J. S. Mill and his father about the secret ballot. We have a social context encouraging small group, face-to-face discussion, so that people offer and respond to reasons. But in the end, we insulate people from social pressure at the moment of decision. These are aspects of the Deliberative Poll that we shall attempt to preserve when we come to the design of Deliberation Day.

Deliberative Polls give us our best glimpse into what a more informed and engaged electorate would be like. It is dramatically different in policy attitudes and in voting intention. But the Deliberative Polls achieve this only for a representative sample. They can have a recommending force for policymakers interested in what the public would have to say if it were more informed. And they can have a modest effect on public opinion through broadcasts and print coverage. But pause for a moment to imagine the powerful effects of a more informed public opinion if it were actually shared throughout the society.

C. The leveraging strategy

Deliberative Polls offer a counterfactual picture of informed and engaged public opinion. Deliberation Day begins to approximate the realization of such a public opinion for the entire society. Not only would the countless holiday conversations change millions of minds; they would change the nature of the larger political environment. Follow the implications of this quasi-utopian thought experiment. In plotting their campaign strategies and advertising, politicians and their consultants would use Deliberation Day as a fundamental reference point. They would no longer automatically suppose that candidates were best sold in eight-second soundbites. Throughout the campaign, their eyes would be fixed firmly on the fact that their messages would be subjected to a day-long dissection – and that millions of votes might swing as a result.

At the very least, this should change the way candidates package their message. There will still be 10-second spots, but they will compete for scarce dollars on different terms than they do today: Will a 5- or 10-minute "infomercial" better survive the rigors of Deliberation Day? As the Day comes closer, the commercials will grow longer, and more discursive – not out of a sudden burst of civic virtue, but from a sober calculation of political self-interest given anticipations of the increased level of information and attention that can be expected from the audience.

This prospect provides the basis of a *leveraging strategy*: By placing Deliberation Day near the end of the campaign, we hope to reshape everything that goes before. Indeed, if we are successful in enhancing the quality of the *ex ante* debate, our intervention might have the paradoxical effect of diminishing the impact of the conversations that take place on Deliberation Day itself. Since more voters will have better information coming into the Day, perhaps fewer of them will find themselves changing their minds on the basis of face-to-face discussions.

But, of course, such an outcome would be a marker of Deliberation Day's success, not failure. It would suggest that, by inserting a formal moment for collective deliberation into the larger process, the community had managed to leverage its entire political conversation onto a higher plane.

II. INSTITUTIONS

A. The day

Imagine Deliberation Day more concretely. Our thought-experiment divides the Day into four deliberative segments. After arriving at neighborhood schools and community centers between 8 and 9 a.m., deliberators will go to randomly assigned groups of 15 for the first event – at which they sit together to watch a live television debate on the leading issues between the principal national candidates.

The organization of this National Issues Debate obviously requires a good deal of thought. We think that the formal process should start two weeks before the main event, with the Debate organizers asking each major candidate to answer one simple question: What are the two most important issues presently confronting the nation?

Within a two-party framework, this query will generate two to four themes that will inevitably serve to structure a good deal of the conversational run-up to Deliberation Day – the candidates' Big Themes will drive lots of talk around the dinner table and on the internet, amongst the pundits and in the newspapers. They will also be the target of a great deal of campaign money. We expect competing "infomercials" devoted to rival presentations of the central facts and values, capped perhaps by a national address from each of the candidates the night before the Day is to begin.

The parties will also be invited to spell out their basic positions on the selected issues in a briefing document suitable for the mass public. Each party will be offered space of a given number of words and both (or all three) positions will receive mass distribution in a single convenient document to serve as an initial basis for discussion. This document will also be put online and made available to the press. While the experience with referendum briefing documents has not been a happy one, citizens preparing to vote in a referendum by secret ballot have little incentive for discussion. However, we believe that citizens anticipating a discussion with diverse groups of fellow citizens will have far more interest in digesting a briefing document. Or, at least, that has certainly been the experience of the Deliberative Polls. In addition, if there are any misleading or inaccurate aspects of the briefing positions provided by one party or another, we can expect those aspects to receive exhaustive dissection by the media in the build-up to the event. Of course, some citizens may not actually read the document or feel comfortable in doing so. But they will have plenty of opportunities to pick up the same facts and arguments in the discussions that follow with fellow citizens who will have read it in preparation for the Day.

In the first phase of the actual Day's proceedings, the candidates will have to rely on their own resources, rather than on their teams of consultants and spin doctors. The format of this first phase will be a familiar one. The first hour of the show will be divided into two to four issue segments. Rather than presenting set speeches, the candidates will be confronted by three of the nation's top journalists – who will try to raise questions to each candidate based on their study of the rival issue presentations during the two week run-up. The candidates will then be given an opportunity, during the last 15 minutes, to elaborate on any of their earlier answers, and address any themes left unresolved by the earlier Q and A.

The TV show ends at 10.15 in the morning: "And now it is your turn, fellow Americans, to take up the debate. But first, let's all take a 15-minute coffee break, during which small group members can introduce themselves to those they haven't had a chance to meet before the National Issues Debate began."

Phase two begins at 10.30 with the small group's first order of business: the deliberators must select a foreman, by majority vote, before they proceed to their main task – which is to prepare their contribution for the large group meeting of 500 that will take place after lunch. During this afternoon session, local representatives of the rival parties will appear before the group and try to answer any questions raised about their parties' television presentations. What, then, should they be asked?

The morning session consists of a roundtable discussion on this issue by the 15 deliberators. Though nobody is obliged to talk, each deliberator will be guaranteed five minutes of floor time. While the foreman serves as moderator, each participant will be provided with a little timer to keep track of her own unelapsed time. Whenever a deliberator talks, she will turn the timer on and off at the beginning and end of her remarks. The foreman cannot call on anybody who has exhausted her initial 5-minute allotment if anybody with free time wishes to speak.

During the 75-minute roundtable, each deliberator is trying to formulate a single question that he thinks should be considered by the large group session in the afternoon. At the end of the conversation, the foreman collects each of the questions, and reads them aloud one last time. After each question is read, group members vote Yes or No on their secret ballots. The foreman then counts the ballots in public and declares which three questions have gained the largest Yes vote. (Ties will be resolved by lot.)

By this point, it will be about 12.15 – lunchtime! But man does not live by bread alone: we expect the school cafeteria, or other such place, to serve as a site for much informal networking and conversation amongst the members of the large group of 500, collecting here for the first time.

For present purposes, we are more interested in describing events that will be going on behind the scenes. Each large group will have its moderator – perhaps a local judge, perhaps a member of a civic group like the League of Women Voters. She will soon be in proud possession of the question lists submitted by each small group foreman. Since there are about 35 small groups, her master list will contain about 100 questions in all – far too many for the afternoon session. During lunch-time, she will be charged with the task of selecting 15 of these questions by lot to serve as the basis of the afternoon's discussion.

But not before she engages in a preliminary sorting operation. Many lists will contain similar questions, and the large group runs a serious risk of a very boring session if the random selection happens to generate a bunch of virtually identical queries. As a consequence, the moderator must first make a common sense sorting judgment – grouping similar questions in a single category. If any of the questions in a particular category are drawn from the hat, she will ignore others from the same category that emerge later on in the process of random selection. This way it will be much more likely that the large group will hear answers to 15 questions that represent most of the themes developed in their morning's discussions.

The moderator will be working out her list of questions in the presence of the local party representatives who will be answering them in the afternoon. While they may observe her in action, she does not have to ask their advice when making her preliminary editorial judgments. Time is of the essence – the key thing is to have a decent list of questions ready for the meeting, and to provide the party representatives with as much notice as possible. If the party reps have any serious complaints about the moderator's fairness, they will have a chance to try to bar her from future Deliberation Days. But they are stuck with her for the present.

The large group meeting will begin at 2 p.m., with the moderator welcoming the two (or three) local party representatives to Deliberation Day. The bulk of the session will, of course, consist of a Q and A – with each representative having about two minutes to answer. But after running the gamut of the 15 questions, each representative should be given a 5-minute opportunity to sum up or raise matters that have been omitted from the list. We reckon that this session will run for about one hour and 45 minutes.

Which brings us to the fourth phase – at 4 p.m., the deliberators have returned to the scene of their morning discussions for a final meeting in their small groups. They follow the same 5-minute protocol, but this time, they are invited by the foreman to share their reactions to the responses by the party representatives at the large group meeting.

Like its morning predecessor, this afternoon roundtable will last 75 minutes. But this time, no votes will be taken, and the foreman will make no effort to draw any substantive conclusions. Group members will simply call it a Day, and bid each other farewell.

B. An assessment

Everything about this four-phase protocol is up for grabs, but it does provide a more concrete sense of what can, and cannot, be expected from Deliberation Day. We organize an initial assessment in terms of four values: information, dialogue, deliberation, and community.

1. Information

The world is full of books and commentaries. The problem is to motivate people to search them out. How will the advent of Deliberation Day affect this process?

Begin with the substantial number – to be generous, let us say one-fifth of Americans – who look upon national politics as (at least) a serious spectator sport, and follow the national news on a regular basis. So far as they are concerned, the run-up to Deliberation Day will largely have a *focusing* effect. By targeting two to four issues for special concern, the national candidates will channel the flow of information in the news media in particular directions – encouraging their regular readers to deepen their acquaintance with the "critical issues" in a way that will encourage more knowledgeable exchange on the Day itself.

The impact on the two political parties will be more profound. As everyone recognizes, the media revolution has shifted campaign resources from the periphery to the center, from locally rooted opinion leaders to media merchants. Deliberation Day will generate a shift back, as some simple political mathematics will suggest.

Assume, for example, that the first Deliberation Day is received rather skeptically by many Americans, and manages to attract "only" half of the current electorate. Since approximately 100 million voters have been recently participating in presidential elections, this still adds up to 50 million deliberators attending 100,000 "large group sessions" in their local communities. Each and every one of them will require the active engagement of a party spokesman, prepared to respond to a broad range of questions in an informed way.

One hundred thousand well informed spokespersons on each side! At first the number may seem staggering, but the human resources already exist in both major parties. They simply remain untapped by the present system. Consider, for example, that there are about 93,000 elected office-holders on local, state and national levels. Almost all of them will find it in their interest to appear before a "large group" on Deliberation Day – as will hundreds of thousands who have office-holding ambitions in the future, together with millions who might think it would be fun to engage in a debate for a day. Add to that the hundreds of thousands of active participants in one or another group with links to the major parties – from union to religious activists. Rather than suffering from scarcity, each party will have a problem discouraging aspirants and selecting spokespersons who will appeal to a cross-section.

But the mobilization and selection of party spokespersons will not be enough. Each national campaign will have new incentives to engage in some serious short-term political education. During the run-up to Deliberation Day, both parties will not only be preparing briefing books for their spokespersons, but will be holding day and evening workshops throughout the land. This is the only way they can expect to field a team of local opinion leaders who are adequate to the challenges of Deliberation Day. If one side or the other fails to make the most of its human resources, they may pay a steep price in the voting booth.

This new effort to recruit informed opinion leaders will have ramifying effects in each local community – opinion leaders, by definition, talk to lots of people, and they will naturally be talking about the themes discussed at the workshops as they prepare themselves for their debate on Deliberation Day. What is more, other local groups may well begin their own campaigns to shape the course of local deliberation. Consider, for example, the likely response of the environmental movement or the right-to-life movement upon learning that the national campaigns have failed to list environmental protection or abortion as one of their National Issues. Rather than meekly accepting this decision from on high, such movements may well urge their members to use their five minutes to urge the broadening of the agenda – and if they encounter like-minded people in their small group, perhaps their proposed questions will win the support necessary to gain serious consideration at the large sessions in the afternoon.

Deliberation Day is a two-way street – while the National Issues Debate gives the national campaigns a great deal of power to set the agenda, they do not deserve a monopoly. If insurgent movements can convince enough of their fellow citizens to place their questions in the "top three" selected by small groups, more power to them. Anticipating these reactions, party workshops will undoubtedly devote some time to considering appropriate responses to likely "community issues" as well as "national issues." No less importantly, the local agitation by ideological movements will increase the anticipatory stir surrounding Deliberation Day, and encourage more indifferent citizens to start paying some attention: What's all this ruckus about anyway?

The level of general interest will be further enhanced by another powerful effect. Those planning to attend Deliberation Day will not want to appear foolish before their peers. Their anxieties on this score will prompt many of them to spend more time than usual on the escalating public conversation Of course, deliberators will be perfectly free to remain silent throughout the small group sessions; but if they expect to use their five minutes to advantage, many of them will prepare in advance. Even if they are uncertain how they will participate, they are likely to become more sensitive to the media, and to discuss issues with friends and family knowing that a given topic will be on the agenda for Deliberation Day. This pattern has been confirmed over and over in the Deliberative Polls. Of course, in Deliberative Polls, the events were televised, which may have increased the interest in preparation. Nevertheless, we can imagine that knowing one will be in a discussion before randomly chosen strangers should be enough to stimulate learning in anticipation of the event. This effect is well known in focus groups if respondents know the topic in advance, and hence, might certainly be expected for an event with national visibility.

Indeed, this "anticipation effect" suggests the possibility of a "virtuous cycle" developing over time. Each Deliberation Day may build on the habits acquired by past citizen engagements – leading to a broadening of the informational base over time.

We do not mean to exaggerate. Many may respond to the risk of looking foolish on Deliberation Day by boycotting the entire event. The payment of $150 will not be nearly enough to compensate them for the anxiety they feel at the prospect of speaking in a small group – or even remaining silent, and thereby seeming to be an "idiot with nothing to say."

Nevertheless, we believe that Deliberation Day will operate as a "self-fulfilling prophecy" – calling into existence the relatively informed citizenry that its successful operation presupposes.

2. Dialogue

Information will, of course, be further enhanced by the dialogue occurring on the Day itself – both in the formal small and large group sessions, and in the informal discussions at lunch and odd moments.

There is more to dialogue than information exchange. The small groups will be the site of face-to-face encounters which will expand the range of each participant's relevant experience and moral reflection. Being in a room with randomly assigned fellow citizens can stimulate understanding across social cleavages. Most of us, when we do talk about politics or policy, talk to people like ourselves. We rarely spend the time to focus on people from other social locations with very different problems. As the media move to more and more narrowcasting, the tendency for people to share viewpoints with those they already agree with will be further enhanced.

When we have serious discussions with people from very different social locations, the effects on policy attitudes can be dramatic. At the National Issues Convention, the Deliberative Poll held prior to the 1996 primary season, an 84-year-old white conservative found himself in a small group discussion of welfare policy with an African-American woman who was, herself, on welfare. At the beginning of the discussion he interjected that she "did not have a family" since a family meant a mother and a father and children in the same household. By the end of the weekend, he came up to her and asked "what are the three most important words in the English language? They are 'I was wrong'." After spending hours in small group discussion with her, he came to appreciate her beyond an impression of soundbites and headlines.

But as with all good things, there is also a downside to dialogue. Since there will be millions and millions of small group meetings, there will be thousands and thousands of small group breakdowns – with passions riding high, meetings will degenerate into shouting matches or brawls, making a mockery of all pretensions to civil deliberation. There can be no hope of eliminating these breakdowns entirely. The question is whether they can be reduced to tolerable limits – to the point where they do not discredit the entire process, discouraging most people from attending Deliberation Days run riot.

The challenge is to create a format for the small groups which reduces the number of predictable petty disputes. By presenting a 5-minute timer to each deliberator, we make it plain that the foreman cannot exclude him from the discussion while his favorites blab on interminably. At the very worst, the foreman may call his favorites first, and allow others to intervene later on in the 75-minute discussions. But after all, this may prove a very doubtful advantage – speakers ignored early may find that a later position in the conversation will allow them to rebut persuasively some of the arguments made earlier on.

Similarly, the Rules of Order should forbid the foreman from ruling any speaker out of order on the ground that his or her contribution is irrelevant to the conversation. In particular, the foreman cannot require speakers to address the National Issues considered in the televised debate that introduces the proceedings. If a citizen believes that other questions are more important, he has the inalienable right to use his five minutes to persuade his fellows to challenge the agenda set by the national campaigns. Though his audience may find his 5-minute ramble tedious or offensive, the rules of order should guarantee him an unconditional right to proceed. After all, five minutes is not such a very long time. Even when the speaker is insulting or obscene, the Rules should urge group members simply to ignore inflammatory remarks, rather than dignify them by a further reply.

Undoubtedly, the group will find it very difficult to restrain its anger at times. Nonetheless, an effort to silence a speaker virtually guarantees an escalation of the conflict, making it almost impossible for the group to return to civil discourse within the short space of a 75-minute conversation. The clear guarantee of an absolute right, and an unconditional obligation of civility on group members, provides the best promise of both civil peace and broad-ranging discussion.

At the same time, it serves to reduce another potential source of conflict – the temptation by some foremen to abuse their momentary power and play the petty tyrant. Once the rules disable the foremen from denying the floor to any participant or suppressing the participant on grounds of irrelevancy, how else might they abuse their power in ways that might provoke a mini-rebellion from the other members of the group?

This is not a rhetorical question – undoubtedly, some foremen will invent new ways of disrupting the conversation or they will simply violate the clear rules limiting their authority. Similarly, civility will sometimes break down as group members react in outrage to one or another conversational provocation. What happens next?

The rules of order should provide an extraordinary mechanism through which a supermajority of members can quickly exclude a nonconforming citizen. Each member has the peremptory right to move for exclusion; without any further debate, the matter will be taken up in a secret ballot, and an affirmative vote of 12 out of 15 members will serve to exclude. If the target of the motion tries to disrupt the vote, any member can leave immediately to call the police contingent assigned to the district.

Undoubtedly some citizens may be excluded unjustly, but we do not think that an elaborate appeals process is worthwhile. The best way to resolve these disputes is by drastically limiting the stakes involved. While citizens found disruptive should lose their $150 stipend, they should be immune from all other sanctions – provided that they did not engage in physical assault, in which case the proceedings should be conducted with all the safeguards and defenses provided by the criminal law.

All this, of course, begs the big question – can the overwhelming majority of Americans avoid the need for invoking this crude control system and conduct their conversations in a civil manner?

The only way to find out is to give Deliberation Day a try.

3. Deliberation

It is one thing to get some information; quite another, to talk and to listen in a mutually respectful fashion; and quite another again to deliberate in a way worthy of a democratic citizen. This involves, first and foremost, asking the right questions.

To grasp the difficulty, reflect upon the multiplicity of social roles characteristic of modern life. We are husbands and wives, parents and children, workers and management, neighbors and coreligionists, friends and enemies, consumers and citizens. Each role carries with it different responsibilities, and only bitter disappointment awaits somebody who confuses one role with another, treating the boss as if he were one's husband, or one's coreligionist as if she were necessarily a friend. The particular role-confusion at stake here is the failure to differentiate one's responsibilities as a citizen from one's stance as a consumer. When entering a marketplace, it is generally acceptable for the consumer to limit herself to a single question when choosing amongst competing products – and that is "Which product do I find most pleasing?" If, for example, he goes to a movie simply because he likes the superstar's good looks, he is within his rights even if he is the first to concede that the movie is a piece of junk otherwise.

But this is not true of citizenship. When you and I get together to choose a new set of leaders, we are not engaged in a private act of consumption, but a collective act of power – one that will profoundly shape the fate of millions of our fellow citizens, and billions more throughout the world. With the stakes this high, it is morally irresponsible to choose the politician with the biggest smile or the biggest handout. Rather than asking the question, "What's good for me?," the good citizen asks "What's good *for the country*?"

Undoubtedly, there may be many occasions when what is good for the country is also good for me personally. But the good citizen recognizes, as the good consumer need not, that this convergence is by no means preordained, and that the task of citizenship is to rise above self-interest and take seriously the nature of the common good.

It is this point about citizenship that motivated John Stuart Mill's anxieties over the secret ballot. Once the voter is liberated from the need to stand up in public for her candidate, she is all too prone to forget the difference between citizenship and consumerism, and vote her personal preferences and interests without bothering to ask whether they are in tension with her considered judgment about public good.

We agree, and it is precisely this point which makes Deliberation Day so valuable. Quite simply, it provides a social context which will make the special obligations of citizenship salient in ordinary life. When talking to one another in their small and large groups, Americans will be not encountering one another as consumers or coreligionists or even friends – but as citizens searching for common ground, engaged in the great task of reconstructing a thin but precious civic bond that ties us all together in a common enterprise.

To be sure, different speakers will disagree, often bitterly, about the nature of our national ideals – as well as the candidates and policies that will best advance them. Nevertheless, the social context will encourage all to take the fundamental question of citizenship seriously. As they rise to speak in turn, few deliberators will treat the issues as if they could be completely resolved by a consumerist reference to merely personal likes and dislikes – and when cynics and skeptics do take the floor, their efforts to scoff at the very notion of a "common good" may often serve to invigorate the larger effort to debate its requirements.

Suppose, then, that a typical American has sat through a typical Deliberation Day. What are the likely effects on her preferences and on her behavior? The Deliberative Polls suggest that the very process of engaging in extended dialogue about shared public problems will produce a greater susceptibility to the public interest – or at least to considerations beyond narrow, short-term self-interest or immediate personal gratification. Consider the experience of a series of Deliberative Polls held in Texas on the apparently mundane issue of electric utility regulation. Respondents were asked to choose among options for providing electric power in their areas – options that ranged from building more fossil fuel plants, to conservation measures (that would limit the need for power), to renewable energy like wind and solar power. As part of this process, they were asked if they would be willing to pay more on their monthly utility bills for purposes such as subsidizing renewable energy (wind and solar power), or conservation measures that would lower the need for power production, or programs that would help the poor. One of the remarkably consistent patterns is that at the end of the Deliberative Polls, overwhelming percentages of the respondents expressed a willingness to pay more on their monthly bills for such purposes. The percentages willing to do so ranged from about two-thirds to four-fifths, and as the result of large increases compared to their positions before deliberation.[7]

These questions were posed as part of a regulatory process conducted with the state Public Utility Commission. The discussions were not designed to increase altruism, but just to pose the public policy problem in all its complexity – cost, effects on the environment, risk, distribution, the uncertainties of investment and of technological change. However, this change in preferences was a consistent by-product of the policy discussions which, as in other Deliberative Polls, took place over the course of a weekend with random and representative samples of the communities in question. As J. S. Mill suggested, the process of discussing public problems together can create a social context where people's preferences change. He called such contexts "schools for public spirit," and hoped that the jury system might constitute such an institution (and he clearly thought public voting offered another). When the private citizen participates in public functions, "He is called upon, while so engaged, to weigh interests not his own; to be guided in case of conflicting claims, by another rule than his private partialities; to apply, at every turn, principles and maxims which have for their reason of existence the general good . . . He is made to feel himself one of the public and whatever is in their interest to be his interest."[8]

We believe Deliberation Day would offer just such a "school for public spirit," but on a massive scale never before undertaken so that the beneficial effects of public discussion would give new content to the office of "citizen" for literally millions of people who occupy that office.

However, we do not need to exaggerate the extent of the required transformation. In stating that the question of citizenship – What is good for the country? – will be far more salient in many more minds, we do *not* suggest that each citizen's answer will be the product of heroic soul-searching. To the contrary, we would be quite alarmed if a single Deliberation Day would provoke lots of participants to rethink their most fundamental values. After all, mature human beings construct their framework of values over the experience of a lifetime, and it would be rather disheartening to learn that they could be deconstructed by a single day's conversation with neighbors.[9] The important point is to emphasize that changing one's vote in politics hardly requires a revolution in ultimate values. It may merely suggest that the deliberator has achieved a more informed appreciation of the complex relationship between ultimate values, the central issues, and the candidates' positions. And he or she may become somewhat more willing to consider the public interest as forming at least one part of the calculation.

Sometimes there are simpler effects of discussion. It can provide crucial facts, strategically located in the web of dialogue, the kinds of facts that change opinion. For example, at the National Issues Convention (an American national Deliberative Poll in 1996), respondents came in, as in other national surveys, wanting to greatly reduce foreign aid. But as in other national surveys at the time, they also thought that foreign aid was one of the largest components of the US budget. During the proceedings, they were given briefing materials that detailed the budget, and these briefings included the fact that foreign aid comprised about 1 percent of the budget. At the end of the weekend, support for foreign aid had firmed up – people no longer wished to eliminate it. One of the Presidential candidates who did not attend the forum, Pat Buchanan, was campaigning partly on the theme that we should balance the budget and get rid of foreign aid. An uninformed public was receptive to such appeals. But the informed participants at the National Issues Convention would not have been. Part of our ambition for changing the public dialogue with Deliberation Day is to empower vast portions of the public with enough information that candidates everywhere will have to make the same calculation – they cannot offer appeals that make sense only when people are ignorant of the facts. Before Deliberation Day they will have to anticipate this effect. After, they will have to live with it.

As they struggle to integrate new factors into their overall voting decisions, citizens will be exercising capacities of critical judgment of the greatest political importance – even if such exercises do not lead them to challenge any of their framework values. Is it utopian to suppose that Deliberation Day will prompt millions upon millions to undertake this effort?

Some may fear that it will have just the opposite effect. A bunch of like-minded neighbors may attempt to browbeat the members of the group holding minority opinions or attributes. Given the millions and millions of small group meetings throughout the country, this will undoubtedly occur sometimes. But the structure of the event will not encourage intimidation. For example, if Deliberation Day were combined with Election Day, it might be tempting for local majorities to browbeat the minority into short-term compliance with its wishes, hoping that this psychological pressure would propel the minority to vote accordingly at the ballot box.

But this strategy is plainly a non-starter when there is a week-long pause between Deliberation and Election. Within this framework, it should be obvious to almost everybody that browbeating will only breed resentment, as dissenting members go home to family and friends to complain about their abusive treatment.

To be sure, there will be zealots who are incapable of acting with respectful concern for the feelings and beliefs of others. But given the week-long cooling-off period, we discount the chance that many small-group meetings will be transformed into ideological pressure cookers. It is even less likely that all the pressure cookers will be pressuring in the same ideological direction – local exercises in psychological coercion will often cancel each other out on a national basis, reducing the problem to a scale that will not undermine the central tendencies of Deliberation Day as a whole.

4. Community

National campaigns have increasingly short-circuited local community organization. To be sure, they carefully stage manage local "media-events" for maximum impact. But this is only one of many means they use to gain direct media access to the voters' living rooms. Rather than emphasizing the need for locally based discussion, the national campaigns seek to shout over the heads of local groups in carefully controlled mass advertising.

To be sure, there still remains a need for locally based organizations on election day itself. So long as voters cannot cast their ballots at home, each campaign still requires lots of local workers to encourage voter turnout. But at this late stage, it is a waste of time for party workers to try to persuade voters on the issues. Their job instead is to identify true believers, and drive every single one of them to the polling place.

Deliberation Day changes this picture. For the first time in a long time, it will no longer make sense for Presidential campaigns to operate independently of local party organizations. How else will they be able to find the 100,000 or more respected local spokespersons to represent the candidate at the afternoon assemblies?

The need to provide these representatives will, moreover, give new life and direction to local party organizations. Quite suddenly, local politicians will have a vital interest in locating the most articulate and thoughtful opinion leaders for their team on Deliberation Day. At the same time, issue activists will have greater interest in involving themselves in local party matters, so as to influence the selection of campaign representatives on Deliberation Day.

All this cannot help but generate a vast increase in the practical involvement of local elites in national politics. But this, of course, only serves to introduce an even more important factor – the active deliberation of tens of millions of Americans, each in his or her local community assembly.

But Deliberation Day will not only provide a forum through which millions will appear to their neighbors in a new capacity – as active citizens presenting their own opinions on matters of mutual concern. It will also serve as a means of enhancing the community's general fund of social capital. We imagine a host of community groups setting up tables at lunchtime, trying to gain the interest and support of deliberators for their activities. Casual connections made during the Day will deepen and grow in countless directions over extended periods.

Over time, dare we say it?, Deliberation Day may come to symbolize a genuine renaissance of civic culture in America.

5. Continuing the conversation

Turn next to consider the day after Deliberation Day. If the events have come off reasonably well, it will naturally provoke a wave of conversation at home and office as deliberators share their experiences. Tens of millions of Americans will ask each other questions that they did not get a chance to raise on the Day itself; and this in turn will provoke much more talking and learning and thinking. Newspaper-reading, newscast-watching, internet-politicking, and old-fashioned conversation will become more intense in the run-up to Election Day – and cascade far beyond those who actually attended Deliberation Day.

At the same time, the media merchants of the national campaigns will not remain idle on the sidelines. They will undoubtedly send an army of observers to a random sample of meetings throughout the country; and when deliberators quit for the day, they will encounter eager exit-pollers seeking to determine how much, and in what ways, public opinion has shifted. This in turn will generate a barrage of last-minute infomercials seeking to channel the path of collective deliberation during the home stretch. These exit polls will, in effect, amplify the deliberative opinions resulting from Deliberation Day. Shifts of opinion, representing the public's more considered judgments, will become widely known. These shifts will, in turn, prompt more conversation, reflection and commentary.

As a consequence, Election Day itself will take on a different social meaning. No longer will voters be proud of the fact that they have roused themselves from the collective apathy to spend half an hour going to the polls. Instead, many will take satisfaction in thinking that they have voted thoughtfully, and with due deliberation, on the fundamental issues of the day; and even the millions who have cast thoughtless ballots will be quietly aware of the fact they have fallen short of their civic duty – and promise themselves to find the time and energy to do a bit better in the future.

III. JUSTIFICATIONS

A. Beyond cost

Is Deliberation Day worth the price?

Unsurprisingly, it all depends on your hopes for democracy.

We have already explained why the payment of a substantial citizen stipend – in the ballpark of $150 – is needed for the successful operation of Deliberation Day. We focus here on the issues raised by the proposal's aggregate price tag and seek to justify the expenditure from two angles. We believe it would be a big mistake to view the annualized cost of $15 billion through the narrow lens of standard cost–benefit analysis. To the contrary, one of the principal benefits of Deliberation Day is that it can provide a new democratic legitimation for the distribution of dollars that are used to measure costs and benefits in the rest of the economy. This large benefit cannot, on pain of grievous intellectual confusion, be reckoned on the same dollar scale as other elements in the cost–benefit equation. Instead of measuring the benefits of Deliberation Day in terms of dollars, we should instead measure the legitimacy of the present distribution of dollars in terms of its capacity to gain the deliberate consent of citizens on Deliberation Day.

Beyond cost benefit analysis there is a second, and deeper, question: How does Deliberation Day help ameliorate some fundamental weaknesses in contemporary democratic theory and practice?

B. Who deliberates? with what opinion?

Let us briefly situate Deliberation Day within the long debate about democracy and thereby show how its introduction may help ameliorate, if not magically resolve, some of the starker compromises in democratic theory and practice.

To begin with, consider a very simple classification of democratic possibilities. At the most fundamental level, any institution that consults the public must answer two questions – "who?" and "what?" Who participates or has their views consulted? What kinds of opinions are solicited or expressed?

The "who" can be most everyone, the mass public, or it can be a select or elite group of some sort. This select or elite group can be elected, appointed, selected by lot, tradition or whatever. The "what" solicited from this group can vary from what we will call "raw public opinion" to opinion that is, to some significant degree, the product of deliberation.

Opinions that are to some significant degree the product of deliberation result from the persons in question having reflected on the merits of competing arguments. Reasons for and against the alternatives at issue need to be voiced and answered. While this process is in theory open-ended, when a discussion gives voice to the major views that people would express were they to focus on the issue, and when those views are answered by others who hold different views, then a minimally adequate level of completeness has been satisfied. This process requires that people make the effort to think about the issue and hopefully to express views about it, and that there be opportunities for reasonably accurate information to enter the dialogue. Some reasonable level of completeness and of accuracy is required for deliberative discussion to take place. For the moment, we will stipulate that we believe that the institutional arrangements we have sketched for Deliberation Day are likely to satisfy at least such minimal levels.

Of course, there are many occasions for deliberation that occur in ordinary life, without any concerted effort at institutional design to bring them about. However, as we have already noted, the overall levels of focus, information and engagement found among mass publics would indicate that under most conditions there is not a great deal of deliberative public opinion being produced at the mass level. We will term public opinion, in the form we normally find it, lacking significant deliberation, "raw."

Hence taking these two distinctions together, there are four basic possibilities:

I   Deliberative mass opinion
II   Deliberative opinion of a select group
III Raw opinion of a select group
IV   Raw mass opinion.

These four possibilities are pictured in figure 1.1. Quadrant I is the possibility that we hope to further with Deliberation Day. As we have seen, we are normally well outside Quadrant I because public opinion tends to be crippled by the incentives for rational ignorance in the large-scale nation-state. There have, however, been *episodic* realizations of this possibility for the mass public – "constitutional moments" in the life history of the Republic when there is such a great crisis, and such an extended public discussion about it, that the public is awakened from its torpor of "normal politics."[10]

But constitutional moments occur only very rarely in the history of a nation. They suggest a picture of what public opinion might be like if Quadrant I were filled out, but they would depend on exceptional historical circumstances to be brought into being. Only with an institutional innovation such as Deliberation Day would there be a continuing basis for realizing the ideal of Quadrant I, the ideal of simultaneously fulfilling both deliberation and mass involvement. Otherwise, we are left with the remaining three possibilities.

Quadrant II is realized whenever there is a select group that deliberates for the rest of us. This can be the representative group that Madison has in mind, in *The Federalist* 10, that "refines and enlarges the public views by passing them through the medium of a chosen body of citizens." It can be the Senate, the Electoral College (in its original aspiration), or a "convention" in the sense meant by the Framers. Using a different method of selection, it can also be the sample in a Deliberative Poll, a select group that serves a representative function in deliberating for the rest of us.

Quadrant III, raw opinion of a select group, is filled out by the participants in poll-directed mass democracy. Ordinary public opinion polls permit select groups of citizens, chosen by random samples, to have their raw, unfiltered preferences

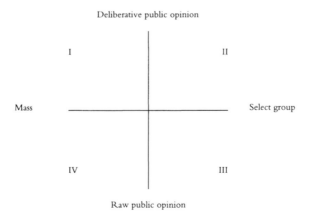

Figure 1.1 :   kinds of public opinion

inserted into the policy process and the public dialogue. To the extent that conventional polls influence politics and policy, we have a realization of Quadrant III — the raw opinions of a select group (chosen by random sampling).

Quadrant IV, raw opinion of the entire mass public, is the realization of plebiscitary democracy. The long-term trajectory of American democracy, and indeed of most democracies around the world, has been to consult the mass public more and more directly. This process has brought power to the people — with referendums and other plebiscites, with primaries in candidate selection, with the elimination of more indirect modes of election of some office-holders, and with expansion of the office-holders who are directly elected, etc. The end result has been that innumerable decisions that were once made in Quadrant II, through a select or elite group deliberating, are now subject to the incentives for rational ignorance on the part of the mass public. Increasingly, we have brought power to the people under conditions where the people have little reason to think about the power we would have them exercise.[11]

Of these four possibilities, Quadrant I has special merit. It is strategically located in the array of democratic possibilities. There are reasons to move north in the diagram, to realize deliberation, and there are reasons to move west in the diagram, to realize mass consent. But our tendency has not been to move north and west, but rather, to move either north-east or south-west. When the founders developed the electoral college, the Senate or the convention, they envisioned decision-making in the north-east direction, believing it was the only way of realizing deliberation. When democratic reformers, from the Populists and Progressives to the post-McGovern–Fraser reformers of the modern American primary system, instituted more democratic consultation, they moved our institutions in the south-western direction, believing it was the only way to realize mass consent.

To encapsulate the problem, we have not been able to move north to further deliberation without also moving east to restrict the process to an elite or select group. Conversely, we have not been able to move west to further mass consent without also moving south to lessen deliberation and increase the input of raw public opinion. Democratic reform has been bedeviled consistently by this kind of forced trade-off. An improvement in one value has consistently meant a sacrifice of another central one.

Deliberation Day is intended to free us from this forced compromise in fundamental democratic values. If we can have *both* deliberation and mass participation, we can infuse the political process, periodically, with what might be called *collective informed consent*. It is the mass consent of most people participating and it is the informed and thoughtful consent that comes from information, thinking, dialogue, and reflection.

All democratic forms should be classifiable within this simple framework, in the sense that all democratic forms need to offer consultation with at least some of the people, so they must offer answers to the question "who?" and to the question "what?" All the other possibilities in the history of democratic practice either have some select group acting as tokens or representatives of the rest of us, acting for us, or they have debilitated, non-deliberative forms of opinion providing the expression of the people's views. Only with an institution such as Deliberative Day could the one most satisfactory alternative among the four actually be realized.

We are not claiming that Deliberative Day is the only possible method of realizing Quadrant I. Instead we are calling for sustained efforts at institutional creativity to realize this possibility. This essay is our contribution to that effort. The fact that there is at least one possibility means that it is not impossible. It does not mean that this is the only way or even the best way. However, it is the best way we have been able to formulate so far and we hope that it will stimulate a dialogue suggesting even more alternatives.

Notes

1   See John Stuart Mill, *Considerations on Representative Government* (New York: Prometheus books, 1991), ch. 10.
2   Mill, p. 207.
3   James Mill *Political Writings*, ed. Terence Ball (Cambridge: Cambridge University Press, 1992) p. 227.
4   For a good overview see Michael Delli Carpini and Scott Keeter, *What Americans Know About Politics and Why it Matters* (New Haven and London: Yale University Press, 1996).
5   Anthony Downs, *An Economic Theory of Democracy* (New York: Free Press, 1957).
6   For an overview of Deliberative Polling, see James S. Fishkin, *The Voice of the People: Public Opinion and Democracy* (New Haven and London: Yale University Press, 1997; expanded ed.).
7   For more on the utility polls see Fishkin, *The Voice of the People*, pp. 200–3 and appendix D. Further data is available from the Center for Deliberative Polling.
8   Mill, *Considerations on Representative Government*, p. 79.
9   In the Deliberative Polls we have found that the items that change are not fundamental values, but rather specific policy attitudes, factual knowledge and what we have called "empirical premises" (typically, assumptions about causal connections between policy choices and valued outputs). Fundamental values seem to have greater stability than any of the items just mentioned.
10   See Ackerman, *We the People*, vols. I, *Foundations*, and II, *Transformations* (Cambridge, MA: Harvard University Press, 1991).
11   For a more extended argument along these lines, see James S. Fishkin, *Democracy and Deliberation: New Directions for Democratic Reform* (New Haven and London: Yale University Press, 1993).

2

Deliberative Democracy Beyond Process

Amy Gutmann and Dennis Thompson

Theories of deliberative democracy consist of a set of principles that are intended to establish fair terms of political cooperation in a democratic society. Some theorists believe that the principles should refer only to the process of making political decisions in government or civil society.[1] The principles of deliberative democracy, they argue, should not prescribe the content of the laws, but only the procedures (such as equal suffrage) by which laws are made and the conditions (such as free political speech) necessary for the procedures to work fairly. These theorists, whom we call pure proceduralists, insist that democratic theory should not incorporate substantive principles such as individual liberty or equal opportunity beyond what is necessary for a fair democratic process. They do not deny that substantive principles such as freedom of religion, nondiscrimination or basic health care are important, but they wish to keep these principles out of their democratic theories.

We argue that this effort to keep democratic theory procedurally pure fails, and that any adequate theory must include substantive as well as procedural principles. Our own theory, presented in *Democracy and Disagreement*, offers one such approach: it includes substantive principles (such as basic liberty and fair opportunity) that extend fairness to persons (for the sake of reciprocity, mutual respect, or fairness itself). Principles of basic liberty and fair opportunity can be defended on many substantive grounds; in that book we argue from a widely recognized principle of reciprocity or mutual justification among persons who are bound by the laws of a democracy.

But our argument here does not depend on accepting the whole theory in that book, or even the specific grounds of reciprocity on which we base the principles. We wish to maintain here that, on a wide range of available grounds, democratic principles must be substantive as well as procedural. A democratic theory that shuns substantive principles for the sake of remaining purely procedural sacrifices an essential value of democracy itself: its principles cannot claim to treat citizens in the way that free and equal persons should be treated – whether fairly, reciprocally, or with mutual respect – in a democratic society in which laws bind all equally.

Pure proceduralists make two kinds of arguments against including substantive principles – one from moral authority and the other from political authority. The argument from moral authority holds that the moral judgment of democratic citizens, not democratic theorists, should determine the content of laws. A theory that contains substantive principles improperly pre-empts the moral authority of citizens. The argument from political authority maintains that substantive principles similarly pre-empt the political sovereignty of citizens, which should be exercised not through hypothetical theoretical reasoning but through actual democratic decision-making. A theory that contains substantive principles unduly constrains the democratic decision-making process, including the process of deliberation itself.

We dispute both of these arguments and defend the inclusion of substantive principles in a theory of deliberative democracy. We agree with those theorists who point out that mere procedures such as majority rule cannot justify outcomes that are unjust according to substantive principles. But these theorists usually neglect the substantive value in the procedures, and assume that an outcome is justified if it is just according to their substantive principles.

In any case, our main argument against pure proceduralism is not the same as the standard objection that procedures can produce unjust outcomes, though we accept this objection. We argue for including substantive principles in a democratic theory for another, generally neglected reason. Such principles should be included so that the theory can explicitly recognize that both substantive and procedural principles are subject to contestation in similar ways. A critical claim in our defense of a deliberative democratic theory that is both procedural and substantive is that the principles are to be treated as morally and politically provisional. This provisionality gives deliberation part of its point. Both procedural and substantive principles are systematically open to revision in an ongoing process of moral and political deliberation. If the principles are understood in this way, the usual objections against including substantive principles lose their force. The provisional status of all its principles thus constitutes a distinctive strength of deliberative democratic theory, and at the same time offers deliberative democrats an effective response to those who would exclude substantive principles from democratic theory.

Although we concentrate here on showing the problems with the form of pure proceduralism that justifies political outcomes by procedural criteria only, our general criticisms also apply against any attempt to segregate procedural and substantive principles in separate theories. Theorists who judge outcomes partly by substantive principles of justice are still pure proceduralists (with respect to their democratic theories) if they assume that the democratic procedures can be justified without reference to some of the same substantive values expressed by their principles of justice. Our argument is intended to show that this kind of sharp separation between procedural and substantive principles and theories is not sustainable.

To illustrate some of the major points in the argument for including both procedural and substantive principles in a deliberative democratic theory, we use a case involving deliberation about health care in the United Kingdom. In 1999, the British Government created a new body, the National Institute for Clinical Excellence (NICE), which is to provide assessments of treatments and clinical guidelines for use by the National Health Service (NHS).[2] The impetus for the new Institute came from the widespread recognition that the NHS could not fund care for all health needs, and needed to find a way to make its difficult decisions in a more public and deliberative manner. By creating a deliberative decision-making body, which includes both expert and lay members, the British Government may also have hoped that it could defuse some of the controversy about the hard choices that must be made. But not surprisingly, shortly after its creation, NICE itself came under criticism in another deliberative forum – the House of Commons. Together these moments of deliberation – the proceedings of NICE and the Commons debate about NICE – are more appropriate for our purposes than cases from the US. They involve an attempt to institutionalize nationwide deliberation about health care priorities in ways that the US has tried only in certain states. Also, the deliberation takes place in a nation in which principles of justice in health care come closer to being satisfied than in the US, and therefore poses a greater challenge to our claim that such principles are necessary in any adequate theory of deliberative democracy. If a theory needs substantive principles when applied to health care in the UK, then *a fortiori* it should need them when applied to similar issues in the US.

1. Why Reciprocity Requires Deliberation

To determine what kind of principles belong in a deliberative democratic theory, we need first to consider the meaning and implications of the fundamental principle of reciprocity. Reciprocity is widely recognized as a core principle of democracy in its many moral variations – liberal, constitutional, procedural, and deliberative – but most theories do not give it the central role that deliberative democracy does. Reciprocity holds that citizens owe one another justifications for the mutually binding laws and public policies they collectively enact. The aim of a theory that takes reciprocity seriously is to help people seek political agreement on the basis of principles that can be justified to others who share the aim of reaching such an agreement.

Mutual justification means not merely offering reasons to other people, or even offering reasons that they happen to accept (for example, because they are in a weak bargaining position). It means providing reasons that constitute a *justification* for imposing binding laws on them. What reasons count as such a justification is inescapably a substantive question. Merely formal standards for mutual justification – such as a requirement that the maxims implied by laws be generalizable – are not sufficient. If the maxim happens to be "maximize self- or group-interest," generalizing it does not ensure that justification is mutual. Something similar could be said about all other conceivable candidates for formal standards. Mutual justification requires reference to substantive values.

We can see more clearly why mutual justification cannot proceed without relying on substantive values by imagining any set of reasons that would deny persons basic opportunities, such as equal suffrage and essential health care. Even if the reasons satisfied formal standards, they could not constitute a mutual justification because those deprived of the basic opportunities could reasonably reject them. Denying some persons suffrage is a procedural deprivation that is inconsistent with reciprocity: we cannot justify coercive laws to persons who had no share in making them. Similarly, denying persons essential health care is a substantive deprivation that cannot be justified to the individuals who need it. That such denials are unacceptable shows that the mutual justification is neither purely formal nor purely procedural.

Because such denials of basic opportunities cannot be mutually justifiable, the principles of a democratic theory must be both procedural and substantive. A democratic theory whose principles would permit some persons to be unnecessarily deprived of a basic opportunity like health care does not take seriously the value of mutual justification implied by the principle of reciprocity. Furthermore, it does not treat persons as free and equal beings. While we argue from the fundamental principle of reciprocity, this principle converges in its implications with the ideal of free and equal personhood, which is the basis of many democratic theories, not only deliberative ones.

The principles of our deliberative democratic theory specify terms of cooperation that satisfy reciprocity. Such terms are similar to what John Rawls calls "fair terms of social cooperation." But the procedural and substantive content of fair terms of social cooperation will vary with different interpretations of what reciprocity requires. A theory is deliberative if the fair terms of social cooperation include the requirement that citizens or their representatives actually seek to give one another mutually acceptable reasons to justify the laws they adopt. The reasons, as we have seen, refer to substantive values no less than to procedural ones.

Although reciprocity is a foundational value in deliberative democracy, it does not play the same role that first principles, such as utility or liberty, play in theories such as utilitarianism or libertarianism. These theories derive all of their other principles from their first principles. Reciprocity is not a first principle from which the rest of justice is derived, but rather a regulatory principle that serves two different roles. First, it guides thinking in the ongoing process in which citizens as well as theorists consider what justice requires in the case of particular laws in specific contexts. Second, it shows the need for other principles to fill out the content of a deliberative democratic theory. Reciprocity points to the need to develop such principles as publicity, accountability, basic liberty, basic opportunity, and fair opportunity, which are necessary for the mutual justification of laws. As the first role of reciprocity suggests, such principles should be developed in an actual ongoing process of mutual justification.

An important implication of reciprocity is that democratic deliberation – the process of mutual reason-giving – is not equivalent to the hypothetical justifications proposed by some social contract theories. Such justifications may constitute part of the moral reasoning to which some citizens appeal, but the reasoning must survive the test of actual deliberation if it is to ground laws that actually bind all citizens. This deliberation should take place not only in the private homes of citizens or the studies of philosophers but in public political forums. In this respect, deliberative theory proposes a political ideal that is process-dependent, even if its content is not exclusively process-oriented.

The requirement that actual deliberation take place is not simply a matter of trying to ensure that citizens feel that their views were taken into account even when they disagree with the outcome. Actual political deliberation at some time is required to *justify* the law for this society at this time. The reason-giving process is necessary for declaring a law to be not only legitimate but also just. The process is necessary to give assurance that (substantive or procedural) principles that may be right in general are right in the particular case or rightly applied to this particular case. No amount of hypothetical reasoning is likely to bring out all the complexities that are relevant to determining whether a law is justified at a particular time in any given society. It would be difficult to decide on the basis of any general principle of basic opportunity whether, for example, NICE was justified in denying coverage for a new anti-flu drug (Zanamivir) marketed as Relenza by the pharmaceutical company Glaxo-Wellcome.[3] What would be missing is not simply factual information but the weighing of facts and the balancing of values in the context of other health care and related decisions that officials as well as citizens need to make.

It may be helpful to think of the requirement of actual deliberation as analogous to a feature of scientific inquiry. Reciprocity is to justice in political ethics what replication is to truth in scientific ethics. A finding of truth in science requires replicability, which calls for public demonstration. A finding of justice in political ethics requires reciprocity, which calls for public deliberation. Deliberation is not sufficient to establish justice, but deliberation at some point in history is necessary. Just as repeated replication is unnecessary once the truth of a finding (such as the law of gravity) has been amply confirmed, so repeated deliberation is unnecessary once a precept of justice (such as equal protection under the laws) has been extensively deliberated. Deliberation may still be desirable, of course, even when justice does not demand it.

The practice of actual deliberation – giving justifying reasons for mutually binding laws to one's fellow citizens – itself both exemplifies and promotes the value of reciprocity. Citizens who have effective opportunities to deliberate treat one another not merely as objects who are to be judged by theoretical principles but also as subjects who can accept or reject the reasons given for the laws that mutually bind them. The reasons are not to be regarded as binding unless they are presented to citizens who have the chance to consider and reject them either directly or indirectly through their accountable representatives in a public forum. In this respect, the creation of NICE supported the value of reciprocity by providing citizens with an example of deliberation in action in which they could assess the justifications their representatives give for policies that will affect their well-being in important ways. The possibility of continuing debate in Parliament about the deliberative practices as well as the decisions of NICE further helps to realize reciprocity.

The process of deliberation also has epistemic value. Decisions are more likely to be morally justifiable if decision-makers are required to offer justifications for policies to other people, including those who are both well informed and representative of the citizens who will be most affected by the decisions. The epistemic value of deliberation is especially great when the justification for a decision must combine factual and evaluative matters, as is the case with most health care decisions, including the kind that NICE makes. While experts may be the best judges of scientific evidence, they have no special claim to finding the right answer about priorities when degrees of risk and trade-offs of costs and benefits are involved.

2. Why Reciprocity Requires Substantive Principles

The practice of deliberation is an ongoing activity of reciprocal reason-giving, punctuated by collectively binding decisions. It is a process of reaching mutually binding decisions on the basis of mutually justifiable reasons. Because the reasons have to be mutually justifiable, the process presupposes some principles with substantive content. It is possible, and sometimes desirable, to distinguish procedural and substantive aspects of principles and theories, but to turn these distinctions into separate principles or distinct theories is to distort both the theory and practice of (deliberative) democracy. Although for convenience we refer to principles and theories as procedural and substantive, strictly speaking democratic principles and theories have both procedural and substantive dimensions, and approaches that force a sharp division are misleading.

The principle of reciprocity itself expresses neither purely procedural nor purely substantive values. A reciprocal perspective is both procedural and substantive because mutual justification cannot proceed without appealing to reasons that refer to both procedures of government and substance of laws, often at the same time. Even philosophers like Stuart Hampshire who seek to exclude substantive justice completely from their procedural political theories acknowledge the need for some substantive values – such as "common decency" – in the very concept of justice.[4] Hampshire says justice is "primarily procedural" – not entirely so.[5] Like other philosophers who want to be pure proceduralists, he never says what constitutes the correct set of procedural principles, and why people who remain subject to tyrannical rule should settle for only procedural principles that permit tyranny.

At a minimum, no one would seriously dispute that justifications should recognize some values expressed by substantive principles such as liberty and opportunity. It would hardly be sufficient for NICE to justify a decision to deny prescription drugs to West Indian immigrants on the grounds that they are not white. Even – or especially – if a large majority of British citizens would accept such reasoning, the justification would not satisfy any adequate standard of reciprocity. Nor would it be any more acceptable to deny prescription drugs to a disadvantaged minority on the grounds that they agreed with the conclusion. They might have agreed simply because they had less power than the groups that prevailed and had no better alternative in a bargaining situation.

To see more clearly why reciprocity requires substantive principles, we might further imagine a situation in which the process of decision-making itself was fair in the sense that the bargaining power of the parties was equitable, but in which the reasoning of the decision-makers was prejudiced (or could only be reasonably interpreted as based on prejudice) against West Indian immigrants or another disadvantaged minority group. The prejudiced reasoning then yields an outcome – supported by the vast majority – that denies critical health care to the disadvantaged minority. This outcome could not be justified on grounds of reciprocity, even if the procedures by which it was reached were otherwise completely fair. The justification for the outcome does not treat members of the minority group as worthy of a justification that they could reasonably accept. Alternatively, one might say that the prejudiced reasoning denies members of the minority group the status of free and equal persons. Given the nature of the reasoning, this would be so no matter how fair the process of decision-making itself might otherwise be.

We can see the principle of reciprocity in action, and the mixture of procedural and substantive values it implies, in the debate about NICE in the House of Commons. The debate had hardly begun when an MP (who is also a physician) challenged the idea that NICE or anyone else has the moral or political authority to ration health care. Another MP responded, saying that rationing was necessary and therefore justifiable: "sometimes some treatments are not available when they would benefit patients or populations, because there simply are not the resources to provide all those treatments on the NHS." Although the debate at first seemed to turn on issues about the legitimacy of the process (who has the authority to decide), most critics (as well as most defenders of the Government) agreed that NICE represented an improvement as far as process was concerned. Most recognized that the new decision-making process is preferable to the old, and much superior to the less deliberative process that prevails in the US.

The challenge instead was directed against the substance of NICE's decision in its first review of a drug. NICE had recommended against the NHS's funding the new anti-flu drug Relenza.[6] The critics worried that this decision would be a precedent that would justify NICE's recommending against funding of other more expensive and effective new drugs, such as beta interferon (which treats the symptoms of multiple sclerosis). The critics argued that decisions denying coverage are likely to deprive less advantaged patients of life-enhancing and life-saving treatments that more advantaged patients receive, and that this unequal opportunity cannot be justified. It leaves the less fortunate without the health care and the life chances that if any citizens enjoy, then all should be entitled to.[7] They appealed to substantive principles, not simply to a claim that the process was unfair, or even that it was not deliberative.

Defenders of NICE's decision rightly realized that they needed to justify the substance of the decision because the deliberative process in which NICE had engaged (and in which they were engaging in the Commons debate) could not in itself be a sufficient justification of the decision. They explicitly invoked substantive standards to defend NICE's decision. They argued, for example, that the decision not to fund Relenza would not adversely affect the basic life chances of any citizen, not even patients who are at high risk of complications from influenza. They called for more research on the effects of Relenza on high-risk patients, and suggested that if there were evidence of Relenza's benefit in reducing the serious secondary complications of influenza in such patients, then they would support NHS funding. Their arguments, whether correct on the merits, were entirely in order, and if correct they were also necessary to justify their conclusion. That they were necessary cannot readily be accommodated in a democratic theory that limits itself to procedural considerations only.

An obvious but no less important virtue of a theory that does not limit itself to procedural principles is that it has no problem with asserting that what the majority decides, even after full deliberation, is wrong. Within a deliberative theory, one should be able to condemn majority tyranny on substantive grounds: one should be able to say that a majority acts wrongly if it violates basic liberty by denying health care on grounds of race, gender, or poverty. Or suppose that the majority, following perfectly deliberative procedures, decides to institute a practice of compulsory organ donation. On a purely procedural conception of deliberative democracy, this law would be justified. If a deliberative theory includes substantive principles such as basic liberty which protect bodily integrity, democrats would be able to object to such a law, without abandoning their commitment to deliberative democracy.

Democrats of course may be mistaken when they assert claims based on substantive principles either because they draw incorrect implications from a correct principle or because they rely on an indefensible principle. Perhaps compulsory organ donation does not violate basic liberty, or perhaps this particular principle of basic liberty is flawed. Our argument for including substantive principles – based on reciprocity – not only allows for both kinds of mistakes; it also incorporates into the theory itself the insight that democratic theorists and citizens may be mistaken about both procedural and substantive principles. Deliberation explicitly deals with the likelihood of mistaken views about principles and their implications by considering the principles of a theory to be provisional, and therefore subject to ongoing deliberation. To point out the possibility of being mistaken about substantive principles is therefore not an argument against including such principles within a deliberative democratic theory.

The conclusions of purely procedural theories sometimes converge with the claims of the substantive standards that reciprocity requires. For example, a procedural theory of democracy may say that racial discrimination in voting is not justified because it excludes a class of human beings from citizenship, and this violates the procedural requirements of democracy, which demand the enfranchisement of all adult persons. This procedural reason is fine as far as it goes. But it does not go far enough in establishing why such discrimination is not justified. Democratic theorists should be able to object that racial discrimination (for example, in the provision of health care by a for-profit HMO) is not justified even if democratic citizenship or no other process values are at stake. Majority tyranny is objectionable on substantive, not only procedural, grounds.

Moreover, this kind of objection should be capable of being made from *within* a deliberative democratic theory. After all, democracy has never meant merely majority rule. Denying basic liberties and opportunities by racially discriminatory policies is either the result of state action or can be remedied by state action, and any such action or inaction requires a justification that could reasonably be accepted by those whose liberties and opportunities are denied. This is a direct implication of the basic requirement of reciprocity. The requirement to give such a justification – to invoke substantive principles in the public forum to justify a mutually binding law or policy – is therefore not an incidental feature of deliberative democracy. The substantive principles are integral to the deliberative process itself.

To say that the principles are integral to the process is not to deny that they may be justifiable outside of that process. Like any theorist of justice (or citizen making a claim about justice), deliberative democrats may put forward principles for consideration which they regard as justifiable – and which indeed may be correct, but simply not yet justified as laws. Deliberative theorists try to justify their substantive principles in a number of familiar ways, some just like those used by any theorist. We justify the substantive principles such as basic liberty in *Democracy and Disagreement*, first and foremost, on their own terms – by identifying core values, convictions, and paradigmatic cases where no one would reasonably deny that they were violated (for example, discrimination on grounds of race). Then by analogy and other forms of reasoning, we try to thicken and extend the principles to apply to more controversial cases. This is also how much of actual political deliberation proceeds.

Certainly, these substantive principles might be rejected, and perhaps even reasonably rejected, in a deliberative process that satisfies the procedural conditions of deliberative democracy. But a precisely parallel argument can be made about procedural principles. Procedural principles may also be rejected by a deliberative democracy (and so may a purely procedural conception of deliberative democracy). Pure proceduralists do not have access to some moral basis, which our conception lacks, on which to claim that the procedural constraints that they recommend for a constitutional deliberative democracy are correct or authoritative.

Some critics who object to including substantive principles in a deliberative democratic theory are themselves not pure proceduralists with respect to justice. They agree that justice requires the protection of basic liberties and opportunities, including perhaps even access to adequate health care. But they still insist that the subject matter of *democratic* theories should be kept distinct from questions of distributive justice. They are pure proceduralists with respect to democracy, but not justice. Democracy, they imply, is supposed to tell us how to decide when we do not agree on what is just; we should not confuse matters by combining principles of justice with the procedures for deciding disputes about those principles.

This argument is not so much substantive as it is definitional: democracy (including deliberative democracy) *means* fair procedures, not right outcomes. The critics cannot rely on ordinary usage or the history of modern democratic theory, because representative democracy has rarely been characterized as exclusively procedural. Ordinary usage of a concept as complex as democracy is enormously varied, as are the conceptions of democracy found in modern democratic theory. And democratic practice itself is full of debates about substantive principles. Why then strain so hard to exclude them from the definition of democracy?

The reason cannot be that democratic theory is somehow internally inconsistent if it contains substantive as well as procedural principles. To be sure, the more principles a theory contains, the more likely there are to be conflicts among them. And including both substantive and procedural principles certainly increases the potential for conflict. But democratic politics itself is rife with conflict among principles, and a democratic theory that tries to insulate itself from that conflict by limiting the range of principles it includes is likely to be less relevant for recognizing and resolving the disagreements that democracies typically confront. When the disagreements mix substantive and procedural values, as so many do in actual democratic practice, theorists who artificially segregate substance and procedure in separate theories of justice and democracy are prone to distort the role of both.

Some pure proceduralists may wish to keep out substantive principles because they are contestable, and democracy is supposed to be a means of resolving disagreement among contestable principles such as basic liberty. But the content of principles that are more procedural, such as majority rule or public accountability, are also contestable. A purely procedural theory does not avoid fundamental disagreement: conflicts among procedural principles are no less severe than among substantive principles. For example, in the debate in Commons about NICE's decision to deny coverage for beta interferon, the MP from North Wiltshire implicitly raised a basic procedural question – to what extent does democratic control require local autonomy – when he argued that his constituents should have access to the drug. He objected that – because of the relative autonomy of regions – some citizens in other parts of the country could get beta interferon from the NHS while his constituents could not. This is "a terrible tragedy for constituents such as mine, who could be prescribed beta interferon if they lived in Bath or Oxford, but not in Wiltshire."[8]

The political debates over health care rationing that are occurring not only in the UK but also in almost every contemporary democracy clearly reveal the need to consider both procedures and outcomes in judging democratic justice. At stake are both the conditions under which these decisions are made and their content. Do the decision-making bodies bring together representatives of all the people who are most affected by the decisions? Are the representatives accountable to all their constituents? These procedural questions cannot be answered in the context of these debates without also asking: to what extent is the substance of the decisions justifiable to all the people who are bound by them? To exclude substantive criteria – such as liberty and opportunity – that judge the justice of decisions would be morally arbitrary and incomplete according to deliberative democracy's own premise of reciprocity. (To exclude substantive criteria would also be morally arbitrary and incomplete according to other premises that are often identified as fundamental to deliberative democracy, such as free and equal personhood or mutual respect.)

To affirm that a democratic theory should include substantive principles does not of course commit one to any particular set of principles. In *Democracy and Disagreement*, we propose a set of principles that are both substantive and procedural, and present arguments for their inclusion as part of the constitution of a deliberative democracy.[9] The arguments we present are intended to be part of a deliberative process itself, and in fact include fragments from actual deliberations. For example, we argue that laws or policies that deprive individuals of the basic opportunities necessary for making choices among good lives cannot be mutually justified as a principle of reciprocity requires. The basic opportunities typically include adequate health care, education, security, work, and income, and are necessary for living a decent life and having the ability to make choices among good lives. We therefore would include a principle of basic opportunity as part of any adequate theory of deliberative democracy.

Critics who object that this principle is not mutually justifiable or that other principles of equality are more mutually justifiable are effectively accepting the idea that democratic theory should include substantive principles. Even while challenging the content of the principles, they are nevertheless accepting that the terms of the argument should be reciprocal. Such challenges are welcome by the terms of the theory itself, which asks for reasons that can be publicly assessed by all those who will be bound by them.[10] This kind of challenge can then become part of the continuing deliberative process. The reason that such a challenge fits within the terms of a deliberative theory itself is that the principles of the theory per se have a morally and politically provisional status.

3. Why the Principles should be Morally Provisional

How is it possible for a theory to propose substantive principles to assess laws while regarding citizens as the final moral judges of the laws they make? The key to deliberative democracy's answer lies in the provisional status of its principles.[11] The principles of deliberative democracy have a different status in deliberative democracy than they do in most moral and political theories. They are morally and politically provisional in ways that leave them more open to challenge and therefore more amenable to democratic discretion. The moral basis of the provisional status of deliberative principles comes from the value of reciprocity. Giving reasons that others could reasonably accept implies accepting reasons that others give in this same spirit. At least for a certain range of views they oppose, citizens should acknowledge the possibility that the rejected view may be shown to be correct in the future.[12] This acknowledgement has implications not only for the way citizens should treat their opponents but also for the way they regard their own views.

The process of mutual reason-giving further implies that each participant involved take seriously new evidence and arguments, new interpretations of old evidence and arguments, including moral reasons offered by those who oppose their decisions, and reasons they may have rejected in the past. "Taking seriously" means not only cultivating personal dispositions (such as open-mindedness and mutual respect) but also promoting institutional changes (such as open forums and sunset provisions) that encourage reconsideration of laws and their justifications. One implication is that citizens and their accountable representatives should continue to test their own political views, seeking forums in which their views can be challenged, and keeping open the possibility of their revision or even rejection.

Deliberative democracy thus expresses a dynamic conception of political justification, in which provisionality – openness to change over time – is an essential feature of any justifiable principles. Provisionality takes two general forms. The principles are *morally* provisional in the sense that they are subject to change through further moral argument; and they are *politically* provisional in the sense that they are subject to change through further political argument.

Morally provisional principles are presented as claims that can be challenged and changed over time in response to new philosophical insights, empirical evidence, or interpretations of both the insights and evidence. They are justified only when they are so presented. Many theories endorse something like this general outlook – for example, by adopting some form of fallibilism, or more simply by expressing general approval of moral and intellectual open-mindedness. But the provisional stance that deliberative democracy takes toward its own claims is distinctive in being integral to the theory. Deliberative democracy supports the means for fundamental change in the content of the theory itself. Deliberative democracy subjects its own principles, as well as other moral principles, to critical scrutiny over time. If as a consequence of such scrutiny, its fundamental principles substantially change – say, from a more egalitarian to a more libertarian orientation (or vice versa) – the theory is appropriately seen as undergoing revision rather than rejection.

Not all principles can be challenged at the same time from within a deliberative democratic theory, but any single principle (or even several principles) may be challenged at a particular time by other principles in the theory. Citizens and accountable officials can revise one principle in a sequential process in which the other principles are held constant. They can alter their understanding of all the principles by applying them in a different context or at a different time. For example, when the NICE Board decided against funding Relenza, it implicitly made the provisional status of its decision clear by limiting its decision to one influenza season only. NICE also recommended that additional trials be conducted and further data be obtained so that its decision could be reassessed in the next influenza season. Particular attention should be paid, the Board said, to finding out whether Relenza has positive effects on reducing serious secondary complications of influenza in high-risk patients. The moral basis for a decision against funding Relenza – the claim that the use of Relenza does not significantly affect anyone's basic opportunity in life – would no longer be defensible if evidence came to light showing that Relenza could significantly reduce serious complications of influenza in high-risk patients. In this way, both the process and the substance of the decision kept open the possibility of revising the recommendation in the future.

The possibility of revision applies not only to substantive principles but also to a principled defense of the practice of deliberation itself. This is why it is misleading to claim that substantive principles should have no place in the theory because they are merely philosophical proposals. Substantive principles are no more or less provisional – and no more or less philosophical proposals – than the case for deliberation itself. It is as possible to question, from within deliberative theory, whether deliberation is justifiable – and what it entails – as it is to question whether basic liberty is justifiable – and what it entails.

Consider the deliberation in the Commons about whether NICE itself – also a deliberative forum – is a justifiable way to make health care decisions. This part of the debate began when several MPs objected that letting NICE make recommendations is "to shield the Government from the very difficult decisions that have to be taken." Should NICE recommend beta interferon, which costs about £10,000 per patient per year and has been judged "marginally effective"? (It treats incurable multiple sclerosis "by reducing the exacerbation rate in patients who have relapsing-remitting disease without important disability."[13]) Should NICE recommend the new taxane drugs for chemotherapy, which do not cure but, as one MP put it, "can add years to life at a cost of about £10,000 per year"? If NICE recommends against prescribing expensive new drugs that can provide some health care benefits to patients, will it thereby be shielding the Government from pressure to increase the total NHS budget? If NICE recommends in favor of the NHS prescribing these drugs, will it thereby be forcing the NHS not to fund some other existing and highly valuable treatments (or pressuring the government to increase funding for the NHS)? The answer to these substantive questions thus depends on taking a position on what the process should be.

Not even the deliberative principle that calls for giving moral reasons in politics is beyond reasonable disagreement. Some critics of deliberation argue that bargaining is not only more common but also preferable as a way of resolving moral disagreements in politics. The claim that self-interested (or group-interested) bargaining processes are better than deliberative ones relies on the premise that interest-based politics is more morally desirable and mutually justifiable than deliberative politics. Whether political bargaining satisfies reciprocity (or any other moral standards) depends in part on the actual consequences of political bargaining in a particular social context. If those consequences can be shown to be mutually justifiable to the people who are bound by them, or more mutually justifiable than the consequences of deliberative processes, then to this extent substituting bargaining for deliberation would satisfy the fundamental aim of deliberative democracy. At least one claim that deliberative democrats often make about the general superiority of deliberation over bargaining would need to be revised – but revised in order to satisfy the demands of deliberative theory itself.

In any actual political context, a general defense of bargaining is not likely to be plausible. The main problem with bargaining as a general substitute for deliberation is that it accepts the current distribution of resources and power as a baseline, the place to begin the negotiations. On the face of it this is not the best site for a moral defense of democratic procedures or outcomes.[14] It is significant that no one defending NICE's rejection of Relenza attempted to justify the decision as the outcome of bargaining. Nor did anyone in the Commons suggest that bargaining should play any role in the process, as they might propose for a labor-management dispute, or a controversy about tax policy.

Is there no limit to what deliberative democrats can treat as provisional? They can encourage reinterpretations of the meaning and implications of deliberative principles, even the guiding principle of reciprocity, but they cannot accommodate the wholesale rejection of the moral justification required not only by reciprocity but many other morally based democratic theories. Deliberative democrats can welcome criticism of any of their principles, including reciprocity, but they cannot accept a general rejection of the requirement that binding political decisions must be justified by moral reasons. The refusal to give up that requirement is not peculiar to deliberative democracy. To reject the idea of moral reasoning in politics *tout court* is to abandon not only deliberative democracy, but also any form of democracy that would claim that its laws are justified to the citizens who are bound by them. Although critics of deliberative democracy sometimes write as if they reject moral reasoning in politics, they rarely face up to what such a rejection would entail either in practice or in theory.

What such rejection would mean – even in a partial form in a particular case – can be illustrated by imagining what would have happened if NICE had made its decision about Relenza on the basis of considerations of bargaining power. The single most powerful agent in this case, the one who stood to gain the most from NICE's decision, was Relenza's manufacturer and distributor, the Glaxo-Wellcome pharmaceutical company. When Glaxo executives learned of the possibility that NICE might recommend against NHS funding of Relenza, they threatened to abandon Glaxo's operations in the UK. They also said they would encourage other pharmaceutical companies to boycott the British economy. As it turned out, NICE stood its ground and Glaxo backed down from its threat. Deliberation and justice coincided in this case, and both prevailed. That would have not been the outcome, given the baseline distribution of power, had NICE sought only to bargain.

Deliberative democrats thus reject – and not just provisionally – any theory that denies the need for moral justification, and therefore also any theory that bases politics only on power. Deliberative democrats are committed – and not just provisionally – to mutually justifiable ways of judging the distribution of power. Deliberative democracy accepts the provisionality of its principles but rejects the provisionality of moral reasoning itself as a way of assessing politics. Theorists who claim that politics is only about power must reject far more than the moral terms and the adjudicative means of deliberative democracy. They must also reject criticism of any current distribution of power, however unjust it may be. Or if they criticize it, they must do so in terms that – on their own view – the persons who would be constrained by the power have no moral reason to accept. If they decline to search for political principles and practices that can be mutually justified, who should listen to them? Certainly no one who is motivated to find fair terms of social cooperation. Their audience can be only people who have themselves already given up on finding mutually defensible reasons. Those who would renounce reciprocal reasons are therefore trying either to persuade the already converted or to reach the unreasonable. In the first case their audience has no need and in the second case no reason to listen.[15]

4. Why the Principles should be Politically Provisional

We are now in a better position to address the second objection against including substantive principles in deliberative democratic theory – that their inclusion usurps the political authority of democratic citizens. A democratic theory that includes substantive principles can declare that a law citizens make is unjust, however correct the procedures by which they make it. It is no comfort to the defender of the authority of citizens to be told that the substantive principles are morally provisional. Even morally provisional principles – if they are the most theoretically justifiable at the time – carry the implication that they should be politically enacted. Acting on this implication denies democratic citizens the authority to determine through a deliberative process what should be politically enacted and why. To respond to this objection, deliberative democracy relies on the second kind of conditional status – political provisionality.

Political provisionality means that deliberative principles and the laws they justify must not only be subject to actual deliberation at some time, but also that they be open to actual reconsideration and revision at a future time. Like the rationale for treating principles as morally provisional, the justification for regarding principles as politically provisional rests on the value of reciprocity. From the perspective of reciprocity, persons should be treated not merely as objects of legislation or as passive subjects to be ruled. They should be treated as political agents who take part in governance, directly or through their accountable representatives, by presenting and responding to reasons that would justify the laws under which they must live together. We showed earlier (in Section 1) why reciprocity requires actual not merely hypothetical deliberation. Because deliberative principles must be justified in an actual deliberative process in which citizens or their accountable representatives take part, the political authority of democratic citizens is to a significant degree respected.

But it still may be objected that once a principle or law is justified in this process, it acts as a constraint on other new laws that citizens may wish to make. Because the body of citizens and their representatives who deliberate about the new laws are never exactly the same as those who enacted the old laws, the democratic authority of citizens at any particular time is held hostage to principles justified at a previous time. Providing such constraints is of course what constitutions are supposed to do, and that may be why some deliberative democrats are wary about regarding their principles as part of a constitution. But if all the principles of deliberative democracy are seen as provisional in the sense of being open to revision over time, these constitutional constraints that embody substantive principle, such as basic liberty and opportunity, are not so threatening to the political authority of citizens.

Deliberative democrats do not favor continual deliberation, but they are committed not only to deliberation about laws at some time but also to the possibility of actually reconsidering them in the future. The extent to which any law is subject to actual reconsideration should depend on the strength of the available moral reasons and empirical evidence (and any other morally relevant considerations) supporting it, which often change over time. In the case of Relenza, part of the reason that NICE's decision was justified is that it called for review after a year's time, an appropriate interval in light of the significant changes that may occur over the course of even a single flu season. A decision by any official body not to fund Relenza, even if otherwise well supported, would not be justified without its providing for the possibility of continuing deliberation in the future. To be sure, at some point a decision is reached, as it was in this case, and it is justifiably enforced. But deliberative theory emphasizes, more than other democratic theories, what happens before the decision and – even more to the point of provisionality – what happens after.

Political provisionality thus goes further than its moral counterpart. It implies that principles should be open to challenge over time in an actual political process that not only permits but encourages revision. Even when a law is rightly enacted today, the practices and institutions of deliberative democracy should ensure that it is subject to the regular reconsideration that is necessary to its justification over time. Deliberative democrats should therefore be especially suspicious of practices that routinely defer to the "intent of the framers" or that make constitutional amendments almost impossible even when the inherited reasons for supporting the laws in question are not compelling. Deliberative democrats should be favorably disposed toward practices that attach sunset provisions to everyday laws and procedures, and require administrators to issue periodic "impact statements" describing the effects of these laws and the regulations that enforce them. We noted earlier that the moral justification for NICE's decision against funding Relenza – the claim that the use of Relenza does not significantly affect anyone's basic opportunity in life – depends in part on evidence that the drug does not significantly reduce complications in high-risk patients. In its deliberations, NICE demonstrated its respect for political provisionality by taking specific institutional measures: limiting their decision to one flu season, providing for continuing review, and recommending further research.

The objection that the presence of substantive principles in a deliberative theory pre-empts democratic authority, it should now be clear, either proves too much or too little. It proves too much if the mere inclusion of substantive principles is taken to imply that these principles must therefore be politically binding on citizens. This objection would apply equally to the inclusion of procedural principles, which may be no less reasonably contestable than substantive principles. If the objection were accepted, it would require democratic theory to exclude *all* reasonably contestable principles, procedural as well as substantive. The objection proves too little if the complaint is only against making provisional judgments (however substantive) that challenge laws enacted by proper procedural methods. Even the critics of deliberative democratic theory could hardly fault it for rendering provisional judgments of this kind. If political theory were disbarred from offering such judgments, it would have little relevance to the democratic politics it purports to criticize.

5. When Moral and Political Judgments Conflict

Ideally, the moral and political judgements that deliberative democracy renders coincide. What deliberative politics decides will satisfy deliberative morality. Indeed, this happy conjunction occurs more often than is usually assumed. In the case of NICE, the decision against funding Relenza, made in a process that was more deliberative than that in which such decisions were made in the past, seems to be morally justified (at least provisionally). The most reliable studies, as reported by NICE, show that the only benefit of Relenza is a one-day reduction of influenza symptoms in the median patient at a direct financial cost to the public of as much as £10.5 million annually. NICE also took into account the cost of the expected increase in visits to doctors by typical influenza patients (most of whom are otherwise healthy), and the risk that the increase would overload the health care system for a very minor health benefit. Furthermore, NICE found no evidence that Relenza reduces any of the serious, life-threatening effects of influenza on high-risk patients.

Nevertheless, there were some critics who raised reasonable moral objections to NICE's decision. In the Commons debate, the physician-MP mentioned earlier complained that the decision not to cover Relenza discriminated against poor people. "When we talk about rationing of NHS treatments, we aren't saying no one in the UK has them. What we are saying is that they aren't available to poor people. The rich and those who can afford it can get these treatments privately."[16] The money saved for all patients would be at the expense of the poor because more affluent citizens could obtain Relenza by means of postcode prescribing. The decision by NICE against funding Relenza would therefore at least appear to be sacrificing the welfare of some poorer citizens in order to save taxpayer money.

Whatever the merits of this MP's criticism, all parties to the dispute over Relenza should be able to agree that he has raised a serious moral question about a decision that was reached by politically justifiable (deliberative) process. Even if under current conditions the NHS cannot do anything about this differential access to drugs such as Relenza, defenders of the decision (and other similarly hard choices) should be prepared to acknowledge the moral costs inherent in a situation in which rich people tend to live in richer districts that provide better health care, and they also can buy any health care treatment on the market while poor people are completely dependent on the NHS for funding those treatments that may be cost-effective for society as a whole.

In this case there was some reasonable disagreement about whether the political judgment conformed to the moral judgment, but in many other cases there may be no doubt that the (procedurally correct) political judgment conflicts with the (philosophically correct) moral judgment. A deliberative process that deliberative democrats recommend may yield an outcome that runs contrary to one or more of the substantive principles of justice that deliberative democrats also wish to defend. This kind of conflict does not seem to be a serious problem for a purely substantive theory, which simply declares the outcome of the process unjust. Similarly, a purely procedural theory faces no serious problem here either; it declares the outcome just, as long as the procedures were proper. But, as we have seen, a deliberative democratic theory should include both procedural and substantive principles because the pure approaches at best neglect and at worst deny the moral complexity of democratic politics. A democratic theory that recognizes what is morally at stake in political decision-making must contain principles that are both substantive and procedural. Moreover, as we have also seen, the basic premise of deliberative democratic theory – reciprocity that calls for mutual justification among free and equal persons – supports both substantive and procedural principles.

Thus, compared to the purer theories, deliberative democracy more fully faces up to the potential conflicts between moral and political deliberation. It does not provide a simple resolution, but instead relies on deliberation itself to deal with the conflicts as they arise. But then the question persists: how can deliberative democrats affirm substantive conclusions about politics and still support the value of actual deliberation, which may or may not produce those same conclusions?

Political philosophers, including deliberative democrats like us, reach substantive conclusions (including conclusions about what procedures are most justifiable) without engaging in any actual political deliberation. This seems to fly in the face of the commitment to actual rather than hypothetical adjudication of political disagreements.

Some critics of deliberative democracy pose this problem as a paradox of deliberative democracy.[17] The critics argue that if, on the one hand, they accept the arguments and conclusions of a substantive deliberative theory (such as the one we present in *Democracy and Disagreement*), they need not bother calling for actual political deliberation. The substantive theory provides all the reasons anyone who accepts it needs for making sound political judgments, and without the aid of any actual deliberation. If, on the other hand, critics reject the arguments and conclusions of the substantive theory, then they should also reject the deliberation that it recommends. Either way, deliberative theory that includes substantive principles seems to eliminate the need for the practice of deliberation.

As our earlier discussion of moral and political provisionality should indicate, this objection does not express a genuine paradox. The procedural and substantive principles (even the political conclusions) that deliberative democrats defend do not pre-empt actual deliberation. According to the very terms of the theory, the (substantive and procedural) principles and conclusions need to be subjected to the rigors of actual deliberation over time; that is part of what it means to treat them as politically provisional. (Moral provisionality also benefits indirectly from political provisionality, because individuals thinking in the privacy of their own homes or offices often draw on ideas, arguments, and perspectives – or respond to challenges – that public deliberations bring to their attention.) Deliberative democrats offer their principles and conclusions not as authoritative philosophical constraints on democratic politics but as provisional contributions to democratic deliberation.

The conclusions that deliberative democrats reach about substantive and procedural principles should be understood as normative hypotheses about political morality. Given certain assumptions about reciprocity, for example, certain principles are the most mutually justifiable. The hypotheses are normative because simply showing that some people, even a majority, in fact reject the principles or their policy implications does not refute them. Restricting coverage for experimental drugs to only those who are willing to participate in random clinical trials, for example, may be the best policy even if a majority of citizens reject it.

But the principles and policies recommended by deliberative theorists are still hypotheses because they may be refuted or refined by showing that there are better arguments for competing principles or conclusions in the same context. And they are hypotheses about political morality – not morality in general – because their confirmation, refutation, or revision calls for public deliberation in the democratic process. Whether a normative hypothesis is confirmed, refuted, or refined, this kind of criticism can succeed only by subjecting rival arguments to the rigors of actual deliberation. Deliberative theorists should of course take into account the imperfections from which any such process suffers in practice. But so should they take account of the imperfections in their own process of reasoning, less obvious though these imperfections may be (to them if not to other theorists).

The problem of the conflict between moral and political judgment is misconceived if it is understood as requiring a choice in general or in advance between substantive and procedural principles. Both kinds of principles are subject to deliberation and are equally provisional in the way we have described. The choice between substantive and procedural principles – when they conflict – is similarly subject to deliberation and should accordingly be regarded as provisional. Neither substantive nor procedural principles have priority even though citizens sometimes justifiably choose one over the other at some particular time.

In the debate about NICE in the Commons, both the critics and the defenders appealed to both substantive and procedural principles. They addressed the justice of the decision (does it violate equal opportunity by hurting poor people?), and the process (does it insulate the Government from demands to increase expenditures for health care?). Even while agreeing that the process was better than in the past, some critics challenged the substance of the decision. And even while agreeing that the substance of the decision was correct, some critics questioned the process. Some criticized and some defended both substance and process. But no one tried to argue that as a general rule one had priority over the other, or that the disagreement should be resolved by deciding once and for all whether substantive or procedural principles should prevail. In this respect the debate in the Commons illustrated the nature of public deliberation in many of the best democratic forums. The debate also captured the moral complexity of democratic politics far better than do theories that seek to resolve the conflict of substance and procedure by excluding one or the other, or declaring one rather than the other trump.

Deliberative democratic theory can and should go beyond process. It can consistently incorporate both substantive and procedural principles. It should go beyond process for many reasons that we have suggested, but above all because its core principle – reciprocity – requires substantive as well as procedural principles. Reciprocity is widely accepted as a core principle of democracy, but even those democrats who do not emphasize this principle argue from ideals such as free and equal personhood, mutual respect or avoidance of majority tyranny, which like reciprocity require both substantive and procedural principles to justify the laws that democracies adopt.

Deliberative democratic theory is better prepared to deal with the range of moral and political challenges of a robust democratic politics if it includes both substantive and procedural principles. It is well equipped to cope with the conflict between substantive and procedural principles because its principles are to varying degrees morally and politically provisional. Deliberative democratic theory can avoid usurping the moral or political authority of democratic citizens – and yet still make substantive judgments about the laws they enact – because it claims neither more, nor less, than provisional status for the principles it defends.

Notes

1   As Jürgen Habermas writes: "all contents, no matter how fundamental the action norm involved may be, must be made to depend on real discourses (or advocatory discourses conducted as substitutes for them)." ["Discourse Ethics," in *Moral Consciousness and Communicative Action*, trans. Christian Lenhardt and Shierry Weber Nicholsen (Cambridge: MIT Press, 1993), p. 94]. For comments and other citations, see our discussion in Amy Gutmann and Dennis Thompson, *Democracy and Disagreement* (Harvard University Press, 1996), pp. 17–18. Other theorists who would also be more inclined to limit deliberative democracy to process considerations and are therefore critical of including substantive principles in its theory include: Jack Knight, "Constitutionalism and Deliberative Democracy," *Deliberative Politics* , ed. Stephen Macedo (Oxford University Press, 1999), pp. 159–69; Cass Sunstein, "Agreement without Theory," in Macedo, pp. 147–8; and Iris Marion Young, "Justice, Inclusion, and Deliberative Democracy," in Macedo, pp. 151–8. For our reply, see Gutmann and Thompson, "Democratic Disagreement," in Macedo, pp. 261–8.

2   See statements by NICE's newly appointed director Michael Rawlins: Richard Horton, "NICE: A step forward in the quality of NHS care," *The Lancet* (March 27, 1999), vol. 353, pp. 1028–9: and Gavin Yamey, "Chairman of NICE admits that its judgments are hard to defend," *British Medical Journal* (November 6, 1999), vol. 319, p. 1222.

3   See "NICE Appraisal of Zanamivir (Relenza)" posted at www.nice.org.uk. For some of the reaction, see Stephen D. Moore, "U.K. Rebuffs Glaxo on New Flu Drug," *Wall Street Journal* (Oct. 11, 1999), p. A19.

4   Stuart Hampshire, *Innocence and Experience* (Cambridge, MA: Harvard University Press, 1989), p. 112.

5   Ibid., p. 112.

6   See "NICE Appraisal of Zanamivir (Relenza)" posted at www.nice.org.uk. For some of the reaction, see Stephen D. Moore, "U.K. Rebuffs Glaxo on New Flu Drug," *Wall Street Journal* (October 11, 1999), p. A19. The Food and Drug Administration approved Relenza for use in the US despite a 13 to 4 vote of an outside panel of experts recommending against approval. Some critics believe that the drug has been over-prescribed during the current flu season. See Sheryl Gay Stolberg, "F.D.A. Warns of Overuse of 2 New Drugs against Flu," *New York Times* (Jan. 13, 2000), p. A18.

7   See House of Commons Debate, Nov. 10, 1999.

8   House of Commons Debate, November 10, 1999. Also see Jo Lenaghan, "The rationing debate: Central government should have a greater role in rationing decisions," *British Medical Journal* (March 29, 1997), vol. 314, pp. 967–1.

9 Gutmann and Thompson, pp. 199–229.

10 Not so welcome are other critics – those who reject the aim of giving substantive content to the claims of reciprocity or who reject the very standard of reciprocity. But neither are their claims cogent. Having rejected the idea of mutual justification, they are hard-pressed to explain how they can justify at all imposing coercive laws and policies on citizens who morally disagree with them. See section 3 below, and Gutmann and Thompson, pp. 352–3.

11 The discussion here of moral and political provisionality draws on our analysis in "Why Deliberative Democracy Is Different," *Democracy*, ed. Ellen Frankel Paul et al. (Cambridge: Cambridge University Press, 2000), pp. 161–80.

12 The range is determined by what we call "deliberative disagreements," which are those in which citizens continue to differ about basic moral principles even though they seek a resolution that is mutually justifiable. The dispute over abortion is an example of a deliberative disagreement because both sides can justify their views within a reciprocal perspective. A dispute about racial segregation is an example of a nondeliberative disagreement because one side can be reasonably rejected within a reciprocal perspective. See Gutmann and Thompson, pp. 2–3, 73-9.

13 E. Rous et al., "A purchase experience of managing new expensive drugs: interferon beta," *British Medical Journal* (Nov. 9, 1996), vol. 313, pp. 1195–6.

14 Gutmann and Thompson, pp. 57–8.

15 Gutmann and Thompson, p. 353.

16 House of Commons Debate, Nov. 10, 1999.

17 Frederick Schauer, "Talking as a Decision Procedure," in Macedo, pp. 17–27.

3

Democratic Deliberation Within

Robert E. Goodin

The focus of deliberative democrats is ordinarily on deliberation in its "external-collective" aspect.[1] That is perfectly understandable. After all, democracy is quintessentially a manner of collective decision-making, in which everyone participates on an equal footing. Deliberation cannot dispense with "the other" without compromising its democratic credentials.

Nevertheless, deliberation also has a familiar "internal-reflective" aspect to it.[2] Deliberation consists in the weighing of reasons for and against a course of action. In that sense, it can and ultimately must take place within the head of each individual. True, the sort of give-and-take involved in that process is fundamentally argumentative, and hence discursive;[3] so perhaps deliberation, even in this internal-reflective mode, is invariably modeled upon, and thus parasitic upon, our interpersonal experiences of discussion and debate. Still, it remains significant how very much of the work of deliberation, even in external-collective settings, must inevitably be done within each individual's head – or so I shall here be arguing.

In their practical political proposals, deliberative democrats naturally concentrate upon ways of democratizing external-collective deliberation. Deliberative democrats seek outcomes which will be regarded as democratically binding and which will thereafter form the basis of (at least partially) "collective intentions."[4] They suppose that outcomes will be democratically legitimate only so far as they emerge through external-collective processes of deliberation involving a free and equal exchange among everyone who will be affected by them.[5]

That ideal seems eminently feasible in small-scale societies where face-to-face interactions are the norm.[6] In large-scale mass societies, they are not and cannot be. Dahl's back-of-the-envelope calculation constitutes a telling *reductio ad absurdum*: "if an association were to make one decision a day, allow ten hours a day for discussion, and permit each member just ten minutes – rather extreme assumptions – then the association could not have more than sixty members."[7] Added to the constraints of time and numbers are the "problems of distance" and the complications arising from the distinctive perspectives associated with

distant others who must be represented in any genuinely democratic deliberation across an extended polity.[8] The challenge facing deliberative democrats is
thus to find some way of adapting their deliberative ideals to any remotely large-
scale society, where it is simply infeasible to arrange face-to-face discussions
across the entire community.[9]

Solutions to that problem are not easily found. After briefly surveying various
flawed attempts to rescue external-collective forms of deliberative democracy
from the problems of time, numbers and distance, I offer a counterproposal. My
suggestion is that we ease the burdens of deliberative democracy in mass society
by altering our focus from the "external-collective" to the "internal-reflective"
mode, shifting much of the work of democratic deliberation back inside the
head of each individual. In defense of that proposal, I recall that such internal
mental processes play a very major role even in ordinary conversational settings.
It is a small step from there to suggesting that empathetic imagining can be an
important supplement to, and at the margins can occasionally substitute for,
interpersonal conversation in the sorts of deliberations which democrats desire
across mass societies.

Deliberation, on this account, is less a matter of making people "conversationally present" and more a matter of making them "imaginatively present" in
the minds of deliberators.[10] This revised understanding of deliberation has the
effect of prioritizing what might otherwise seem peripheral to modern democratic theory. No doubt democrats always regard it as a presumptively good
thing to democratize all corners of society, the arts along with everything else.
But seeing empathetic imaginings as central to the deliberative processes of mass
democracies sensitizes us to conditions surrounding the production and distribution of crucial aids to those imaginings, conspicuously among them the literary, visual and performing arts. Ensuring the broad representativeness and
generalized uptake of those representations is, on the model of democratic deliberation propounded here, of capital importance.

Internal-reflective modes of deliberation can never literally replace external-
collective ones. For one thing, in practice the two modes are inextricably inter-
twined. Making others imaginatively present is essential to understanding what
they are saying to us; so too can making them conversationally present constitute a powerful impetus for making them imaginatively present, as well. Politically, a deliberation conducted entirely within people's imaginations, however
expansive it may be, would still lack the sort of ratification by others required for
it to count as fully democratic. Conversely, a procedure in which people fail to
internalize the perspective of one another qualifies as democratic only in the
most mechanical of ways: without properly registering what each other is saying, it will be not an exchange of reasons but merely a count of votes.

Thus, internal-reflective deliberation is an important supplement and com-
plement to external-collective deliberation in the political realm. To be prop-

erly democratic, its results must at some point or another be validated through procedures of the external-collective sort. Still, appreciating the proper role that internal-reflective deliberation may and indeed must play in deliberation can help to relieve many of the burdens plaguing external-collective deliberation in modern mass societies.

I. Unsuccessful Adaptations

Previous solutions to the problems posed by large-scale mass society for deliberative democracy rely upon one or another of four basic strategies. One pair works by limiting the *number of people* with whom you have to deliberate, a second pair by limiting the *level of inputs from others* with which you have to deal. Both seem likely to fail, for one reason or another.

A. Seriality: disjointed deliberation

If we are too numerous to deliberate together all at the same time, then one solution is Aristotle's suggestion that we "deliberate, not all in one body, but by turns."[11] Here is one way. Break us down into groups sufficiently small to allow genuine deliberation within each of them; and then let the upshots of those deliberations serve as inputs to subsequent deliberations among other groups, similarly constituted. Let us call this a model of "serial" or "disjointed deliberation."

That is how the "common law" has supposedly been discovered by English juries since the twelfth century.[12] A variation on that model appeals to certain sorts of post-modernists, whose preferred solution to the increasingly fractured social world is a "directly-deliberative polyarchy" involving "a plurality of modes of association."[13]

The trick with this general approach lies, of course, in somehow articulating all those separately deliberating bodies' judgments with one another. Many ways of doing so are not particularly democratic. The deliberations of local English assizes were rendered into a unified common law across the realm by having the same small set of judges (25 in all) travel up and down the country presiding over all proceedings. Sir Matthew Hale was pleased to report that

> those men who are employed as justices . . . have had a common education in the study of law. . . . [I]n term-time . . . they daily converse and consult with one another; acquaint one another with their judgements, sit near one another in Westminster Hall, whereby their judgements are necessarily communicated to one another.... [B]y this means their judgements and their administrations of common justice carry a constancy, congruity and uniformity one to another. . . .[14]

Deliberative democrats are unlikely to share Hale's enthusiasm. From their perspective, whatever directly deliberative gains were secured by introducing juries in the first place would be largely nullified by entrusting to such a small and closed elite the task of blending all those lower-level deliberations into a single nationwide common law.

The upper English judiciary constitutes only the most dramatic instance of a problem plaguing models of disjointed deliberation quite generally. Most of them seem to aggregate the inputs of highly democratic groups at the ground level through a hierarchy whose own directly-democratic deliberative credentials are substantially less secure. Habermas, for example, proposes that the "oppositional public sphere" serve as the source of deliberatively-democratic inputs which are then fed into, and coordinated through, the ordinary political sphere – which Habermas himself, of course, regards as itself being very far indeed from directly deliberatively democratic.[15] Or for another example, consider Cohen and Sabel's proposal for the outputs of "directly deliberatively democratic polyarchies" at the local level to be fed into a "peak-level" meta-deliberation among all those groups: once again, however equal the groups might be within that meta-deliberation, the incorporation of that extra layer of deliberation itself makes that scheme less "directly deliberative," and hence less democratic in that sense.[16] Much the same might be said about the various other mediating institutions – ranging from political parties to legislative subcommittees to high courts – which have from time to time been proposed as key agents in the deliberative process.[17]

I can see only one way in which the inputs of a plurality of groups could be blended together in a fashion that genuinely would be both directly and deliberatively democratic. Suppose each of us is a member of many different "groups." (Nothing hangs on the nature of those groups: they might, as with juries, be nothing more than random sortitions of the population.) Suppose furthermore that each of us overlaps any given other in only a small fraction of our group memberships.[18] Then there might be a "web of group affiliations" which links (indirectly: perhaps very indirectly) everyone with everyone else in a dialogue which effectively straddles the entire community.[19] Thus, for example, if each of us were a member of just 5 groups containing 20 others each, and none of us overlapped any other more than once, then our judgments would on these assumptions be merged directly or indirectly with those of 20^5 or 3,200,000 others.

That way of linking all the groups could, in principle, be both deliberatively and directly democratic. In practice, however, the crucial presuppositions underlying that model are unlikely to be met. Whereas the model of overlapping group affiliations presupposes that everyone is a member of some (indeed, several) groups, each of which approximates the deliberative ideal, in the real world altogether too many people are "socially excluded," participating in no such groups at all. Others are "socially segregated," participating in only the same small sets of deliberative groups with the same other people, over and over again. Insofar as either is the case, there will be no "serial deliberation" indirectly linking all members of the community.

B. Substitution: ersatz deliberation

The first strategy of "disjointed deliberation" substituted deliberation within partial, overlapping groups for deliberation across the entire community. A second strategy, which I dub "ersatz deliberation," instead substitutes deliberation within a *subset* of the community for deliberation across the *whole* of the community.[20]

How the subset is identified and how the substitution is justified are interconnected issues. The subset is supposed to be representative – typical, "a fair sample," "a microcosm"[21] – of the larger set. Substituting its judgment for that of the larger is justified, in turn, on the grounds that the considered views reached through deliberation within that smaller group will be representative (an accurate reflection) of the views that would have been reached had similar processes been feasible within the larger group.[22]

The clearest example of this sort of "ersatz deliberation" – the substitution of deliberation within a smaller group for that within an unwieldily large one – is of course representative democracy.[23] Legislatures are regularly styled as "deliberative assemblies," in contrast to "popular" ones (and even within the legislature, the less numerous house is standardly styled the "deliberative" chamber[24]). But recent innovations like "citizens' juries" and "deliberative polling" are other instances of the same broad class of model.[25]

All these models of ersatz deliberation involve, at root, substituting a subset for the whole and letting the subset deliberate on behalf of the whole. The generic problem with all of those schemes lies in ensuring the *continuing* representativeness of the subset, once the deliberation gets underway. Naturally, people change their minds over the course of the deliberation (it would hardly be a genuine deliberation at all if they did not, at least sometimes[26]). The question is whether people who started out being representative of the wider community, in all the ways we can measure, are also representative of that wider community in the ways in which they *change* over the course of the deliberation.

On the face of it, that seems unlikely. From everyday life we know that different conversations with different participants (or with the same participants interjecting at different points) proceed in radically different directions.[27] Given the path dependency of conversational dynamics, and the sheer creativity of conversing agents, it beggars belief that any one group would come to exactly the same conclusions by exactly the same route as any other.[28] (Lawyers say it is a "well-known secret" that "no two juries and no two judges are alike."[29]) Yet that is what strong advocates of ersatz deliberation must be claiming to be at least approximately true, in insisting that deliberations within a representative subset will genuinely mirror, and can therefore substitute for, deliberations across the whole community.[30]

C. Restricting inputs: emaciated deliberation

Whereas the first pair of strategies cope with the problem of mass society by reducing the *number of people* deliberating together, the second pair of strategies cope with the problem by reducing *how much they communicate* to one another. The first variation on this model is one of "emaciated deliberation," which facilitates mass deliberation by reducing the density of the signals and hence the deliberative load each participant has to bear.

Legislative assemblies, for one familiar example, streamline their proceedings by imposing limits on the length or number of speeches.[31] One effect (among others) is to limit how much speakers can say, and hence to restrict how much input deliberators have to take into account. Rules of "germaneness," of course, serve even more directly to filter the quantity (as well, obviously, as the quality) of inputs into legislative deliberations.[32]

Another version of this same basic strategy is "mediated deliberation," where some intermediary filters what messages get passed along to others within the larger community. In international negotiations, intermediaries facilitate agreement by restricting the messages passed among parties to the negotiation.[33] In modern mass society, much the same sort of "mediated deliberation" occurs through the agency of the mass media, which strictly limits how much information anyone can impart to (or impose upon) everyone else.[34]

Facilitating mass deliberations by "restricting inputs" into them poses some obvious problems, however. Unless we have some reason for supposing that we are screening out only inputs which are irrelevant or superfluous,[35] restricting inputs leaves us deliberating more or less in ignorance. Our cognitive capacities, which rely upon informational inputs, are more or less undernourished. (Hence the term "emaciated deliberation.") In the limiting case of a "democracy of soundbites," we are deliberating on the basis of so little as to make it hardly a case of deliberation – of seriously reflective "weighing and judging reasons" – at all.

D. Selective uptake: blinkered deliberation

Participants in Habermas' "public sphere" are ideally supposed to "engage" with one another.[36] Maybe they actually did in the coffee-houses of eighteenth-century London.[37] Most of the institutions of the contemporary public sphere, however, are more like Habermas' other great paragon of the early public sphere, the broadsheet newspaper. "When Addison and Steele published the first issue of *The Tatler* in 1709," Habermas tells us, "the coffee-houses were already so numerous and the circles of their frequenters already so wide that contact among these thousandfold circles could only be maintained through a journal."[38] At that point, participants in the public sphere were no longer engaging directly with one another at all.

The problem is not merely that their interactions were mediated through the broadsheet, with the consequent problems as already sketched. There is a further problem. Contributors to broadsheets – and, come to that, people holding forth in coffee-houses as well – are not so much "talking to one another" as they are "posting notices for all to read." Others might (or might not) take note of them, and reply. Insofar as they reply in like fashion, they too are essentially just posting other notices for all to note (or not), in turn.

What we find in the public sphere, in short, is not so much "public deliberation" as "deliberation *in public*." Beijing's "Wall of Democracy" provided democracy of a sort. And democracy of that sort – the free broadcasting of opinions – might be one important precondition of any genuinely deliberative democracy. But merely posting notices on billboards or the internet, or shouting out opinions from a soapbox in Hyde Park, does not in and of itself constitute communication, much less full-blown deliberative democracy.[39]

There must also be uptake and engagement – other people must hear or read, internalise and respond – for that public-sphere activity to count as remotely deliberative.[40] Furthermore, for that public sphere to count as particularly democratic, it must be the case that most people are actively engaged in this sort of give-and-take with most other people.

Theorists of the public sphere, in short, solve the problem of how to deliberate democratically in mass societies by compromising the conditions that make the processes deliberative. In guaranteeing the free and equal expression of opinions in the public sphere, they guarantee everyone a voice but no one a hearing.

II. Another Approach: Deliberation Within

All of those previous proposals for making deliberative democracy work in the context of mass society focus on the "external-collective" side of deliberation. They all suppose that the key to making democracy deliberative is making everyone "communicatively present," in some sense or another. But in any large society, it is impossible to do that literally, and none of the substitutes suggested so far seems very satisfactory. My proposal is to try to make the "internal-reflective" aspect of deliberation do more of the work for us.

A. Understanding one another

Begin by recalling how very much of what goes on in a genuine face-to-face conversation is actually contained inside the head of each of the participants, anyway. Language itself must be public rather than private, to be sure. But the point remains that most of the work in interpreting the utterances of others – decoding the literal meaning, and enriching that literal meaning pragmatically in light of contextual information – is actually done within the hearer's own head.

When trying to understand what others are saying, we start by assuming that they are trying to talk sense. We assume, at least as a first approximation, that they mean by their utterances roughly what we ourselves would have meant by them.[41] We are prepared to treat provisionally as true, for the purposes of any given conversation, that set of propositions which seem to constitute the most coherent way of construing the background assumptions underlying the assertions our interlocutor is making.[42]

In ordinary conversation, people do not tediously elaborate complete syllogisms. (Nobody listens, if they do.) Instead, people characteristically talk more or less "loosely."[43] They make more-or-less cryptic allusions to more full-blown arguments. "Catching the other's drift" in ordinary conversation is substantially a matter of completing the other's syllogism in your own mind, working out the various "implicatures" contained within the other's utterances.[44]

How exactly we make sense of "other minds" is a large and philosophically contentious issue.[45] But whatever more particular story we tell, the general idea is invariably that we make sense of others, their utterances and their actions, by mentally "putting ourselves in the other's place" in some sense or another. "Simulation theorists" envisage us "understanding other minds from the inside" in a lightly theorized way.[46] "Theory theorists," as the name implies, envisage us doing so in a much more theoretically laden manner, through a "folk psychology" perhaps.[47] Either way, much of the work involved in making sense of what others are saying in ordinary discourse necessarily goes on in the hearer's own head.

B. Discourse and imagination

Discourse theorists know perfectly well that this is how ordinary conversation proceeds. Indeed, they make much of the fact. Habermas, for the most famous example, describes discourse ethics as "rest[ing] on . . . a joint process of 'ideal role taking'" in which "everyone is required to take the perspective of everyone else, and thus project herself into the understandings of self and world of all others."[48] That is how he hopes to secure the sort of "intersubjectivity" that is so central to his larger project.

It is precisely that process of imagining yourself into the place of the other which discourse theorists hope that interpersonal discourse will set in motion. But note well: The process which discourse theorists valorize is this "internal-reflective" one. The "external-collective" process of discourse and debate is, even for discourse theorists, merely a means of setting this other more "internal-reflective" process in motion.[49]

Having to answer to another in person might well be one good way of getting that process going. But it is hardly the only. Sometimes "answering to oneself" might sometimes suffice, instead. Suppose our imagination has been fired by some film or fiction; we have been led by those artifices to imagine vividly what it would be like to be *them,* or to be in *that* situation; we ask ourselves, "What would we say, *then?*"

C. Firing the imagination

The precise mechanisms by which that works is the subject of much debate in literary theory and art criticism.[50] The fact that some such process does seem to be at work seems incontrovertible enough, though, judging simply from our own everyday experience as readers, viewers and listeners.[51]

One particularly striking example is the way in which "slave narratives" – autobiographical accounts by freed slaves, vividly evoking their experiences in bondage – served the abolitionist cause.[52] Perhaps there are only a very few fictions which could literally be said to have changed the course of history, *Uncle Tom's Cabin* being one and *Passage to India* perhaps another.[53] But some such "expanding of people's sensibilities" occurs in all good writing.[54] Literary theorists regard it as something of a commonplace that "historical and social events as mirrored in the plots of Stendhal, Dickens or Tolstoy had a realness, an authenticity deeper than that conveyed by the journalist or professional historian. . . . The art of Balzac is a *summa mundi,* an inventory of contemporaneous life. A man can learn half a dozen professions by reading Zola."[55] And so on.

It is not just that fiction (and art more generally) might, and often does, contain allusions to social, economic, political and historical facts, and in that way might serve certain didactic purposes. The larger point is that those lessons come packed with more emotional punch and engage our imagination in more effective ways than do historical narratives or reflective essays of a less stylized sort. "Artists," John Dewey says, "have always been the real purveyors of news, for it is not the outward happening in itself which is new, but the kindling by it of emotion, perception and appreciation. . . . Democracy," he continues, "will have its consummation when free social inquiry is indissolubly wedded to the art of full and moving communication."[56]

That is not just to say that novelists are more evocative writers than historians or essayists (true though that may be, too). Rather, they fix their focus on the particular – one person or one action or one period – and they introduce generalities by way of anecdotes, episodes viewed from that particular perspective.[57] That vivid evocation of the particular, in turn, has important consequences for the uptake of works of art. Inevitably, we find it relatively easy to project ourselves imaginatively into the place of some specific (fictitious but grounded) other. It is necessarily harder to project ourselves imaginatively into the inevitably underdescribed sorts of amorphous and abstract others which are the stock-in-trade of historians and social scientists.[58]

That fiction "takes us out of ourselves" in this way is intrinsic rather than incidental to the enterprise:

> The very form of the novel arises from and embraces conflicts of character, values, interests, circumstances and classes. And . . . that only seems to work well, as Sartre pointed out in his *What is Literature?*, when the author . . . can empathize with and portray plausible social diversity. Where, he asked, is there a great totalitarian novel? That was not just a contradiction in terms but a psychological impossibility.[59]

George Steiner no doubt exaggerates when talking about how "a major work of fiction or philosophy, of imagination or doctrine . . . may come to possess us so completely that we go, for a spell, in fear of ourselves. . . ."[60] Discount such rhetorical excesses as you will, the fact nonetheless remains that the "unique value of fiction" lies in its "relatively cost-free offer of trial runs. . . . In a month of reading, I can try out more 'lives' than I can test in a lifetime."[61]

Poets from Wordsworth to Eliot have harbored some such ambitions, aspiring to produce work that "enlarges our consciousness or refines our sensibility."[62] Some such role has been played, from time to time, by social realist art, by photojournalism and by radio plays. Nowadays it is played most commonly by what one critic dubs "the imagination of the new media of direct knowledge and graphic reproduction": television, film and video.[63]

D. Imaginary deliberations and the deliberative imagination

My proposal is simply that we make use of those familiar phenomena to enhance democratic deliberations in large-scale societies. No doubt there is much more we can do to make everyone else "communicatively present," even in such settings. Ultimately, however, there are strict limits to the extent to which everyone really can be communicatively present all at once in large-scale mass societies.

Rather than merely bemoaning that fact, let us instead try harder to make everyone else "imaginatively present" in the minds of each of the deliberators. Private fictions, I submit, can serve important public functions. Through the exercise of a suitably informed imagination, each of us might be able to conduct a wide-ranging debate within our own heads among all the contending perspectives.

Such internal dialogues can never wholly substitute for public ones. However well informed our imaginings, we will always need to crosscheck the views we attribute to others against those views they actually profess themselves holding. However astute our imaginings and extensive our internal dialogues, at some point or another we must let others speak, and vote, for themselves if our deliberations are to carry any genuinely democratic warrant.

Still, where society is not small enough to allow genuine conversational exchanges among all the relevant public, internal-reflective dialogues can be a useful aid in helping to inform external-collective ones. Certainly they seem at least as helpful as the other suggestions offered by deliberative democrats for overcoming the constraints of time, numbers and distance in large-scale society.

Furthermore, precisely because they do not require people to speak for themselves, internal-reflective deliberations might hope to secure better representation of the communicatively inept or the communicatively inert than external-collective deliberations ever could. Consider as a limiting case future generations.[64] Our actions and choices today clearly affect them, and according to ordinary democratic canons everyone affected ought have a say in our deliberations. But the unborn, by nature, cannot speak for themselves; and others who purport to speak for them will inevitably be asked by what authority they do so. Internal-reflective deliberations encounter no such problems. They do not need future people to be physically present in order for them to be imaginatively present; and since the whole process proceeds by everyone imagining themselves into the place of others, no special warrant is required for each of us to imagine ourselves into the place of people in the future.

III. Dangers of Internal Deliberation

Internal-reflective deliberations suffer many obvious drawbacks compared to external-collective ones. One is the obvious absence of an insistent "other" who is pressing her perspective upon you.[65] Some people and their perspectives might be ignored altogether; others might end up being more or less parodied because the too-pat representations of them we have inside our heads pass unchallenged. People whose situations are prototypical and familiar may be represented tolerably well in our internal deliberations; those whose situations are peculiar in some way often will not.[66] And so on.

All of that is true enough. That is why external-collective deliberation is superior to purely internal-reflective deliberation, where society is sufficiently small to make external-collective deliberation genuinely possible. But where societies are of a size such that genuinely democratic collective deliberations are not possible, anyway, we are operating in a world of "second-best." The alternative strategies for making external-collective decision procedures more directly deliberatively democratic all suffer from various drawbacks as well. My hope is merely that, by supplementing external-collective deliberations with internal-reflective ones, some of the errors and omissions inevitable in each mode might compensate for and cancel out one another.

A. Attending to the other

Consider the many ways in which internal-reflective deliberations seem necessarily inferior to ideal-case external-collective ones. We might, for example, be worried over "who is included" in the deliberations. In external-collective settings, deliberative democrats are at pains to ensure that everyone who will be affected is a party to the deliberations. With internal-reflective deliberations, in contrast, each deliberator inevitably populates her own imaginary internal universe as she will.

Of course we might exhort her to be as inclusive as she can, to try very hard to engage imaginatively with as many different sorts of people as might genuinely be affected by the decision. We might even send her a pile of books or photos or videos, as an aid to that process. But there seems little that we can do from the outside to *make* the full range of others present to her mind's eye, in the way we might hope to make all appropriate others physically present in external-collective deliberations of the more ordinary sort.

Remember, however, the context of my present argument. I have suggested we turn to internal-reflective deliberation precisely because (or, rather, insofar as) the group of people affected is too large literally to make them all physically present and still have a meaningful deliberation. Thus, what we should be comparing is, on the one hand, the representativeness of the population which we would conjure up in our mind's eye with, on the other hand, the (effective) representativeness of the second-best methods of external-collective deliberation surveyed above.

No doubt our imagination will always be imperfect, and some people will be left out of deliberations based on internal-reflective processes alone. By the same token, however, those other second-best methods of external-collective deliberation are imperfect too; and some people or positions will always be unrepresented or inadequately represented in them as well. All these second-best mechanisms run analogous risks in that respect. We can only hope that the voices omitted by the one can be captured by the other when we use internal-deliberative processes to supplement external-collective ones in these settings.

Even where others are physically present in external-collective deliberations, of course, that does not necessarily mean that we will be genuinely responsive to them and their concerns. We can always shrug our shoulders or walk away.[67]

We can always turn a blind eye or deaf ear.[68] Input is no assurance of uptake. Indeed, recalling how heavily ordinary conversation depends on internal representations, one might even say that "internal presence" is just as much a precondition of effective representation in external-collective deliberations as it is in internal-reflective ones.

B. Understanding the other

In real conversations between real people, there is a constant crosschecking and renegotiation of meanings.[69] That facilitates interlocutors' understanding of one another. People who are merely overhearing a conversation sometimes find it hard to understand what is going on, precisely because they cannot interject into the conversation to cross-check their own understandings of what others mean to be saying.[70]

In real conversations, a code of dyadically-shared meanings emerges. That simply cannot happen in imaginary conversations with imagined people of the sort that occur in the "internal-reflective" deliberative mode. There, we are essentially having a conversation with ourselves. If we are sufficiently imaginative, we might envisage our "imaginary other" correcting us in ways akin to those in which actual others might. But inevitably that is a pale shadow of the vigorous sort of cross-checking and cross-fertilization which occurs in any actual conversation. No single individual's imagination, however rich, will be able to mimic what occurs in the perfectly ordinary course of events in conversations among real people with genuinely different perspectives.

Much the same is true of mass deliberations as well, though. In dyadic conversations, each speaker can sensitize the other to her own particular perspective, one-on-one. In mass deliberations, what typically happens is that some speak and many listen. Hopefully those who speak are broadly typical of many others who do not.[71] But in any moderately large group there can be no realistic hope of each person individually negotiating meanings with each particular other, anyway.

Thus, while "internal-reflective" deliberations may look seriously deficient in the sorts of shared understandings they nurture when compared with conversational dynamics in dyads or small groups, once again that is not the relevant comparison. The proposal here is to let internal-reflective deliberations inform and supplement external-collective ones in large groups. In settlings of that sort, discursive dynamics are very different from conversational dyads anyway. There, the sorts of intensely negotiated meanings which we find emerging in conversational dyads will be largely missing. There, external representations risk being just as stylized, just as oriented toward the prototypical, as are the representations which figure in people's internal imaginary reconstructions of social life.[72] Once again, we can only hope that by allowing internal-reflective mechanisms to supplement external-collective ones, their respective errors and omissions might compensate and correct for one another's.

C. Representing the other

As if in direct reply to my proposal to let internal deliberation do much of the work of external, reading doing much of the work of talking, Montaigne protests:

> Studying books has a languid feeble motion, whereas conversation provides teaching and exercise all at once. If I am sparring with a strong and solid opponent he will attack me on the flanks, stick his lance in me right and left; his ideas send mine soaring. Rivalry, competitiveness and glory will drive me and raise me above my own level.[73]

Certainly we can sympathize with that sentiment. Playing chess against yourself is far less satisfactory than playing against someone else (or even a good computer). Everything is too pat, too devoid of surprise. That seems as true of cooperative games like conversation as of competitive games like chess. No one can imagine someone else's interests, position and perspective as richly as that person herself experiences them. There is therefore a compelling case, pragmatically as well as symbolically, for the "politics of presence": for all different sorts of people being physically present during deliberations that affect their interests, rather than just having their interests "represented" by others.[74]

Once again, however, that ideal seems to be compromised by the realities of large-scale societies. The circumstances here in view – the circumstances under which I envisage external-collective deliberation being importantly supplemented by internal-reflective – are circumstances in which there are too many different people involved for all of them to be effectively present in deliberations.

At best, we might (through what I have called "ersatz deliberation") substitute one or a few members of the group for all other members of that group.[75] Such a substitution might be satisfactory if the groups were so homogeneous that a few members really were representative of the group as a whole. (In the limiting case if each were a literally identical token of the type, utterly interchangeable with every other, then a single representative from each group would suffice.) Most theorists of group difference would baulk at the sort of "essentialism" implied by that, however.[76] They shun the "generalized" in favor of the "concrete other."[77] And one implication of that is that no small set of representatives can truly stand in for groups as a whole, as the politics of presence would require.

How much this will impinge on external-collective deliberative processes depends in part on how many different groups there are to be represented and in part on how many individuals it takes to represent tolerably well each of those groups in its full complexity. But in any large-scale society, we can probably assume moderately high levels both of inter-group pluralism and of intra-group heterogeneity. And that multiplicity would be compounded yet again if geographical situatedness itself proves to be an important dimension of identity and difference, as theorists of the "politics of place" contend.[78]

The upshot would seem to be, once again, that in any large-scale society external-collective deliberations are necessarily very far from ideal. That deliberation cannot effectively give every distinct voice a hearing: second-best short cuts of one sort or another will inevitably be required; and something will inevitably be lost in the process. Something would also inevitably be lost in trying to replicate some such conversation within one's own mind, in internal-reflective mode. But once again, hopefully the omissions and errors of the one might cancel and correct those of the other, when we supplement external-collective deliberations with internal-reflective ones.[79]

D. Finding time for the other

Finally it might be argued that, in any large-scale mass society, internal-reflective deliberative processes would fall prey to the same pressures on time and attention as do external-collective deliberative processes. In the latter case, the problem is that we lack the time to *have* the requisite conversations with all others. In the former case, it might be said, there is a perfectly parallel problem: we lack the time to *imagine* those conversations, either.

Certainly it is true that "attention" is a strictly limited resource, imposing severe constraints on our deliberative capacities.[80] But those constraints have greater impact on external-collective methods of deliberation. The mechanism by which we attend to others in that way is through oral or written communications, and we can listen to only one speaker or read only one thing at a time. That makes the external-collective deliberative process a more radically serial process than is internal-reflective deliberation.

Suppose we manage successfully to "internalize" the perspectives of various others, through having imaginatively projected ourselves into their position on some previous occasion. Then perhaps we might even be able to "see" the situation from those many different perspectives at once without any conscious effort. If those other perspectives have been internalized in some strong way, applying them is "second nature" to us. No deliberate act of will is required to evoke them; no deliberate focusing of our attention on them is involved. "Seeing" things from all those other perspectives might then be more like the "parallel" processes which Simon describes governing the eyes and the ears than it is like the "serial" process of consciously directing attention first here and next there.

Again, there is no guarantee that people will "internalize" any (much less all) other relevant perspectives in this strong way.[81] The point is merely that they might. If they do, that would significantly ease the cognitive constraints involved in attending to many others, once again making internal-reflective deliberation an invaluable supplement to external-collective modes.

IV. Informing the Democratic Imagination

Important practical consequences follow from recognizing all these ways in which internal, imaginary discourses can serve as important aids to democratic deliberation. Concerns which might otherwise seem peripheral to our democratic theory – concerns to do with the production and consumption of the representations and images upon which our imaginings work – suddenly become central.

On the one side are familiar questions about access to means of modern mass communication. On the other side are equally familiar questions about "for whom does one write?"[82] Who is the audience, the reference group? Who are the subjects, and how are they represented?[83]

Those are not just arcane disputes within cultural studies. Instead, they are absolutely crucial issues for democracy as it is inevitably practiced in modern large-scale societies, where (as I have been arguing) representations inside the head can count for almost as much as representation within the legislative chamber. The art forms out of which we construct those representations are potentially as potent, politically, as are the elections out of which we construct legislative majorities.

Some of the public policy implications of that insight are rather banal. Of course democracy naturally requires well-stocked public libraries and public funding of the arts.[84] Art and literature are at least partly public goods which would be undersupplied by ordinary market forces; we ought therefore subsidize creativity, insofar as we can.[85] Turning from the production to the consumption side of the cultural equation, of course we ought to "take art to the people" rather than locking it away. Precisely because "artistic creations shape political conceptions," it is important that public museums ought to function as "forums, not temples."[86] All of that is obviously important in generating and disseminating the sorts of representations which will serve as crucial aids to the sorts of internal-reflective deliberations that I am here proposing.

Equally importantly, though, we must ensure the representativeness of those representations. When supplementing external-collective deliberations with internal-reflective ones, we are in effect enfranchising images. If we want that process to serve democratic ends, we obviously need to ensure that the images thus enfranchised are as extensive as required really to represent the diversity of experiences extant across the communities to be affected by those deliberations.[87]

Not all of those experiences are pretty. Not all are intellectually edifying or morally uplifting. Some will be sad or depressing or downright obnoxious. Still, all deserve a voice in the democratic cultural space, insofar as that feeds into internal-reflective deliberation – or anyway all do, to just the same extent that they deserve a literal voice in the political space of external-collective democratic deliberations. Insofar as we have good democratic grounds for censoring "hate speech," we ought to be prepared to ban its other cultural manifestations as well.[88] But from the present perspective, we have no more grounds for confining our public concern, and public subsidies, purely to more "elevated" forms of cultural expression than we do for confining our political attention purely to the expression of "elevated" opinion.

Merely producing diverse representations is not enough, though. We must also ensure that those diverse representations are widely diffused throughout the deliberative community. "Despite . . . the emphasis on artistic multiculturalism in the United States, it sometimes appears that Asian-American literature is being read by Asian-Americans, Afro-American literature by Afro-Americans, and Euro-American literature by Euro-Americans."[89] Narrow-band imaginings thereby fostered will hardly aid the cause of genuinely democratic deliberation.

That is to specify a set of desiderata for cultural policy in a deliberative democracy. How exactly those desiderata might best be met undoubtedly varies from place to place and from one period to the next. In inter-war Britain, cheap Penguins and the BBC performed broadly this function with some considerable success; and it has long been hoped that some combination of public broadcasting and public subsidies for the performing arts might have a similarly "broadening" function elsewhere around the world. Social mixing within primary and secondary schools, through "comprehensive" schools in postwar Britain and integrated schools in post-*Brown* America, were similarly championed in no small part for the "lessons in diversity" that they would impart.

How these models might be adapted to the peculiar circumstances of contemporary broadcasting and schooling, and how they might be extended beyond those realms, constitute major policy challenges. The first step in addressing those challenges, however, lies in recognizing the many and varied purposes which were supposed to be served by those older social forms and what exactly it therefore is that we are wanting to recreate in some new guise. Mechanisms for informing and extending our social imaginings are, I suggest, one of the things that we as deliberative democrats ought to be seeking in whatever new social arrangements are proposed.

V. From Democratic Deliberation to Democratic Legitimacy

Deliberation is supposed to have an *end*, it is supposed to *resolve* something.[90] Occasionally deliberation yields a decision directly, as when a genuine consensus has emerged. But deliberative assemblies even of the most ideal sort more typically have to force a decision, announcing an end to the deliberations and calling for a vote.

That final show of hands is what is crucial in conferring democratic legitimacy on the decision. However free and equal the preceding discussion may have been, the democratic credentials of the ultimate decision would be deeply suspect had it merely been left to the chairperson of the meeting to summarize the "sense of the meeting," with no ratification from others.[91] But however crucial that that distinctly non-deliberative final show of hands may be in providing *democratic legitimacy* for the decision, it is the preceding discussion which renders that decision a *democratically deliberative* one.

Thus, even in the most pristine directly-democratic deliberative assemblies, democratic legitimacy typically derives from one source and democratic deliberativeness from another. Internal-reflective and external-collective deliberative processes, I submit, stand in a similar relation to one another.

Internal-reflective deliberations are not a substitute for, but rather an input into, external-collective decision procedures. That is so, in the first instance, because internal deliberations cannot in and of themselves yield any collective determinations. Beyond that necessary analytic truth stands another deeper democratic one. Purely private acts of internal deliberation, however expansive or empathetic they may be, can never have a fully democratic warrant until they have secured public validation of one sort or another. Democratizing our internal reflections – rendering them more expansive and more empathetic – contributes to the democratic quality of the process as well, making it more democratically deliberative. But some external-collective act is eventually required to confer democratic legitimacy on any conclusions we reach.

Just as in a small assembly the requirements of deliberative democracy may be met by a free-ranging discussion of the issues culminating in a distinctly non-deliberative show of hands, so too in large-scale mass societies the requirements of deliberative democracy may be met by expansive internal-reflective deliberations culminating in a distinctly non-deliberative visit to the poll booth. And the more democratically deliberative our internal reflections manage to be, the less it will matter that external-collective decision procedures can never be as directly deliberatively democratic as we might like in large-scale mass societies.

Notes

An earlier version was read to the "Deliberating about Deliberation" conference, University of Texas Law School, February 2000. I am particularly grateful for comments then and later from Louise Antony, Josh Cohen, Martin Davies, John Dryzek, Dave Estlund, Cynthia Farrer, Jim Fishkin, Dick Flathman, Amy Gutmann, Peter Laslett, Martha Nussbaum, Philip Pettit, Cass Sunstein, Dennis Thompson, Iris Young and the Editors of *Philosophy & Public Affairs*.

1   Represented by Aristotle's "deliberative speaking" (*Rhetoric*, bk 1, chs 3–4).
2   Found in, for example, Aristotle's *Nicomachean Ethics*, bk 4 and Hobbes's *Leviathan*, ch. 6.
3   Stuart Hampshire, *Justice Is Conflict* (Princeton, NJ: Princeton University Press, 2000).
4   Amy Gutmann and Dennis Thompson, *Democracy and Disagreement* (Cambridge, MA: Harvard University Press, 1996), pp. 4–5. Henry Richardson, "Democratic intentions," *Deliberative Democracy*, ed. James Bohman and William Rehg (Cambridge, MA: MIT Press, 1997), pp. 349–82.
5   Bernard Manin, "On legitimacy and political deliberation," *Political Theory*, 15 (1987), 338–68. Joshua Cohen, "Deliberation and democratic legitimacy," *The Good Polity*, ed. Alan Hamlin and Philip Pettit (Oxford: Blackwell, 1989), pp. 17–34 at pp. 21–3 and "Procedure and substance in deliberative democracy," *Democracy and Difference*, ed. Seyla Benhabib (Princeton, NJ: Princeton University Press, 1996), pp. 95–119 at pp. 99–100. Seyla Benhabib, "Deliberative rationality and models of democratic legitimacy," *Constellations*, 1 (no. 1: April 1994), 26–52. John S. Dryzek, *Discursive Democracy* (Cambridge: Cambridge University Press, 1990) and *Deliberative Democracy and Beyond* (Oxford: Oxford University Press, 2000).
6   As in Peter Laslett, "The face to face society," *Philosophy, Politics and Society,* ed. Peter Laslett, 1st series (Oxford: Blackwell, 1956), pp. 157–84.
7   Robert A. Dahl, *After the Revolution?* (New Haven, Conn.: Yale University Press, 1970), pp. 67–8.
8   Contenting ourselves with getting all the positions on the table, as distinct from all persons to the podium, is one way of mitigating these problems. My proposals below can be seen as one way of doing that.
9   James Madison thought that "a democracy . . . must be confined to a small spot" whereas "a republic may be extended over a large region," precisely because "in a democracy the people meet and exercise government in person" whereas "in a republic they administer it by their representatives and agents" (*The Federalist* no. 14). See similarly Robert A. Dahl and Edward R. Tufte, *Size and Democracy* (Stanford, CA: Stanford University Press, 1973) and Jane J. Mansbridge, *Beyond Adversary Democracy* (New York: Basic Books), chs 19–20. Even face-to-face assemblies cease being deliberative when they become too large, with speech-making replacing conversation and rhetorical appeals replacing reasoned arguments. As Madison (or perhaps Hamilton) wrote in *The Federalist* no. 55, "In all very numerous assemblies, of whatever characters composed, passions never fail to wrest the sceptre from reason. Had every Athenian assembly been a Socrates, every Athenian assembly would still

have been a mob." Cf. Cicero, *De Officiis*, II.48 and Madison, *The Federalist* no. 62 and 63.

10   After the fashion of Benedict Anderson's *Imagined Communities* (London: Verso, 1983). See, more generally, Gilbert Ryle, "Imagination," *The Concept of Mind* (London: Hutchinson, 1949), ch. 8.

11   Aristotle, *Politics*, 1298a13.

12   Harold J. Berman, *Law and Revolution: The Formation of the Western Legal Tradition* (Cambridge, MA: Harvard University Press, 1983), pp. 448–9. Even today, juries are virtually the sole institution which "regularly calls upon ordinary citizens to engage each other in a face-to-face process of debate"; Jeffrey Abramson, *We, the Jury* (New York, Basic, 1994), p. 8.

13   Joshua Cohen and Charles Sabel, "Directly-deliberative polyarchy," *European Law Journal* 3 (no. 4: Dec 1997): 313–42. See similarly: Joshua Cohen and Joel Rogers et al., *Associations and Democracy*, ed. E. O. Wright (London: Verso, 1995); Paul Hirst, *Associative Democracy* (Oxford: Polity, 1994); Seyla Benhabib, "Deliberative rationality and models of democratic legitimacy," p. 35; and Iris Marion Young, "Communication and the other: beyond deliberative democracy," *Intersecting Voices* (Princeton, NJ: Princeton University Press, 1997), pp. 60–74.

14   Sir Matthew Hale, *The History of the Common Law of England* (1716), quoted in A. W. B. Simpson, "The common law and legal theory," *Oxford Essays in Jurisprudence*, 2nd series, ed. A. W. B. Simpson (Oxford: Clarendon Press, 1973), pp. 77–99 at p. 96. See also Berman, *Law in Revolution*, p. 449.

15   Jürgen Habermas, *Between Facts and Norms*, trans. William Rehg (Oxford: Polity, 1996; originally published 1992), ch. 8. See similarly John S. Dryzek, "Political inclusion and the dynamics of democratization," *American Political Science Review*, 90 (1996), 475–87.

16   Cohen and Sabel, "Directly-deliberative polyarchy," p. 326.

17   See, respectively: Cohen, "Deliberation and democratic legitimacy," pp. 31–2; Joseph M. Bessette, *The Mild Voice of Reason: Deliberative Democracy and American National Government* (Chicago: University of Chicago Press, 1994), esp. ch. 6; and John Uhr, *Deliberative Democracy in Australia* (Cambridge: Cambridge University Press, 1998), esp. ch 4.

18   Something like this is suggested by Iris Marion Young, "Together in difference: transforming the logic of group political conflict," *The Rights of Cultural Minorities*, ed. Will Kymlicka (Oxford: Oxford University Press 1995), pp. 155–77 at p. 157.

19   Georg Simmel, *Conflict and the Web of Group Affiliations*, trans. Kurt H. Wolff and Reinhard Bendix (Glencoe, Ill.: Free Press, 1955), esp. pp. 125–95.

20   To be sure, deliberators genuinely deliberate in these processes. The only question – which is what is meant to be signaled by calling the process "ersatz" – is the extent to which the deliberations of the subset can adequately substitute for those of the whole.

21   John Stuart Mill, *Considerations on Representative Government* (1861), ch. 5, in Richard Wollheim, *John Stuart Mill, Three Essays* (Oxford: Clarendon Press, 1975), pp. 142–423 at p. 228. In Lord Boothby's delightful formulation, "Ideally, the House of Commons should be a social microcosm of the nation. The nation includes a great many people who are rather stupid, and so should the house," quoted in A. H.

Birch, "The nature and functions of representation," *The Study of Politics,* ed. Preston King (London: Frank Cass, 1977), pp. 265–78 at p. 268.

22   Thus, for example, in their deliberations behind the closed doors of the Philadelphia Convention the Founding Fathers self-consciously couched their arguments in terms of what "ought to occur to a people deliberating on a Government for themselves . . . in a temperate moment, and with the experience of other nations before them"; James Madison, *Notes of Debates in the Federal Convention of 1787* (New York: Norton, 1966; originally published 1840), entry for 26 June 1787, pp. 193–4.

23   Hanna F. Pitkin, *The Concept of Representation* (Berkeley: University of California Press, 1967). Bernard Manin, *Principles of Representative Government* (Cambridge: Cambridge University Press, 1997), esp. ch. 6.

24   Madison, *The Federalist* no. 62 and 63.

25   James S. Fishkin, *Democracy and Deliberation: New Directions for Democratic Reform* (New Haven, Conn.: Yale University Press, 1991) and *The Voice of the People: Public Opinion and Democracy* (New Haven, Conn.: Yale University Press, 1995). Anna Coote and Jo Lenaghan, *Citizens' Juries: Theory into Practice* (London: Institute for Public Policy Research, 1997).

26   Jon Elster, "Introduction," *Deliberative Democracy*, ed. J. Elster (Cambridge: Cambridge University Press, 1998), pp. 8–9.

27   James Tully, "The agonic freedom of citizens," *Economy & Society*, 28 (no. 2: May 1999), 101–22.

28   Cf. Fishkin's *Voice of the People*, p. 220 report of deliberative polls done for three different local public utilities in Texas. There he is pleased to report that in all three cases the shift in opinion, pre- to post-deliberation, was in the same *direction*. But the *absolute numbers* nonetheless diverged wildly. In one case, half the respondents thought post-deliberation that "investing in conservation" was the "option to pursue first," whereas in another case under a third thought so. In one case, over a third still thought post-deliberation that "renewable energy" should be the top option, whereas in another case less than a sixth thought so. Clearly, these deliberating groups ought not be regarded as interchangeable. Neither, in consequence, does this evidence inspire confidence in the general strategy of "ersatz deliberation," treating smaller deliberative groups as microcosms capable of literally "substituting" for deliberation across the whole community.

29   Harry Kalven, Jr., and Hans Zeisel, *The American Jury* (Chicago: University of Chicago Press, 1966), p. 474. Even where mock juries come to the same verdicts, as Cass Sunstein tells me they often do, they do so through very different lines of collective reasoning.

30   At most, they might be taken as "recommendations" to be fed back into those broader community-wide deliberations (Fishkin, *Voice of the People*, p. 162).

31   Limiting the length of interventions is the more modern way, limiting the number of them the older. British parliamentary practice traditionally was that "none may speak more than once to the matter"; Thomas Jefferson, *Parliamentary Pocket-Book*; sec. 180, reprinted in *Jefferson's Parliamentary Writings,* ed. Wilbur Samuel Howell, 2nd series (Princeton, NJ: Princeton University Press, 1988), pp. 47–162 at p. 89.

32   Ibid., pp. 89–90.

33   Omitting gratuitous insults, groundless threats and so on; see Oran R. Young, *The*

Intermediaries: Third Parties in International Crises (Princeton, NJ: Princeton University Press, 1967).

34   Benjamin I. Page, *Who Deliberates? Mass Media in Modern Democracy* (Chicago: University of Chicago Press, 1996). "Seconds" played a similar role in the old *code dueletto.*

35   As arguably we do with germaneness rules in the legislative case, for example.

36   Habermas, *The Structural Transformation of the Public Sphere,* trans. Thomas Burger and Frederick Lawrence (Oxford: Polity, 1989; originally published 1962), esp. pp. 31–43; "The public sphere" (trans. S. and F. Lennox), *New German Critique,* 3 (1964), 49–55; and *Between Facts and Norms,* esp. chs 7–8. See also Charles Taylor, "Modernity and the rise of the public sphere," *Tanner Lectures on Human Values,* 14 (1993), 203–60.

37   Even there they engaged directly but not particularly deeply, judging from William Hazlitt's contemporaneous account, "On coffee-house politicians," *Table Talk, or Original Essays* (New York: Chelsea House, 1983; originally published 1869), pp. 261–83. There he writes that coffee-house politicians "are like an oyster at the ebb of the tide, gaping for fresh *tidings*" (p. 263). Among them, "The Evening Paper is impatiently expected and called for at a certain critical minute: the news of the morning becomes stale and vapid by the dinner-hour. . . . It is strange that people should take so much interest at one time what they so soon forget: – the truth is, they feel no interest in it at any time, but it does for something to talk about. Their ideas are served up to them, like their bill of fare, for the day" (p. 262). In coffee-houses, "People do not seem to talk for the sake of expressing their opinions, but to maintain an opinion for the sake of talking. . . . It is not conversation, but rehearsing a part" (pp. 268–9). "Men of education and men of the world . . . know what they have to say on a subject, and come to the point at once. Your coffee-house politician balances between what he heard last and what he shall say next; and not seeing his way clearly, puts you off with circumstantial phrases, and tries to gain time for fear of making a false step" (p. 269).

38   Habermas, *Structural Transformation,* p. 42.

39   British parliamentary practice prohibits reading out of written speeches for precisely that reason: "When orators confine themselves to reading out what they have written in the silence of their study, they no longer discuss, they amplify. They do not listen, since what they hear must not in any way alter what they are going to say. They wait until the speaker whose place they must take has concluded. They do not examine the opinion he defends, they count the time he is taking and which they regard as a delay. In this way there is no discussion.... Everyone sets aside whatever he has not anticipated, all that might disrupt a case already completed in advance. Speakers follow one another without meeting; if they refute one another it is simply by chance. They are like two armies, marching in opposite directions, one next to the other, barely catching a glimpse of one another, avoiding even looking at one another for fear of deviating from a route which has already been irrevocably traced out." Benjamin Constant, "Principles of politics applicable to all representative governments," *Political Writings,* trans. and ed. Biancamaria Fontana (Cambridge: Cambridge University Press, 1988; originally published 1815), ch. 7, p. 222.

40   On uptake see J. G. A. Pocock, "Verbalizing a political act: toward a politics of

speech," *Political Theory*, 1 (1973), 27–45.

41   J. L. Austin, "Other minds," *Philosophical Papers*, ed. J. O. Urmson and G. J. Warnock, 3rd edn (Oxford: Oxford University Press, 1979), pp. 76–116 at p. 115. Donald Davidson, *Inquiries into Truth and Interpretation* (Oxford: Clarendon Press, 1984).

42   David Lewis, "Scorekeeping in a language game," *Journal of Philosophical Logic*, 8 (1979), 339–59.

43   Dan Sperber and Deidre Wilson, "Loose talk," *Proceedings of the Aristotelian Society*, 86 (1986), 153–71.

44   That is how "conversational implicature" works: G. Paul Grice, "Logic and conversation," *The Logic of Grammar*, ed. Donald Davidson and Gilbert Harman (Encino, CA: Dickenson Publishing Co., 1975), pp. 64–75 and *Studies in the Way of Words* (Cambridge, MA: Harvard University Press, 1989), esp. pp. 22–40, 138–44, 269–82.

45   On related disputes in cognitive science, see: Gregory Currie, *Meeting of Minds: Thought, Imagination & Perception* (Oxford: Oxford University Press, 1999); Christopher Peacocke, ed., *Simulation and the Unity of Consciousness: Current Issues in the Philosophy of Mind*, Proceedings of the British Academy no. 83 (Oxford: Oxford University Press for the British Academy, 1994), esp. Martin Davies, "The mental simulation debate," pp. 99–127; Martin Davies and Tony Stone, "Folk psychology and mental simulation," *Current Issues in the Philosophy of Mind*, ed. Anthony O'Hear (Cambridge: Cambridge University Press, for the Royal Institute of Philosophy, 1998), pp. 53–82.

46   Jane Heal, "Understanding other minds from the inside," *Current Issues in the Philosophy of Mind*, ed. O'Hear, pp. 83–100. "Lightly theorized," but still nonetheless theorized: we need some grounds for supposing they are like us in relevant respects, for example.

47   Ned Block, ed., *Readings in the Philosophy of Psychology* (Cambridge, MA: Harvard University Press, 1980). "Folk psychologists" assume we attribute to others the same sort of psychology of beliefs and desires which, upon introspection, we find that we ourselves have; and we assume that they will act on their peculiar beliefs and desires in standard sorts of ways, under standard sorts of provocations, just as we ourselves would do. See Frank Jackson and Philip Pettit, "In defense of folk psychology," *Philosophical Studies*, 57 (1990), 7–30; Philip Pettit, *The Common Mind*, 2nd edn (New York: Oxford University Press, 1996), esp. chs 1–2, 4 and postscript; and David Braddon-Mitchell and Frank Jackson, *The Philosophy of Mind and Cognition* (Cambridge, MA: Blackwell, 1996).

48   Habermas elaborates: "Discourse ethics rests on the intuition that the application of the principle of universalization, properly understood, calls for a joint process of 'ideal role taking.' It interprets this idea of G. H. Mead in terms of a pragmatic theory of argumentation. Under the pragmatic presupposition of an inclusive and noncoercive rational discourse among free and equal participants, everyone is required to take the perspective of everyone else, and thus project herself into the understandings of self and world of all others." See Jürgen Habermas, "Reconciliation through the public use of reason: remarks on John Rawls's *Political Liberalism*," *Journal of Philosophy*, 92 (March 1995), 109–31 at p. 117.

49   As Iris Marion Young aptly remarks, *a propos* Habermas, it is not just a matter of

intellectually registering the perspective of the others but rather of "imaginatively" projecting oneself into their position; "Asymmetrical reciprocity: on moral respect, wonder and enlarged thought," *Intersecting Voices*, pp. 38–59 at p. 39.

50 For philosophical treatments, see: Richard Wollheim, *The Thread of Life* (Cambridge: Cambridge University Press, 1984), esp. chs 3–4 ; Gregory Currie, *Image and Mind: Film, Philosophy and Cognitive Science* (Cambridge: Cambridge University Press, 1995); and Elaine Scarry, "On vivacity: the difference between daydreaming and imagining-under-authorial-instruction," *Representations*, no. 52 (Fall 1995), 1–26.

51 It may well be that one's own "sense of oneself" is similarly constructed out of some such internal narrative. See, e.g., Charles Taylor, *Sources of the Self* (Cambridge: Cambridge University Press, 1989), esp. ch. 2, and Alasdair MacIntyre, *After Virtue* (Notre Dame, IN: University of Notre Dame Press, 1981).

52 Kimberly K. Smith, "Storytelling, sympathy and moral judgment in American abolitionism," *Journal of Political Philosophy*, 6 (1998), 356–77.

53 Such is the claim of Elaine Scarry, "The difficulty of imagining other people," *For Love of Country*, ed. Joshua Cohen (Boston: Beacon Press, 1996), pp. 98–110 at p. 105.

54 This, and the political implications flowing from it, form recurring themes in the writings of Martha Nussbaum: *Love's Knowledge: Essays on Philosophy and Literature* (New York: Oxford University Press, 1990); *Poetic Justice: The Literary Imagination and Public Life* (Boston: Beacon Press, 1995); and *Cultivating Humanity* (Cambridge, MA: Harvard University Press, 1997).

55 George Steiner, "Literature and post-history," *Language and Silence* (London: Faber & Faber, 1967), pp. 413–24 at p. 420.

56 John Dewey, *The Public and Its Problems* (Chicago: Swallow Press, 1954; originally published 1927), ch. 5, p. 184.

57 Aristotle, *Poetics*, 1459a17–1459b8.

58 Conduct the experiment for yourself. Is it not ever so much easier to imagine yourself Jean Valjean, given what all Hugo has told us about him, than it is to imagine yourself a generic "prisoner of the Bastille" on the basis of what historians have told us about that place and its denizens? Intellectually, generalizations may be easier both to convey and to grasp; but emotionally and imaginatively we respond better to more fully described particulars than to generalities which abstract from the details that make those particulars more evocative.

59 Bernard Crick, *Essays on Politics and Literature* (Edinburgh: Edinburgh University Press, 1989), p. 17.

60 Steiner, "Humane literacy" (1963), *Language and Silence*, pp. 21–9 at p. 29.

61 Wayne C. Booth, *The Company We Keep: An Ethics of Fiction* (Berkeley: University of California Press, 1988), p. 485. Cf. Scarry's claim that "it is impossible to hold rich multitudes of imaginary characters simultaneously in the mind." She may well be right that, "presented with the large number of characters one finds in Dickens or in Tolstoi, one must constantly strain to keeep them sorted out" ("The difficulty of imagining other people," p. 104). But it is not at all hard to recall a large number of characters and situations, drawn from many different novels. We all do that all the time.

62 T. S. Eliot, "The social function of poetry," *On Poetry and Poets* (London: Faber &

Faber, 1958; originally published 1943), pp. 15–25. Eliot goes on to claim that poetry conveys "some fresh understanding of the familiar, or the expression of something we have experienced but have no words for, which enlarges our consciousness or refines our sensibility" (p. 18). "The genuine poet . . . discovers new variations of sensibility which can be appropriated by others. . . . In expressing what other people feel he is also changing the feeling by making it more conscious; he is making people more aware of what they feel already, and therefore teaching them something about themselves" (p. 20). See similarly William Wordsworth, "Observations prefixed to 'Lyrical Ballads'" (1820), *What Is Art?* ed. Alexander Sesokske (New York: Oxford University Press, 1965), pp. 261–74.

63   Steiner, "Literature and post-history," p. 420.

64   Peter Laslett and James S. Fishkin, eds, *Justice Between Generations: Philosophy, Politics and Society,* 6th series (Oxford: Blackwell, 1992). Other communicatively inert interests which we arguably ought take into account might include those of other peoples and other species. Robert E. Goodin, "Enfranchising the earth, and its alternatives," *Political Studies,* 44 (Dec. 1996), 835–49.

65   As Alan Ryan writes, "In the absence of a real, physically present interlocutor . . . you the reader are at the mercy of my ideas about what this conversation is about. . . . [Y]ou cannot redirect the conversation as you would wish"; "In a conversational idiom," *Social Research,* 65 (Fall 1998), 473–89 at p. 473.

66   Michael F. Schober, "Conversational evidence for rethinking meaning," *Social Research,* 65 (Fall 1998), 511–34. Seyla Benhabib, "The generalized and the concrete other: the Kohlberg–Gilligan controversy and moral theory," *Situating the Self* (Oxford: Polity, 1992), pp. 148–77. Note that it is not just the "peculiar" that presents a challenge, though: any departure from our own way of thinking requires a stretch of the imagination which is, to some greater or lesser extent, difficult to achieve.

67   Ryan, "In a conversational idiom," p. 473.

68   As Averell Harriman famously did, in ostentatiously switching off his hearing aid when Soviet negotiators launched into one of their standard harangues. I owe this anecdote to my old friend and teacher, Robert Ferrell.

69   As in Charles Tilly's representation of conversation as necessarily involving "continuously negotiated communication"; "Contentious conversation," *Social Research,* 65 (Fall 1998), 491–510 at p. 495.

70   Michael F. Schober and Herbert H. Clark, "Understanding by addressees and overhearers," *Cognitive Psychology,* 21 (1989), 211–32, confirming a speculation by Jean-Paul Sartre, *What Is Literature?,* trans. Bernard Frechtman (London: Methuen, 1950), p. 50.

71   If only in their atypicality: in a representative sample, the fact of diversity ought be represented even if not all the diverse components can be individually represented.

72   They inevitably reflect the "generalized" more than the "concrete" other, in all the other's concrete forms, in the terms of Benhabib, "The generalized and the concrete other."

73   Michel de Montaigne, "On the art of conversation," *The Essays of Michel de Montaigne,* trans. and ed. M. A. Screech (Harmondsworth: Allen Lane/Penguin, 1991; originally published 1580), bk 3, essay 8, pp. 1044–69 at p. 1045.

74   Anne Phillips, *The Politics of Presence: Democracy and Group Representation* (Oxford:

Clarendon Press, 1995).

75 That is precisely what Phillips calls for: "group representation." See esp. *Politics of Presence*, ch. 6.

76 Young, "Together in difference."

77 Benhabib, "The generalized and the concrete other."

78 J. E. Malpas, *Place and Experience* (Cambridge: Cambridge University Press, 1999).

79 True, in situations of great heterogeneity we might find it hard to imagine ourselves in a very different other person's position: but that compromises our capacity for understanding what the other is asserting, in external-collective deliberations, just as much as it compromises our capacity for imagining ourselves her for internal-reflective deliberative purposes.

80 Herbert A. Simon, "Human nature in politics: the dialogue of psychology and political science," *American Political Science Review*, 79 (1985), 293–304.

81 And if they internalize some but not all other perspectives, there is of course then a risk that their internal-reflective deliberations will be biased accordingly.

82 Sartre, *What Is Literature?* ch. 3.

83 In terms of democratizing culture (or, rather, of enlisting cultural artifacts in the service of democracy), it is not so much a matter of "high culture" against "low" as it is of "broad" against "narrow."

84 Amy Gutmann, *Democratic Education* (Princeton, NJ: Princeton University Press, 1987), ch. 8. Dick Netzer, *The Subsidized Muse: Public Support for the Arts in the United States* (Cambridge: Cambridge University Press, 1978). Edward C. Banfield, *The Democratic Muse: The Visual Arts and the Public Interest* (New York: Basic Books, 1984). Carnegie Commission on the Future of Public Broadcasting, *A Public Trust* (New York: Bantam, 1979).

85 Ronald Dworkin, "Can a liberal state support art?," *A Matter of Principle* (Cambridge, MA: Harvard University Press, 1985), pp. 221–33.

86 Murray Edelman, *From Art to Politics: How Artistic Creations Shape Political Conceptions* (Chicago: University of Chicago Press, 1995). Robert McC. Adams, "Forums, not temples," *American Behavioral Scientist*, 42 (1999), 968–76.

87 Harry Brighouse, "Neutrality, publicity and public funding of the arts," *Philosophy and Public Affairs*, 24 (1995), 36–63 and Dworkin, "Can a liberal state support art?"

88 Karl Lowenstein, "Legislative control of political extremism in European democracies," *Columbia Law Review,* 38 (1938), 591–622, 725–74.

89 Scarry, "The difficulty of imagining other people," p. 104.

90 Hobbes, *Leviathan*, ch. 6.

91 As, lore has it, was the traditional practice of the Cabinet Secretary in Britain.

4

The Law of Group Polarization

Cass R. Sunstein

Consider the following events:

- Affirmative action is under attack in the state of Texas. A number of professors at a particular branch of the University of Texas are inclined to be supportive of affirmative action; they meet to exchange views and to plan further action, if necessary. What are these professors likely to think, and to do, after they talk?
- After a nationally publicized shooting at a high school, a group of people in the community, most of them tentatively in favor of greater gun control, come together to discuss the possibility of imposing new gun control measures. What, if anything, will happen to individual views as a result of this discussion?
- A jury is deciding on an appropriate punitive damage award in a case of recklessly negligent behavior by a large company; the behavior resulted in a serious injury to a small child. Before deliberating as a group, individual jurors have chosen appropriate awards, leading to an average of $1.5 million and a median of $1 million. As a statistical generalization, how will the jury's ultimate award tend to compare to these figures?
- A group of women are concerned about what they consider to be a mounting "tyranny of feminism." They believe that women should be able to make their own choices, but they also think that men and women are fundamentally different, and that their differences legitimately lead to different social roles. The group decides to meet every two weeks to focus on common concerns. After a year, is it possible to say what its members are likely to think?

Every society contains innumerable deliberating groups. Church groups, political parties, women's organizations, juries, dissident organizations, legislative bodies, regulatory commissions, multimember courts, faculties, student organizations, those participating in talk radio programs, Internet discussion groups, and others engage in deliberation. It is a simple social fact that sometimes people enter discussions with one view and leave with another, even on political and moral questions. Emphasizing this fact, many recent observers have embraced the traditional American aspiration to "deliberative democracy," an ideal that is designed to combine popular responsiveness with a high degree of reflection and exchange among people with competing views.[1] But for the most part, the resulting literature has not been empirically informed. It has not much dealt with the real-world consequences of deliberation, and with whether what generalizations hold in actual deliberative settings, with groups of different predispositions and compositions.

My principal purpose is to investigate a striking but largely neglected statistical regularity – that of **group polarization** – and to relate this phenomenon to underlying questions about the role of deliberation in the "public sphere" of a heterogeneous democracy. In brief, group polarization means that **members of a deliberating group predictably move toward a more extreme point in the direction indicated by the members' predeliberation tendencies**.[2] Thus, for example, members of the first deliberating group are likely to become more firmly committed to affirmative action; the second group will probably end up favoring gun control quite enthusiastically; the punitive damages jury will likely come up with an award higher than the median, perhaps higher than the mean as well, and very possibly as high as or higher than that of the highest predeliberation award of any individual member; the group of women concerned about feminism is likely to become very conservative indeed on gender issues. Notably, groups consisting of individuals with extremist tendencies are more likely to shift, and likely to shift more (a point that bears on the wellsprings of violence and terrorism); the same is true for groups with some kind of salient shared identity (like Republicans, Democrats, and lawyers, but unlike jurors and experimental subjects). When like-minded people are participating in "iterated polarization games" – when they meet regularly, without sustained exposure to competing views – extreme movements are all the more likely.

Two principal mechanisms underlie group polarization. The first points to social influences on behavior and in particular to people's desire to maintain their reputation and their self-conception. The second emphasizes the limited "argument pools" within any group, and the directions in which those limited pools lead group members. An understanding of the two mechanisms provides many insights into deliberating bodies. Such an understanding illuminates a great deal, for example, about likely processes within multimember courts, juries, political parties, and legislatures – not to mention ethnic groups, extremist organizations, terrorists, criminal conspiracies, student associations, faculties, institutions engaged in feuds or "turf battles," workplaces, and families. At the same time, these mechanisms raise serious questions about deliberation from the normative point of view. If deliberation predictably pushes groups toward a more extreme point in the direction of their original tendency, whatever it may be, do we have any reason to think that deliberation is producing improvements? A sensible answer would emphasize the importance of paying far more attention to the circumstances and nature of deliberation, not merely to the fact that it is occurring.

One of my largest purposes is to cast light on *enclave deliberation*, a process that I understand to involve deliberation among like-minded people who talk or even live, much of the time, in isolated enclaves. I will urge that enclave deliberation is, simultaneously, a potential danger to social stability, a source of social fragmentation or even violence, and a safeguard against social injustice and unreasonableness. As we will see, group polarization helps to cast new light on the old idea that social homogeneity can be quite damaging to good deliberation. When people are hearing echoes of their own voices, the consequence may be far more than support and reinforcement. But there is a point more supportive of enclave deliberation: Participants in heterogeneous groups tend to give least weight to the views of low status members[3] – in some times and places, women, African-Americans, less educated people. Hence enclave deliberation might be the only way to ensure that those views are developed and eventually heard. Without a place for enclave deliberation, citizens in the broader public sphere may move in certain directions, even extreme directions, precisely because opposing voices are not heard at all. An ambivalent lesson is that deliberating enclaves can be breeding grounds for *both* the development of unjustly suppressed views and for unjustified extremism, indeed fanaticism. A less ambivalent lesson involves the need, not to celebrate or to challenge deliberation as such, but to design institutions so as to ensure that when individuals and groups move, it is because of the force of the arguments, not because of the social dynamics that I will emphasize here.

I. How and Why Groups Polarize

A. The basic phenomenon

Group polarization is among the most robust patterns found in deliberating bodies, and it has been found all over the world and in many diverse tasks. The result is that groups often make more extreme decisions than would the typical or average individual in the group (where "extreme" is defined solely internally, by reference to the group's initial dispositions). Note that in the experimental work, both extremism and tendencies are measured not by reference to anything external, or to a normative standard, but by reference to the particular scale that is brought before the individuals who compose the group. Thus, for example, people might be asked, on a scale of −5 to 5, how strongly they agree or disagree with a particular statement (white racism is responsible for the disadvantages faced by African-Americans, the government should increase regulation of nuclear power, America should increase foreign aid). We shall see that the experimental literature is closely connected to real-world phenomena.

Though standard, the term "group polarization" is somewhat misleading. It is not meant to suggest that group members will shift to the poles, nor does it refer to an increase in variance among groups, though this may be the ultimate result. Instead the term refers to a predictable shift *within* a group discussing a case or problem. As the shift occurs, groups, and group members, move and coalesce, not toward the middle of antecedent dispositions, but toward a more extreme position in the direction indicated by those dispositions. The effect of deliberation is both to decrease variance among group members, as individual differences diminish, and also to produce convergence on a relatively more extreme point among predeliberation judgments.

Consider some examples of the basic phenomenon, which has been found in over a dozen nations.[4] (a) A group of moderately profeminist women will become more strongly profeminist after discussion.[5] (b) After discussion, citizens of France become more critical of the United States and its intentions with respect to economic aid.[6] (c) After discussion, whites predisposed to show racial prejudice offer more negative responses to the question whether white racism is responsible for conditions faced by African-Americans in American cities.[7] (d) After discussion, whites predisposed not to show racial prejudice offer more positive responses to the same question.[8] As statistical regularities, it should follow, for example, that that those moderately critical of an ongoing war effort will, after discussion, sharply oppose the war; that those who believe that global warming is a serious problem are likely, after discussion, to hold that belief with considerable confidence; that people tending to believe in the inferiority of a certain racial group will become more entrenched in this belief as a result of discussion; that those tending to condemn the United States will, as a result of discussion, end up condemning the United States with some intensity.

There have been two main explanations for group polarization, both of which have been extensively investigated.

1. *Social comparison.* The first, involving social comparison, begins with the claim that people want to be perceived favorably by other group members, and also to perceive themselves favorably. Once they hear what others believe, they adjust their positions in the direction of the dominant position. The result is to press the group's position toward one or another extreme, and also to induce shifts in individual members. People may wish, for example, not to seem too enthusiastic or too restrained in their enthusiasm for, affirmative action, feminism, or an increase in national defense; hence their views may shift when they see what other group members think. The result will be group polarization.

The dynamic behind the social comparison explanation is that most people may want to take a position of a certain socially preferred sort – in the case of risk-taking, for example, they may want to be perceived (and to perceive themselves) as moderate risk-takers, and their choice of position is partly a product of this desire. No one can know what such a position would be until the positions of others are revealed. Thus individuals move their judgments in order to preserve their image to others and their image to themselves.

2. *Persuasive arguments*. The second explanation, emphasizing the role of persuasive arguments, is based on a common sense intuition: that any individual's position on an issue is partly a function of which arguments presented within the group seem convincing. The choice therefore moves in the direction of the most persuasive position defended by the group, taken as a collectivity. Because a group whose members are already inclined in a certain direction will have a disproportionate number of arguments supporting that same direction, the result of discussion will be to move individuals further in the direction of their initial inclinations. The key is the existence of a limited argument pool, one that is skewed (speaking purely descriptively) in a particular direction. Members of a group will have thought of some, but not all, of the arguments that justify their initial inclination; consider the question whether to fear global warming or not to do so. In discussion, arguments of a large number of individuals are stated and heard, but the total argument pool will be tilted in one or another direction, depending on the predispositions of the people who compose the group. Hence there will be a shift in the direction of the original tilt.

There is a related possibility, not quite reducible to either of the two standard arguments, but using elements of each. In their individual judgments, people are averse to extremes; they tend to seek the middle of the relevant poles.[9] It is possible that when people are making judgments individually, they err on the side of caution, expressing a view in the direction that they really hold, but stating that view cautiously, for fear of seeming extreme. Once other people express supportive views, the relevant inhibition disappears, and people feel free to say what, in a sense, they really believe. There appears to be no direct test of this hypothesis, but it is reasonable to believe that the phenomenon plays a role in group polarization and choice shifts.

B. Refinements – and depolarization

I now turn to some refinements, complicating the basic account of group polarization. For purposes of understanding the relationship between that phenomenon and democracy, the central points are twofold. *First*, it matters a great deal whether people consider themselves part of the same social group as the other members; a sense of shared identity will heighten the shift, and a belief that identity is not shared will reduce and possibly eliminate it. *Second*, deliberating groups will tend to depolarize if they consist of equally opposed subgroups and if members have a degree of flexibility in their positions. Both of these findings have great relevance to any account of the relationship between group polarization and democratic institutions, as we will see.

1. *Statistical regularities.* Of course not all groups polarize; some groups end up in the middle, not toward either extreme. Nor is it hard to understand why this might be so. If the people defending the original tendency are particularly unpersuasive, group polarization is unlikely to occur. If the outliers are especially convincing, groups may even shift away from their original tendency and in the direction held by few or even one.

Sometimes, moreover, external constraints or an external "shock" may prevent or blunt group polarization. Group members with well-defined views on a certain issue (gun control, separation of church and state, intervention in foreign nations) may be prone to polarize, but in order to maintain political effectiveness, even basic credibility, they will sometimes maintain a relatively moderate face, publicly or even privately. Groups that have started to polarize in an extreme direction may move toward the middle in order to promote their own legitimacy or because of new revelations of one kind or another. Readers are likely to be able to identify their own preferred examples.

2. *Affective factors, identity, and solidarity.* Affective factors are quite important in group decisions, and when manipulated, such factors will significantly increase or decrease polarization. If group members are linked by affective ties, dissent is significantly less frequent.[10] The existence of affective ties thus reduces the number of divergent arguments and also intensifies social influences on choice. Hence people are less likely to shift if the direction advocated is being pushed by unfriendly group members; the likelihood of a shift, and its likely size, are increased when people perceive fellow members as friendly, likeable, and similar to them.[11] In the same vein, physical spacing tends to reduce polarization; a sense of common fate and intragroup similarity tend to increase it, as does the introduction of a rival "outgroup."

In a refinement of particular importance to social deliberation and the theory of democracy, it has been found to matter whether people think of themselves, antecedently or otherwise, as part of a group having a degree of solidarity. If they think of themselves in this way, group polarization is all the more likely, and it is likely too to be more extreme.[12] Thus when the context emphasizes each person's membership in the social group engaging in deliberation, polarization increases. This finding is in line with more general evidence that social ties among deliberating group members tend to suppress dissent and in that way to lead to inferior decisions.[13] This should not be surprising. If ordinary findings of group polarization are a product of social influences and limited argument pools, it stands to reason that when group members think of one another as similar along a salient dimension, or if some external factor (politics, geography, race, sex) unites them, group polarization will be heightened.

3. *Depolarization and deliberation without shifts.* Is it possible to construct either groups that will depolarize – that will tend toward the middle – or groups whose members will not shift at all? Both phenomena seem to be real in actual deliberating bodies. In fact the persuasive arguments theory implies that there will be depolarization if and when new persuasive arguments are offered that are opposite to the direction initially favored by group members. There is evidence for this phenomenon.[14] Depolarization, rather than polarization, will also be found when the relevant group consists of individuals drawn equally from two extremes.[15] And "familiar and long-debated issues do not depolarize easily."[16] With respect to such issues, people are simply less likely to shift at all. And when one or more people in a group know the right answer to a factual question, the group is likely to shift in the direction of accuracy.

C. Actual deliberation within identifiable groups: iterated "polarization games"

Studies of group polarization involve one-shot experiments. We will turn shortly to group polarization in the real world. But let us notice an intriguing implication of the experiments, an implication with special importance for democratic deliberation involving people who meet with each other not once, but on a regular basis.

If participants engage in repeated discussions – if, for example, they meet each month, express views, and take votes – there should be repeated shifts toward, and past, the defined pole. Thus, for example, if a group of citizens is thinking about genetic engineering of food, or the minimum wage, or the World Trade Organization, the consequence of their discussions, over time, should be to lead in quite extreme directions. In these iterated "polarization games," deliberation over time should produce a situation in which individuals hold positions more extreme than those of any individual member before the series of deliberations began. In fact the idea of iterated polarization games seems far more realistic than the processes studied in one-shot experiments. There appears to be no study of such iterated polarization games. But it is not difficult to think of real-world groups in which the consequence of deliberation, over time, appears to be to shift both groups and individuals to positions that, early on, they could not possibly have accepted.

D. Rhetorical asymmetry and the "severity shift": a pervasive phenomenon?

In a noteworthy qualification of the general literature on group polarization, the previously mentioned study of punitive damage awards by juries found a striking pattern for dollar awards.[17] For *any* dollar award above zero, the general effect of deliberation was to increase awards above those of the median voter. This was a kind of "severity shift." Dollar awards did not simply polarize; while higher awards increased dramatically, as compared to the median of predeliberation votes, low awards increased as well. Why is this?

Both the original experiment and a follow-up experiment suggest that the severity shift is a product of a "rhetorical asymmetry" that favors, other things being equal and in any contest, the person or persons urging higher awards. In our culture, and in light of existing social norms, the person favoring the higher amount for punitive damages appears likely to be more convincing than the person favoring the lower amount. It is important to emphasize that this asymmetry operates independently of any facts about the individual case. The reason appears to be that with respect to dollar awards involving a corporate defendant, stronger arguments – "we need to deter this kind of conduct," "we need to send a powerful signal," "we need to attract their attention" – tend to have comparatively greater weight.

Undoubtedly there are many other contexts containing rhetorical asymmetry, and undoubtedly the asymmetry can affect outcomes in democratic institutions, as it did in the jury study. Legislative judgments about criminal punishment may, for example, involve an asymmetry of exactly this kind; those favoring greater punishment for drug-related offenses appear to be at a systematic advantage over those favoring lesser punishment. In certain settings, those favoring lower taxes, or more aid for scholarship students, or greater funding for environmental protection may have a similar rhetorical advantage. Much remains to be explored here. For present purposes the point is that when there is an initial distribution of views in a certain direction, and when existing norms give a more extreme movement in that direction a rhetorical advantage, quite extreme shifts can be expected.

II. Polarization and Democracy

In this section I discuss evidence of group polarization in legal and political institutions, and I trace some implications of that evidence for participants in a deliberative democracy. I will deal with normative issues below; my purpose here is to cast a new light on social practices.

A. Polarizing events and polarization entrepreneurs

Group polarization has a large effect on many deliberating groups and institutions; its effects are hardly limited to the laboratory. Consider, for example, the political and social role of religious organizations. Such organizations tend to strengthen group members' religious convictions, simply by virtue of the fact that like-minded people are talking to one another. Religious groups amplify the religious impulse, especially if group members are insulated from other groups, and on occasion, the result can be to lead people in quite bizarre directions. Whether or not this is so, political activity by members of religious organizations is undoubtedly affected by cascade-like effects and by group polarization. In a related vein, survey evidence shows that dramatic social events, like the assassination of Martin Luther King and civil rights disturbances, tend to polarize attitudes, with both positive and negative attitudes increasing within demographic groups.[18] The point emphatically holds for the terrorist attacks in New York City and Washington DC on September 11, 2001.

In fact it is possible to imagine "professional polarizers," or "polarization entrepreneurs," that is, political activists who have, as one of their goals, the creation of spheres in which like-minded people can hear a particular point of view from one or more articulate people, and also participate, actually or vicariously, in a deliberative discussion in which a certain point of view becomes entrenched and strengthened. For those seeking to promote social reform, an extremely promising strategy is to begin by promoting discussions among people who tend to favor the relevant reform; such discussions are likely to intensify the underlying convictions and concerns. Social reformers of all stripes may qualify as polarization entrepreneurs; the category includes those fighting communism in Eastern Europe and apartheid in South Africa, as well as terrorist leaders and those involved in criminal conspiracies of many kinds.

B. "Outgroups"

Group polarization has particular implications for insulated "outgroups" and (in the extreme case) for the treatment of conspiracies. Recall that polarization increases when group members identify themselves along some salient dimension, and especially when the group is able to define itself by contrast to another group. Outgroups are in this position – of self-contrast to others – by definition. Excluded by choice or coercion from discussion with others, such groups may become polarized in quite extreme directions, often in part because of group polarization. It is for this reason that outgroup members can sometimes be led, or lead themselves, to violent acts.

The tendency toward polarization among outgroups helps explain special concern about "hate speech," where group antagonisms can be heightened, and it simultaneously raises some questions about the idea that certain group discussions produce "consciousness raising." It is possible, at least, that the consequence of discussion is not only or mostly to raise consciousness (an ambiguous idea to be sure), but to produce group polarization in one direction or another – and at the same time to increase confidence in the position that has newly emerged.

This does not mean that consciousness is never raised; undoubtedly group discussion can identify and clarify problems that were previously repressed, or understood as an individual rather than social product. But nothing of this sort is established by the mere fact that views have changed and coalesced, and are held, post-discussion, with a high degree of confidence.

C. Feuds, ethnic and international strife, and war

Group polarization is inevitably at work in feuds, ethnic and international strife, and war. One of the characteristic features of feuds is that members of feuding groups tend to talk only to one another, fueling and amplifying their outrage, and solidifying their impression of the relevant events. Informational and reputational forces are very much at work here, producing cascade effects, and group polarization can lead members to increasingly extreme positions. It is not too much of a leap to suggest that these effects are sometimes present within ethnic groups and even nations, notwithstanding the usually high degree of national heterogeneity. In America, sharp divergences between whites and African-Americans, on particular salient events or more generally, can be explained by reference to group polarization. The same is true for sharp divergences of viewpoints within and across nations. Group polarization occurs within Israel and among the Palestinian Authority; it occurs within the United States and among those inclined to support, or at least not to condemn, terrorist acts. A large part of the perennial question, "Why do they hate us?" lies not in ancient grievances or individual consciences but in the social influences emphasized here. Of course the media play a large role, as we shall now see.

D. The internet, communications policy, and mass deliberation

Many people have expressed concern about processes of social influence on the mass media and the Internet. The general problem is said to be one of fragmentation, with certain people hearing more and louder versions of their own pre-existing commitments, thus reducing the benefits that come from exposure to competing views and unnoticed problems. With greater specialization, people are increasingly able to avoid general interest newspapers and magazines, and to make choices that reflect their own predispositions. The Internet is making it possible for people to design their own highly individuated communications packages, filtering out troublesome issues and disfavored voices. Long before the Internet, it was possible to discuss the "racial stratification of the public sphere," by reference to divergences between white and African-American newspapers.[19] New communications technologies may increase this phenomenon.

An understanding of group polarization explains why a fragmented communications market may create problems.[20] A "plausible hypothesis is that the

Internet-like setting is most likely to create a strong tendency toward group polarization when the members of the group feel some sense of group identity."[21] If certain people are deliberating with many like-minded others, views will not be reinforced but instead shifted to more extreme points. This cannot be said to be bad by itself – perhaps the increased extremism is good – but it is certainly troublesome if diverse social groups are led, through predictable mechanisms, toward increasingly opposing and ever more extreme views.

III. Deliberative Trouble

I now turn to normative issues, involving the relationship among group polarization, democratic theory, and legal institutions. I focus in particular on the implications of group polarization for institutional design, with special reference to the uses of heterogeneity and the complex issues presented by deliberation inside particular "enclaves." Should enclave deliberation count as deliberation at all? If deliberation requires a measure of disagreement, this is a serious question. But even like-minded people will have different perspectives and views, so that a group of people who tend to like affirmative action, or to fear global warming, will produce some kind of exchange of opinion. I will urge that in spite of this point, enclave deliberation raises serious difficulties for the participants and possibly for society as a whole. But there are many complexities here. In some cases, enclave deliberation will be a defective form for the participants, but will serve to foster a diversity of views for the wider public, and will therefore be desirable from the social point of view.

The central problem is that widespread error and social fragmentation are likely to result when like-minded people, insulated from others, move in extreme directions simply because of limited argument pools and parochial influences. As an extreme example, consider a system of one-party domination, which stifles dissent in part because it refuses to establish space for the emergence of divergent positions; in this way, it intensifies polarization within the party while also disabling external criticism. In terms of institutional design, the most natural response is to ensure that members of deliberating groups, whether small or large, will not isolate themselves from competing views – a point with implications for multimember courts, open primaries, freedom of association, and the architecture of the Internet. Here, then, is a plea for ensuring that deliberation occurs within a large and heterogeneous public sphere, and for guarding against a situation in which like-minded people are walling themselves off from alternative perspectives.

But there is a difficulty with this response: A certain measure of isolation will, in some cases, be crucial to the development of ideas and approaches that would not otherwise emerge and that deserve a social hearing. Members of low-status groups are often quiet within heterogeneous bodies, and thus deliberation, in such bodies, tends to be dominated by high-status members. Any shift – in technology, norms, or legal practice – that increases the number of deliberating enclaves will increase the diversity of society's aggregate "argument pool" while also increasing the danger of extremism and instability, ultimately even violence. Terrorism itself is a product, in part, of group polarization. Shifts toward a general "public sphere," without much in the way of enclave deliberation, will decrease the likelihood of extremism and instability, but at the same time produce what may be a stifling uniformity. And shifts toward more in the way of enclave deliberation will increase society's aggregate "argument pool," and hence enrich the marketplace of ideas, while also increasing extremism, fragmentation, hostility, and even violence.

No algorithm is available to solve the resulting conundrums. But some general lessons do emerge. It is important to ensure social spaces for deliberation by like-minded persons, but it is equally important to ensure that members of the relevant groups are not isolated from conversation with people having quite different views. The goal of that conversation is to promote the interests of those inside and outside the relevant enclaves, by subjecting group members to competing positions, by allowing them to exchange views with others and to see things from their point of view, and by ensuring that the wider society does not marginalize, and thus insulate itself from, views that may turn out to be right, or at least informative.

A. Doubts and questions

1. *Why deliberate?* If the effect of deliberation is to move people toward a more extreme point in the direction of their original tendency, why is it anything to celebrate? The underlying mechanisms do not provide much reason for confidence. If people are shifting their position in order to maintain their reputation and self-conception, before groups that may or may not be representative of the public as a whole, is there any reason to think that deliberation is making things better rather than worse? To the extent that shifts are occurring as a result of partial and frequently skewed argument pools, the results of deliberative judgments may be far worse than the results of simply taking the median of predeliberation judgments.

The most important point here is that those who emphasize the ideals associated with deliberative democracy tend to emphasize its preconditions, which include political equality, an absence of strategic behavior, full information, and the goal of "reaching understanding."[22] In real-world deliberations, behavior is often strategic, and equality is often absent in one or another form. But the existence of a limited argument pool, strengthening the existing tendency within the group, will operate in favor of group polarization even if no individual behaves strategically. By itself this will produce group polarization whether or not social influence is operating. On the other hand, the social context of deliberation can make a large difference, and under certain conditions, group polarization need not occur. The nature of the deliberative process, and the characteristics of the deliberating participants, can matter a great deal. I will return to this issue below.

In any case social influences need not be inconsistent with the effort to produce truth and understanding; when people attempt to position themselves in a way that fits with their best self-conception, or their preferred self-presentation, nothing has gone wrong, even from the standpoint of deliberation's most enthusiastic defenders. Perhaps group polarization could be reduced or even eliminated if we emphasized that good deliberation has full information as a precondition; by hypothesis, argument pools would not be limited if all information were available. But that requirement is extremely stringent, and if there is already full information, the role of deliberation is greatly reduced. In any case the group polarization phenomenon suggests that in real-world situations, deliberation is hardly guaranteed to increase the likelihood of arriving at truth. The trick is to produce an institutional design that will increase the likelihood that deliberation will lead in sensible directions, so that any polarization, if it occurs, will be a result of learning, rather than group dynamics.

2. *Movements right and wrong.* Of course we cannot say, from the mere fact of polarization, that there has been a movement in the wrong direction. Perhaps the more extreme tendency is better; recall that group polarization is likely to have fueled the antislavery movement and many others that deserve to meet with widespread approval. In the context of punitive damage awards, perhaps a severity shift produces good outcomes. Extremism should hardly be a word of opprobrium; everything depends on what extremists are arguing *for.* In addition, group polarization can be explained partly by reference to the fact that people who are confident are likely to be persuasive; and it is sensible to say that as a statistical matter, though not an invariable truth, people who are confident are more likely to be right. But when group discussion tends to lead people to more strongly held versions of the same view with which they began, and when social influences and limited argument pools are responsible, there is little reason for great confidence in the effects of deliberation.

We can go further. If it is possible to identify a particular viewpoint as unreasonable, it is also possible to worry about group discussion among people who share that viewpoint. If the underlying views are unreasonable, it makes sense to fear that these discussions may fuel increasing hatred and extremism (used here in an evaluative sense). This does not mean that the discussions can or should be regulated in a system dedicated to freedom of speech. But it does raise questions about the idea that "more speech" is necessarily an adequate remedy.

B. The virtues of heterogeneity

The simplest lesson here involves both individual susceptibility and institutional design. For many people, mere awareness of the role of limited argument pools and social influences might provide some inoculation against inadequately justified movements of opinion within groups. More important, institutions might well be designed to ensure that when shifts are occurring, it is not because of arbitrary or illegitimate constraints on the available range of arguments. This is a central task of constitutional design, and in this light a system of checks and balances might be defended, not as an undemocratic check on the will of the people, but as an effort to protect against potentially harmful consequences of group discussion.

To explore some of the advantages of heterogeneity, imagine a deliberating body consisting of all citizens in the relevant group; this may mean all citizens in a community, a state, a nation, or the world. By hypothesis, the argument pool would be very large. It would be limited only to the extent that the set of citizen views was similarly limited. Social influences would undoubtedly remain. Hence people might shift because of a desire to maintain their reputation and self-conception, by standing in a certain relation to the rest of the group. But to the extent that deliberation revealed to people that their private position was different, in relation to the group, from what they thought it was, any shift would be in response to an accurate understanding of all relevant citizens, and not a product of an accidentally skewed group sample.

This thought experiment does not suggest that the hypothesized deliberating body would be ideal. Perhaps all citizens, presenting all individual views, would offer a skewed picture from the normative point of view; in a pervasively unjust society, a deliberating body consisting of everyone may produce nothing to celebrate. Perhaps weak arguments would be made and repeated and repeated again, while good arguments would be offered infrequently. As we will see below, it is often important to ensure enclaves in which polarization will take place, precisely in order to ensure the emergence of views that are suppressed, by social influences or otherwise, but reasonable or even right. But at least a deliberating body of all citizens would remove some of the distortions in the group polarization experiments, where generally like-minded people, not exposed to others, shift in large part because of that limited exposure. Hence the outcomes of these deliberations will not be a product of the arbitrariness that can be introduced by skewed argument pools.

C. Enclave deliberation and suppressed voices

The discussion has yet to focus on the potential vices of heterogeneity and the potentially desirable effects of deliberating "enclaves," consisting of groups of like-minded individuals. It seems obvious that such groups can be extremely important in a heterogeneous society, not least because members of some demographic groups tend to be especially quiet when participating in broader deliberative bodies. In this light, a special advantage of what we might call "enclave deliberation" is that it promotes the development of positions that would otherwise be invisible, silenced, or squelched in general debate. While this is literally dangerous in numerous contexts, it can also be a great advantage; many desirable social movements have been made possible through this route. The efforts of marginalized groups to exclude outsiders, and even of political parties to limit their primaries to party members, can be justified in similar terms. Even if group polarization is at work – indeed *because* group polarization is at work – enclaves can provide a wide range of social benefits, not least because they greatly enrich the social "argument pool."

The central empirical point here is that in deliberating bodies, high-status members tend to initiate communication more than others, and their ideas are more influential, partly because low-status members lack confidence in their own abilities, partly because they fear retribution.[23] For example, women's ideas are often less influential and sometimes are "suppressed altogether in mixed-gender groups,"[24] and in ordinary circumstances, cultural minorities have disproportionately little influence on decisions by cultural mixed groups.[25] Interestingly, there is evidence that with changes in gender norms, some tasks show no gender differences in influence on groups; this evidence confirming the claim that people's role in group deliberation will be influenced by whether social norms produce status hierarchies. In these circumstances, it makes sense to promote deliberating enclaves in which members of multiple groups may speak with one another and develop their views.

But there is a serious danger in such enclaves. The danger is that through the mechanisms of social influence and persuasive arguments, members will move to positions that lack merit but are predictable consequences of the particular circumstances of enclave deliberation. In the extreme case, enclave deliberation may even put social stability at risk (for better or for worse). And it is impossible to say, in the abstract, that those who sort themselves into enclaves will generally move in a direction that is desirable for society at large or even for its own members.

There is no simple solution to the dangers of enclave deliberation. Sometimes the threat to social stability is desirable. From the standpoint of institutional design, the problem is that any effort to promote enclave deliberation will ensure group polarization among a wide range of groups, some necessary to the pursuit of justice, others likely to promote injustice, and some potentially quite dangerous. In this light we should be able to see more clearly the sense in which Edmund Burke's conception of representation – rejecting "local purposes" and "local prejudices" in favor of "the general reason of the whole"[26] – is not contingently but is instead *essentially* conservative (speaking purely descriptively, as a safeguard of existing practices). The reason is that the submersion of "local purposes" and "local prejudices" into a heterogeneous "deliberative assembly" will inevitably tend to weaken the resolve of groups – and particularly low-status or marginalized groups – whose purely internal deliberations would produce a high degree of polarization.

Hence James Madison – with his fear of popular passions producing "a rage for paper money, for an abolition of debts, for an equal division of property, or for any other improper or wicked project"[27] – would naturally be drawn to a Burkean conception of representation, favoring large election districts and long length of service[28] to counteract the forces of polarization. By contrast, those who believe that "destabilization" is an intrinsic good, or that the status quo contains sufficient injustice that it is worthwhile to incur the risks of encouraging polarization on the part of diverse groups, will, or should, be drawn to a system that enthusiastically promotes insular deliberation within enclaves.

In a nation in which most people are confused or evil, enclave deliberation may be the only way to develop a sense of clarity or justice, at least for some. But even in such a nation, enclave deliberation is unlikely to produce change unless its members are eventually brought into contact with others. In democratic societies, the best response is to ensure that any such enclaves are not walled off from competing views, and that at certain points there is an exchange of views between enclave members and those who disagree with them. It is total or near-total self-insulation, rather than group deliberation as such, that carries with it the most serious dangers, often in the highly unfortunate (and sometimes deadly) combination of extremism with marginality.

D. The public sphere and appropriate heterogeneity

1. *The public sphere*. A reasonable conclusion would return to the need for full information, not only about facts but also about relevant values and options, and suggest that for a designer or leader of any institution, it makes sense to promote ample social space both for enclave deliberation and for discussions involving a broad array of views, including those who have been within diverse enclaves. The idea of a "public sphere," developed most prominently by Jürgen Habermas, can be understood as an effort to ensure a domain in which multiple views can be heard by people with multiple perspectives.[29] Of course any argument pool will be limited. No one has time to listen to every point of view. But an understanding of group polarization helps shows that heterogeneous groups are often a far better source of good judgments, simply because more arguments will be made available.

2. *A new look at group representation*. The point very much bears on the continuing debate over proportional or group representation.[30] On one approach,

political groups should be allowed to have representation to the extent that they are able to get more than a minimal share of the vote. On another approach, steps would be taken to increase the likelihood that members of disadvantaged or marginal groups – perhaps African-Americans, religious minorities, gays and lesbians, women – would have their own representatives in the deliberating body. The decision whether to move in one or another direction depends on many factors, and an understanding of group polarization is hardly sufficient. But at least it can be said that proportional or group representation draws strength from the goal of ensuring exposure to a diverse range of views. On the one hand, group representation should help counteract the risks of polarization, and susceptibility to cascade effects, that come from deliberation among like-minded people. On the other hand, group representation should help reduce the dangers that come from insulation of those in the smaller enclave, by subjecting enclave representations to a broader debate. For these purposes, it might well be insufficient that representatives, not themselves members of any enclave, are electorally accountable to constituents who include enclave members. The point of group representation is to promote a process in which those in the enclave hear what others have to say, and in which those in other enclaves, or in no enclaves at all, are able to listen to people with very different points of view.

3. *Appropriate heterogeneity.* The principal qualification here is that the real question is how to ensure *appropriate* heterogeneity. For example, it would not make sense to say that in a deliberating group attempting to think through issues of affirmative action, it is important to allow exposure to people who think that slavery was good and should be restored. The constraints of time and attention call for limits to heterogeneity; and – a separate point – for good deliberation to take place, some views are properly placed off the table, simply because time is limited and they are so invidious, implausible, or both. This point might seem to create a final conundrum: To know what points of view should be represented in any group deliberation, it is important to have a good sense of the substantive issues involved, indeed a sufficiently good sense as to generate judgments about what points of view must be included and excluded. But if we already know that, why should we not proceed directly to the merits? If we already know that, before deliberation occurs, does deliberation have any point at all?

The answer is that we often do know enough to know which views count as reasonable, without knowing which view counts as right, and this point is sufficient to allow people to construct deliberative processes that should correct for the most serious problems potentially created by group deliberation. What is necessary is not to allow every view to be heard, but to ensure that no single view is so widely heard, and reinforced, that people are unable to engage in critical evaluation of the reasonable competitors.

E. The deliberative opinion poll: a contrast

In an interesting combination of theoretical and empirical work, James Fishkin has pioneered the idea of a "deliberative opinion poll," in which small groups, consisting of highly diverse individuals, are asked to come together and to deliberate about various issues. Deliberative opinion polls have now been conducted in several nations, including the United States, England and Australia. Fishkin finds some noteworthy shifts in individual views; but he does not find a systematic tendency toward polarization. In his studies, individuals shift both toward and away from the median of predeliberation views.

In England, for example, deliberation led to reduced interest in using imprisonment as a tool for combating crime.[31] The percentage believing that "sending more offenders to prison" is an effective way to prevent crime went down from 57 percent to 38 percent; the percentage believing that fewer people should be sent to prison increased from 29 percent to 44 percent; belief in the effectiveness of "stiffer sentences" was reduced from 78 percent to 65 percent. Similar shifts were shown in the direction of greater enthusiasm for procedural rights of defendants and increased willingness to explore alternatives to prison. In other experiments with the deliberative opinion poll, shifts included a mixture of findings, with larger percentages of individuals concluding that legal pressures should be increased on fathers for child support (from 70 percent to 85 percent) and that welfare and health care should be turned over to the states (from 56 percent to 66 percent). Indeed, on many particular issues, the effect of deliberation was to create an increase in the intensity with which people held their pre-existing convictions. These findings are consistent with the prediction of group polarization. But this was hardly a uniform pattern, and on some questions deliberation increased the percentage of people holding a minority position (with, for example, a jump from 36 percent to 57 percent of people favoring policies making divorce "harder to get"). These are not the changes that would be predicted by group polarization.

There appear to be several factors distinguishing the deliberative opinion poll from experiments on group polarization. First, Fishkin's deliberators did not vote as a group, and opinions were collected both individually and confidentially; while group polarization is observed when no group decision is expected, the extent of polarization is likely to decrease, simply because members have not been asked to sign onto a group decision as such. Second, Fishkin's experiments involve random sampling of the population, designed to create a diverse and representative microcosm (note, though, that group polarization can and does occur within diverse groups). Third, the relevant experiments contained balanced panels of experts, able to respond to questions from small group discussions. Fourth, Fishkin's groups were overseen by moderators, trained to make sure that no one dominates the discussion, to ensure general participation, and to ensure a level of openness likely to alter some of the dynamics discussed here. Fifth, Fishkin's studies presented participants with a set of written materials that attempted to be balanced and that contained detailed arguments on both sides. The likely consequence would be to move people in different directions from those that would be expected by simple group discussion, unaffected by external materials inevitably containing a degree of authority. Indeed, the very effort to produce balance should be expected to shift large majorities into small ones, pressing both sides closer to 50 percent representation; and this is in fact what was observed in many of the outcomes in deliberative opinion polls.

In short, the external materials and expert panels shift the argument pool available to the deliberators and are also likely to have effects on social influence. Once certain arguments are on the table, it is harder to say how one or another position will affect a group member's reputation. Taken as a whole, a significant amount of Fishkin's data nonetheless seems consistent with the group polarization hypothesis. What does not is probably a product of some combination of moderator behavior, effects of external presentation, and deviations produced by convincing arguments from members of the particular groups involved. The most sensible conclusion is that the existence of monitors, an absence of a group decision, the great heterogeneity of the people involved in Fishkin's studies, together with the external arguments, makes the deliberative opinion poll quite different from the group polarization studies, in which small groups of deliberators have relatively clear antecedent tendencies in one or another direction.

There are large lessons here about appropriate institutional design for deliberating bodies. Group polarization can be heightened, diminished, and possibly even eliminated with seemingly small alterations in institutional arrangements. To the extent that limited argument pools and social influences are likely to have unfortunate effects, correctives can be introduced, perhaps above all by exposing group members, at one point or another, to arguments to which they are not antecedently inclined. To the extent that institutional proposals are intended to increase public participation by promoting deliberation by ordinary people, they would do well to incorporate an understanding of these facts, which are sometimes neglected. The value of deliberation, as a social phenomenon, depends very much on social context – on the nature of the process and the nature of the participants. Here institutions are crucial. One of the most important lessons is among the most general: It is desirable to create spaces for enclave deliberation without insulating enclave members from those with opposing views, and without insulating those outside of the enclave from the views of those within it.

Notes

An earlier version of this essay, designed for a legal audience, appeared as "Deliberative Trouble? Why Groups Go To Extremes," *Yale Law Journal*, 110 (2000), 71–119. The present essay draws extensively on materials there, but also represents a significant revision and reorientation of the argument. I am especially grateful to James Fishkin for valuable comments on a previous draft.

1   See Amy Gutmann and Dennis Thompson, *Democracy and Disagreement* (Cambridge, MA: Harvard University Press, 1997), pp. 128–64; Jon Elster, ed., "Deliberative Democracy" (Cambridge: Cambridge University Press, 1998); Jürgen Habermas, *Between Facts and Norms* Oxford: Polity Press, 1996), pp. 274–328; Cass R. Sunstein, *The Partial Constitution* (Cambridge, MA: Harvard University Pres, 1993) pp. 133–45.

2   Note that this statement has two different implications. First, a deliberating group, asked to make a group decision, will shift toward a more extreme point in the direction indicated by the median predeliberation judgment. Second, the tendency of individuals who compose a deliberating group, if polled anonymously after discussion, will be to shift toward a more extreme point in the direction indicated by the median predeliberation judgment. Frequently these two phenomena are collapsed in the empirical literature, and I will not always distinguish between them here. But for some purposes it is important to distinguish them, and hence some work refers to the movement of groups as "choice shifts" and the movement of individuals as "group polarization." See Joahnnes A. Zuber et al., "Choice Shift and Group Polarization: An Analysis of the Status of Arguments and Social Decision Schemes," *Journal of Personality and Soc. Psychology*, 62 (1992), 50–61 at pp. 50, 59.

3   Caryn Christenson and Ann Abbott, *Team Medical Decision Making, in Decision Making in Health Care*, ed. Gretchen Chapman and Frank Sonnenberg (New York: Cambridge University Press, 2000), at pp. 267, 273–6.

4   R. Brown, *Social Psychology*, 2nd edn (New York: Free Press, 1986) p. 222. These include the United States, Canada, New Zealand, Germany and France. See, e.g., Johannes A. Zuber et al., "Choice Shift and Group Polarization," *Journal of Personality and Social Psychology*, 62 (1992), 50–61(Germany); Dominic Abrams et al., "Knowing What To Think By Knowing Who You Are," British Journal of Social Psychology, 29 (1990), 97–119 at p. 112 (New Zealand). Of course it is possible that some cultures would show a greater or lesser tendency toward polarization; this would be an extremely interesting area for empirical study.

5   See D. G. Myers, "Discussion-Induced Attitude Polarization," *Human Relations*, 28 (1975), p. 699.

6   Brown, p. 224.

7   D. G. Myers and G. D. Bishop, "Enhancement of Dominant Attitudes in Group Discussion," *Journal of Personality and Social Psychology*, 20 (1971), 386–91.

8   See ibid.

9   See, e.g., Mark Kelman et al. "Context Dependence in Legal Decision Making," *Behavioral Law and Economics*, ed. Cass R. Sunstein (New York: Cambridge University Press, 2000), pp. 61, 71–6.

10 See Brooke Harrington, "The pervasive effects of embeddedness in organizations" (unpublished manuscript 2000), p. 24.

11 See Hermann Brandstatter, "Social Emotions in Discussion Groups," *Dynamics of Group Decisions,* ed. Hermann Brandstatter et al.) Beverly Hills: Sage Publications, 1978).

12 See Russell Spears, Martin Lea and Stephen Lee, "De-Individuation and Group Polarization in Computer-Mediated Communication," *British Journal of Social Psychology,* 29 (1990), 121–34; Dominic Abrams et al., "Knowing What To Think By Knowing Who You Are," *British Journal of Social Psychology,* 29 (1990), 97–119 at p. 112; Patricia Wallace, *The Psychology of the Internet* (Cambridge: Cambridge University Press), pp. 73–6.

13 See Lee Roy Beach, *The Psychology of Decision Making in Organizations* (Thousand Oaks, CA: Sage Publications, 1997); Harrington, "The pervasive effects of embeddedness in organizations."

14 A third possibility is that hearing other similar opinions produces greater confidence in individual positions, opening members to a more extreme judgment in the same direction raised recently by Heath and Gonzales. See Chip Heath and Richard Gonzales, "Interaction with others increases decision confidence but not decision quality: evidence against information collection views of interactive decision making," *Organizational Behavior and Human Decision Processes,* 61 (1997), 305–26.

15 See H. Burnstein, "Persuasion as argument processing, in group decision making," ed. H. Brandstatter, J. H. Davis and G. Stocker-Kreichgauer (London: Academic press, 1982).

16 Brown, p. 226.

17 See David Schkade, Cass R. Sunstein and Daniel Kahneman, "Deliberating about dollars," Columbia Law Review, 100 (2000, 1139–75).

18 See R. T. Riley and T. F. Pettigrew, "Dramatic events and attitude change," Journal of Personality and Social Psychology, 34 (1976), 1004–15.

19 Ronald N. Jacobs, *Race, Media and the Crisis of Civil Society* (New York: Cambridge University Press, 2000), p. 144.

20 See Cass R. Sunstein, *Republic.com* (Princeton, NJ: Princeton University Press, 2001).

21 Wallace, pp. 73–84.

22 See Jürgen Habermas, *A Theory of Communicative Action* (Boston: Beacon Press, 1984), p. 99. Thus Habermas distinguishes between strategic and communcative action and stresses "the cooperatively pursued goal of reaching understanding"; compare the treatment in Gutmann and Thompson, *Democracy and Disagreement,* pp. 52–94, emphasizing the idea of reciprocity, which emphasizes the desire to justify one's position by reference to reasons.

23 See Christenson and Abbott, "Team medical decision making", p. 273.

24 Ibid. p. 274.

25 C. Kirchmeyer and A. Cohen, "Multicultural groups: their performance and reactions with constructive conflict," *Group and Organization management,* 17 (1992), p. 153.

26 See "Speech to the Electors (Nov. 3, 1774)," reprinted in *Burke's Politics,* ed. R. J. S. Hoffman and P. Levack (New York: Knopf, 1949), p. 116.

27 See *The Federalist*, No. 10.

28 See Cass R. Sunstein, "Interest groups in American public law," *Stanford Law Review*, 38 (1985), 29–87 at p. 42.

29 See Jürgen Habermas, *The Structural Transformation of the Public Sphere* (Oxford: Polity, 1991), pp. 231–50.

30 See Anne Phillips, *The Politics of Presence* (Oxford: Oxford University Press, 1995); Iris Young, *Justice and the Politics of Difference* (Princeton, NJ: Princeton University Press, 1994), pp. 183–91; Cass R. Sunstein, "Beyond the republican revival," *Yale Law Journal*, 97 (1988), 1539–90 at pp. 1585–9.

31 See James Fishkin, *The Voice of the People* (New Haven, CN: Yale University Press, 1995).

5

Activist Challenges to Deliberative Democracy

Iris Marion Young

Screen and song celebrate social justice movements that protested in the streets when they were convinced that existing institutions and their normal proce-dures only reinforced the status quo. Many rights have been won in democratic societies by means of courageous activism – the eight-hour day, votes for women, the right to sit at any lunch counter. Yet contemporary democratic theory rarely reflects on the role of demonstration and direct action.[1] Indeed, it might be thought that one of the major strains of contemporary democratic theory, the theory of deliberative democracy, should be critical of typical tactics of activism as such street marches, boycotts, or sit-ins, on the grounds that their activities confront rather than engage in discussion with people the movement's members disagree with.

This essay constructs a dialogue between two "characters" with these differ-ing approaches to political action, a deliberative democrat and an activist.[2] A dialogue between them is useful because their prescriptions for good citizenship clash in some respects. I aim through this exercise to bring out some of the limitations of at least some understandings of deliberatively democratic norms, especially if they are understood as guiding practices in existing democracies where structural inequalities underlie significant injustices or social harms. At the same time I aim to foreground some of the virtues of non-deliberative politi-cal practices for democratic criticism. The "characters" of the deliberative demo-crat and the activist I construct as ideal types. Many political theorists and citizens doubtless sympathize with both, and the stances often shift and mix in the politi-cal world.

As I construe her character, the deliberative democrat claims that parties to political conflict ought to deliberate with one another and through reasonable argument try to come to an agreement on policy satisfactory to all. The activist is suspicious of exhortations to deliberate, because he believes that in the real world of politics, where structural inequalities influence both procedures and outcomes, democratic processes that appear to conform to norms of deliberation are usually biased toward more powerful agents.[3] The activist thus recommends that those who care about promoting greater justice should engage primarily in critical oppositional activity, rather than attempt to come to agreement with those who support or benefit from existing power structures.

In the dialogue I construct, the deliberative democrat claims that the activist does not adopt a stance of reasonableness. After answering these commonly heard charges on behalf of the activist, I consider four challenges the activist brings to the recommendation that responsible citizens should follow norms of deliberative democracy as the best form of political engagement. I find that the early challenges are easier for the deliberative democrat to answer than the later.

The purpose of the dialectic is not to recommend one side over the other, because I think that both approaches are valuable and necessary to democratic practice that aims to promote justice. Bringing the approaches into critical relation with one another in this way, however, helps sound a caution about trying to put ideals of deliberative democracy into practice in societies with structural inequalities. This dialogue also reveals tensions between the two stances that cannot be thoroughly resolved.

I. The Characters

For the purposes of this essay, I understand deliberative democracy as both a normative account of the bases of democratic legitimacy, and a prescription for how citizens ought to be politically engaged. The best and most appropriate way to conduct political action, to influence and make public decisions, is through public deliberation. In deliberation, parties to conflict, disagreement and decision-making propose solutions to their collective problems and offer reasons for them; they criticize one another's proposals and reasons, and are open to being criticized by others. Deliberative democracy differs from some other attitudes and practices in democratic politics in that it exhorts participants to be concerned not only with their own interests, but to listen to and take account of the interests of others insofar as these are compatible with justice. Practices of deliberative democracy also aim to bracket the influence of power differentials in political outcomes, because agreement between deliberators should be reached on the basis of argument, rather than as a result of threat or force.

The theory of deliberative democracy thus expresses a set of normative ideals according to which actual political processes are evaluated and usually found wanting. Political decisions ought to be made by processes that bring all the potentially affected parties or their representatives into a public deliberative process. Deliberators should appeal to justice and frame the reasons for their proposals in terms they claim that others ought to accept. Doing so rules out the assertion of simple partisan interest, or the attempt to compel assent by means of threats and sanction.

As I construct the character of the deliberative democrat here, however, she not only finds in the ideals of deliberative democracy means to criticize political processes. She also advocates processes and action to implement deliberative procedures in actually existing democracy, with all its conflict, disagreement, economic, social and political inequality. The deliberative democrat thinks that the best way to limit political domination and the naked imposition of partisan interest and the best way to promote greater social justice through public policy is to foster the creation of sites and processes of deliberation among diverse and disagreeing elements of the polity. She thus attributes several dispositions to the good citizen. The politically engaged citizen aiming to promote social justice seeks to criticize and debate with those with whom she disagrees or those with whom her interests initially conflict in public settings where she tries to persuade others that some policies or interests have unjust or harmful aspects or consequences. Through critical argument that is open to the point of view of others, she aims to arrive at policy conclusions freely acceptable by all involved.

Like that of the deliberative democrat, the stance of the activist offers itself as a model of citizen virtue. The activist is committed to social justice and normative value, and that politically responsible persons ought to take positive action to promote these. He also believes that the normal workings of the social, economic and political institutions in which he dwells enact or reproduce deep wrongs – some laws or policies have unjust effects, or social and economic structures cause injustice, or non-human animals and things are wrongly endangered, and so on. Since the ordinary rules and practices of these institutions tend to perpetuate these wrongs, we cannot redress them within those rules. The activist opposes particular actions or policies of public or private institutions, as well as systems of policies or actions, and wants them changed. Sometimes he also demands positive policies and action to reduce injustice or harm.

Besides being motivated by a passion for justice, the activist is often also propelled by anger or frustration at what he judges is the intransigence of people in power in existing institutions, who behave with arrogance and indifference toward the injustices the activist finds they perpetuate, or flatly deny them and rationalize their decisions and the institutions they serve as beneficent. Since many of his fellow citizens are ignorant of these institutional harms, or accept them with indifference or resignation, the activist believes it important to express outrage at continued injustice, in order to motivate others to act.

Typically the activist eschews deliberation, especially deliberation with persons wielding political or economic power and official representatives of institutions he believes perpetuate injustice or harm. He finds laughable the suggestion that he and his comrades should sit down with those whom he criticizes, and whose policies he opposes, to work out an agreement through reasoned argument they all can accept. The powerful officials have no motive to sit down with him, and even if they did agree to deliberate, they would have the power unfairly to steer the course of the discussion. Thus the activist takes other action which he finds more effective in conveying his criticism and furthering the objectives he believes right: picketing, leafleting, guerilla theater, large and loud street demonstrations, sit-ins, and other forms of direct action, such as boycotts. Often activists make public noise outside when deliberation is supposedly taking place on the inside.[4] Sometimes activists invade the houses of deliberation and disrupt their business by unfurling banners, throwing stink bombs, or running and shouting through the aisles. Sometimes they are convinced that an institution produces or perpetuates such wrong that the most morally appropriate thing for them to do is to try to stop its business – by blocking entrances, for example.

Morally acceptable tactics are much disputed by activists. Should they be strictly nonviolent or not, and precisely what does being nonviolent mean? Is being annoying and insulting acceptable, or should the activist be respectful? Is it acceptable to destroy or damage property as long as one does not hurt people or animals? I do not here wish to enter these debates. For the purposes of this characterization, I will assume that the activist believes that intentional violence directed at others is neither morally or politically acceptable, but that he has the right physically to defend himself if he is physically attacked. I will assume that the activist rejects tactics of intentionally producing serious damage to property – such as bombing or burning. Less damaging forms of defacement or breakage, especially as by-products of protest actions, need not be condemned.

II. Deliberative Judgment of Activism

Theories of deliberative democracy rarely mention political activities such as those I have made typical of activism, and thus we cannot derive from them a direct account of the extent to which political virtue as understood by deliberative democrats stands opposed to political virtue as I have characterized it for the activist. Nevertheless, we do know that many responsible political participants routinely condemn activists, claiming they are irrational nihilists who bring a bad name to good causes.

From the point of view of principles of deliberative democracy, what reasons might they have? We can reconstruct two kinds of reasons, I suggest. Some who see themselves guided by norms of deliberative democracy might say that activists engage in interest group politics rather than orienting their commitment to principles all can accept. They might also say that the stance of the activist is flatly unreasonable. Here I review such possible criticisms of activism from the point of view of deliberative democracy, and answer them on behalf of the activist.

As I construe her for the purposes of this encounter, the deliberative democrat judges the approach to democracy the activist takes as little different from the pressure group interest-based politics that she thinks should be transcended in order to achieve workable agreement and legitimate policy outcomes. An interest group approach to politics encourages people to organize groups to promote particular ends through politics and policy by pressuring or cajoling policy makers to serve those interests. By means of lobbying, buying political advertisements, contributing funds to parties and candidates, mobilizing votes for or against candidates who hold positions on certain issues, interest groups further their goals and defeat their opponents. They feel no obligation to discuss issues with those with whom their interests conflict in order to come to an agreement they all can accept. They simply aim to win the most for their group and engage in power politics to do so.

To this charge the activist responds that his stance differs from that of simple interest advocacy because he is committed to a universalist rather than partisan cause. There is a significant difference, he claims, between self-interest or group interest and an interest in redressing harm and injustice. The good citizen activist is not usually motivated by personal gain nor by the gain of groups he defends at an unfair expense of others. He sacrifices his time, career advancement, and money for the sake of the causes to which he is committed. He does indeed seek to bring pressure, the power of collective action, disruption and shame to effect change in the direction of greater justice. The power he and his comrades exert in the streets, however, is usually a mere David to the Goliath of power wielded by the state and corporate actors whose policies he opposes and aims to change. The deliberative democrat who thinks that power can be bracketed by the soft tones of the seminar room is naive.

While he is suspicious of the claim that he ought to engage in deliberation with the powerful agents he believes perpetuate injustice and harm or with those who support them, moreover, the activist does not reject discussion altogether. The promulgation and exchange of information and ideas is a major part of his political work, both within his activist organizations, and more broadly among other citizens whom he aims to convince that there are serious harms and injustices that they should protest and resist. When social, economic and political institutions produce unjust structural inequalities and other serious social and environmental harms, insists the activist, it is important for citizens to try to avoid complicity with the workings of those institutions. Activities of protest, boycott, and disruption are most appropriate for getting citizens to think seriously about what until then they may have found normal and acceptable. Activities of deliberation, on the contrary, tend more to confer legitimacy on existing institutions and effectively silence real dissent.

The deliberative democrat might claim that the stance of the activist is *unreasonable*. Reasonable political engagement, on this account, consists in the willingness to listen to those whom one believes are wrong, to demand reasons from them and to give arguments oneself aimed at persuading them to change their views. For the most part, the activist declines so to engage persons he disagrees with. Rather than on reason, according to this deliberative democrat, the activist relies on emotional appeal, slogans, irony and disruptive tactics to protest and make his claims.

It is common in the political life of many democracies thus to label an activist stance unreasonable and even "extremist". One can interpret such blanket labeling itself as a power ploy whose function is to rule out of bounds all claims that question something basic about existing institutions and the terms in which they put political alternatives. It is important, therefore, to consider the activist answer to the charge of being an irrational extremist: it relies on far too narrow an understanding of what is reasonable.

By "reasonable" here I mean having a sense of a range of alternatives in belief and action, and engaging in considered judgment in deciding among them. The reasonable person thus is also able and willing to justify his or her claims and actions to others. As I have constructed the stance of the activist, he is principled and reasonable in this sense. He reflects on some of the wrongs that come to people and non-human things and has an account of some of the social causes of those wrongs that he believes are alterable. He considers alternative means for bringing attention to those wrongs and calling upon others to help redress them, and he is usually quite prepared to justify the use of specific means on specific occasions, both to his comrades and to others, such as television reporters. While his principles often lead him to protest outside of or disrupt the meetings of powerful people with whom he disagrees, one of his primary reasons for such protest is to make a wider public aware of institutional wrongs and persuade that public to join him in pressuring for change in the institutions. While not deliberative, then, in the sense of engaging in orderly reason-giving, most activist political engagements aim to *communicate* specific ideas to a wide public. They use slogans, humor and irony to do so because discursive arguments alone are not likely to command attention or inspire action.[5]

In the real world of politics there are some nihilistic and destructive persons who demonstrate and protest from blind rage or because they get pleasure from destruction. Such a nihilistic stance describes few activists, however; activists are often more self-conscious than other political actors about having good reasons for what they do and disciplining their fellow to follows rules in their collective actions. The common rhetorical move of official powers to paint all protest action with the tar of "extremism" should be resisted by anyone committed to social justice and reasonable communication.

Now that the activist has answered the deliberative democrat's suspicion that he is not worth talking to, we can hear his criticism of deliberative recommendations for political engagement and citizen virtue. I will present these challenges in four steps, giving the deliberative democrat the opportunity to respond to each.

108 Iris Marion Young

III. Deliberative Procedures are Exclusive

Exhorting citizens to engage in respectful argument with others they disagree with is a fine recommendation for the ideal world that the deliberative democrat theorizes, says the activist, where everyone is included and are the political equals of one another. This is not the real world of politics, however, where powerful elites representing structurally dominant social segments have significant influence over political processes and decisions.

Deliberation sometimes occurs in this real world. Officials and dignitaries meet all the time to hammer out agreements. Their meetings are usually well organized within structured procedures, and those who know the rules are often able to further their objectives through them by presenting proposals and giving reasons for them, which are considered and critically evaluated by the others, who give their own reasons. Deliberation, the activist says, is an activity of boardrooms and congressional committees, and sometimes even parliaments. Elites exert their power partly through managing deliberative settings. Among themselves they engage in debate about the policies that will sustain their power and further their collective interests. Entrance into such deliberative settings is usually rather tightly controlled, and the interests of many affected by the decisions made in them often receive no voice or representation. The proceedings of these meetings, moreover, are often not open to general observation and often they leave no public record. Observers and members of the press come only by invitation. Deliberation is primarily an activity of political elites who treat one another with cordial respect and try to work out their differences. Insofar as deliberation is exclusive in this way, and insofar as the decisions reached in such deliberative bodies support and perpetuate structural inequality, or otherwise have unjust and harmful consequences, says the activist, then it is wrong to prescribe deliberation for good citizens committed to furthering social justice. Under these circumstances of structural inequality and exclusive power, good citizens should be protesting outside these meetings, calling public attention to the assumptions made in them, the control exercised, and the resulting limitations or wrongs of their outcomes. They should use the power of shame and exposure to pressure deliberators to widen their agenda and include attention to more interests. As long as the proceedings exercise exclusive power for the sake of the interests of elites and against the interests of most citizens, then politically engaged citizens who care about justice and environmental preservation are justified even in taking actions aimed at preventing or disrupting the deliberations.

Many of the thousands who filled the streets of Seattle in December 1999, it seems to me, assumed just this account of the relation between deliberation and protest. Heads of state or other high officials came from all over the world to a meeting of the World Trade Organization (WTO) to deliberate and try to agree on a new round of global trade rules. Protestors criticized the meeting and many thought it should simply be stopped. They protested the exclusive methods of the WTO, that the proceedings of its commission are closed, and that the Seattle meeting itself was not public. They claimed that the WTO is a tool of transnational corporate power, and that its deliberations give little attention to the effects of the free trade regime on average citizens, especially the world's poorest people. The deliberations of the WTO are not legitimate and the agenda of the organization is morally wrong. As I write this some of my fellow citizens prepare to protest similar deliberations on agreement for free trade in the Americas. Not only are the meetings exclusive, but even the document they will discuss is not public. There is no alternative to protest and disruption, the activist thinks, when decisions affecting so many people are made by so few and almost in secret.

The advocate of deliberative democracy as a prescription for political processes and the behavior of good citizens has an easy answer to this criticism of deliberation. She agrees with many things the activist says. Insofar as the proceedings of elite meetings are exclusive and nonpublic, they are not democratic, even if they are deliberative. The norms of deliberative democracy call not only for discussion among parties who use the force of argument alone and treat each other as equals. They also require publicity, accountability and inclusion.[6] To be democratically legitimate, policies and actions decided on by means of deliberation ought to include representation of all affected interests and perspectives. The deliberations of such inclusively representative bodies ought to be public in every way. The people who speak and vote in such deliberative settings, finally, ought to be accountable to their fellow citizens for their opinions and decisions. The deliberative democrat will likely join the activist to protest outside exclusive and private deliberations. She exhorts the activist to join her call for deliberations whose proceedings are public, accountable and inclusive, and she allies with the activist in regarding deliberative processes as illegitimate unless they meet these conditions. She may consider activist protest a healthy means of deepening democracy, of creating open and inclusive settings of deliberative democracy.

IV. Formal Inclusion is not Enough

Criticism of political processes of discussion and decision-making which include only powerful insiders and take place behind closed doors is frequent and often effective in democratic politics. In response to such criticisms, official deliberative bodies have sometimes taken steps to make their processes more public and inclusive. They open their doors to observation by press and citizens, publish their proceedings and evaluations of their operations. Some legislative and other official bodies have discussed and implemented measures intended to open their

seats to a wider diversity of representatives, including campaign finance regulation, electoral process reform, or even quotas in party lists for under-represented
groups. In the United States, in the last thirty years norms of inclusiveness and
publicity have been taken more seriously than before. Public agencies and even
some powerful private agencies hold hearings to discuss policy proposals at which
members of the public are invited to testify. Influenced by some of the ideas of
James Fishkin, some local officials or non-government organizations have organized "citizen juries" that aim to be broadly representative of the profile of the
electorate.[7] Members of these panels listen to and question political candidates
on issues and then deliberate among themselves, often also receiving phone and
email contributions from citizens listening to proceedings on the radio. Many
students of democracy have commended the broadly participatory process of
public deliberation the state of Oregon undertook in the 1990s in its process of
restructuring its low income health care program. Another notable example of a
heroic effort to make public deliberation inclusive is the consultative process the
government of South Africa ran to discuss the new constitution which became
law in 1996. Not only did the constitutional commissioners invite comment on
the draft constitution by mail and email, but they conducted public meetings for
those unable to read the draft, explaining to attendees its content and inviting
response.

The deliberative democrat endorses measures such as these. She thinks the
good citizen should vigorously advocate for creative ways to expand the publicity of deliberations about problems and policy proposals and make them inclusive. If they have the opportunity to participate in such consultative deliberative
processes, they should do so, and if they are invited to help design them, they
should accept.

The activist is more suspicious even of these deliberative processes that claim
to give all affected by projected policies, or at least representatives of everyone,
the opportunity to express their opinions in a deliberative process. In a society
structured by deep social and economic inequalities, he believes that formally
inclusive deliberative processes nevertheless enact structural biases in which more
powerful and socially advantaged actors have greater access to the deliberative
process, and therefore are able to dominate the proceedings with their interests
and perspectives.

Under conditions of structural inequality normal processes of deliberation
often in practice restrict access to agents with greater resources, knowledge or
connections to those with greater control over the forum. We are familiar with
the many manifestations of this effective exclusion from deliberation. Where
radio and television are major fora for further deliberation, for example, citizens
either need the money or connections to get air time. Even when a series of
public hearings are announced for an issue, people who might wish to speak at
them need to know about them, be able to arrange their work and child care

schedule to be able to attend, be able to get to them, and have enough under-standing of the hearing process to participate. Each of these abilities is unevenly present among members of a society.

Some have argued that such differential access and participation characterized both of the ostensibly inclusive public deliberative processes I cited above: the Oregon medicaid process and the deliberations about the South African consti-tution. In the first case, participants in the consultative process turned out to be largely white, middle-class, able-bodied people, despite the fact that the pro-gram specifically was to serve lower income people. Many citizens of South Africa understood too little about the meaning of a constitution, or their lives were too occupied by survival, for them to become involved in that deliberative process.

The activist thus argues that citizens who care about justice should continue to criticize processes of public deliberation from the outside, even when the latter have formal rules aimed at producing wide participation. To the extent that structural inequalities in the society operate effectively to restrict access to these deliberative processes, their deliberations and conclusions are not legiti-mate. Responsible citizens should remain at least partially outside, protesting the process, agenda, and outcome of these proceedings, and demonstrating against the underlying relations of privilege and disadvantage that condition them. They should aim to speak on behalf of those *de facto* excluded, and attempt to use tactics such as strikes, boycotts and disruptive demonstrations to pressure these bodies to act in ways that respond to the needs and interests of those effectively excluded. If we participate in these formally inclusive processes, the activist says, we help confer undeserved legitimacy on them, and fail to speak for those who remain outsiders.

The recent World Trade Organization meetings offer another example of an attempt at a more inclusive process that most activists there rejected as illegiti-mate. In response to the advance criticism of the WTO as an exclusive forum dominated by corporate interests in the service of Northern hemispheric econo-mies, some of its officials hastily organized a meeting to take place the day before the official WTO meeting, to which representatives of non-governmental or-ganizations were invited. Many activists considered this gesture an absurd at-tempt to coopt and dampen an opposition to the WTO proceedings, which even before they began had been very effective in bringing issues of transpar-ency and global inequality before a world public; they demonstrated outside the NGO meetings. Some of the NGO representatives who decided to attend the meeting, moreover, were sorely disappointed. They found the agenda already decided, and that they were passively listening to the WTO head, the US trade secretary, and other powerful figures, with only minimal time available to ques-tion their speeches or make speeches of their own. When the agents of exclusion try to reform political processes to be more publicly inclusive, it seems, they fall far short of providing opportunity for real voice for those less privileged in the social structures. Given these realities, the activist says, the most responsible stance for the citizen who cares about justice is to expose this manipulative power and express the legitimate demands of those suffering under structural injustices, whether or not the powerful will listen to them.

The deliberative democrat agrees with the activist's exposure and critique of the way that structural inequalities effectively limit access of some people to formally inclusive deliberative settings. Unlike the activist, however, she thinks that the responsible citizen should engage and argue with those who design and implement these settings to persuade them that they should devote thought and resources to activities that will make them more inclusive and representative of all the interests and perspectives potentially affected by the outcome of policy discussions. In a polity that claims to be committed to democracy, it should be possible to persuade many members of a formally inclusive deliberative public that special measures may need to be taken to facilitate voice and representation for segments of the society subject to structural disadvantages. Protesting and making demands from the outside may be an effective way to bring attention to injustices that require remedy, says the deliberative democrat, but on their own they do not propel the positive institutional change that would produce greater justice. Those who believe such change is necessary must enter deliberative proceedings with those indifferent or hostile to them in an effort to persuade a democratic public of their rightness.[8]

The activist's first two challenges have focused on the publicity and inclusiveness of the deliberative public, rather than on the terms and content of deliberations. So far the deliberative democrat and the activist perspective are rather close on the issues of morally legitimate political processes, inasmuch as both criticize formal and *de facto* exclusions from deliberations. The difference between them may reduce to how optimistic they are about whether political agents can be persuaded that there are structural injustices, the remedy for which an inclusive deliberative public ought to agree on. Once we turn to analyze issues of the terms and content of deliberations, however, we see more divergence between the deliberative democrat and the activist.

V. Constrained Alternatives

Let us suppose that by some combination of activist agitation and deliberative persuasion some deliberative settings emerge that approximately represent all those affected by the outcome of certain policy decisions. Given the world of structural inequality as we know it, the activist believes such a circumstance will be rare at best, but is willing to entertain the possibility for the sake of this argument. The activist remains suspicious of the deliberative democrat's exhortation to engage in reasoned and critical discussion with people he disagrees with, even on the supposition that the public where he engages in such discussion really includes the diversity of interests and perspectives potentially affected by policies. That is because he perceives that existing social and economic structures have set unacceptable constraints on the terms of deliberation and its agenda.

Problems and disagreements in the real world of democratic politics appear and are addressed against the background of a given history and sedimentation of unjust structural inequality, says the activist, which helps set agenda priorities and constrains the alternatives that political actors may consider in their deliberations. When this is so, both the deliberative agenda and the institutional constraints it mirrors should themselves be subject to criticism, protest and resistance.[9] Going to the table to meet with representatives of those interests typically served by existing institutional relations, to discuss how to deal most justly with issues that presuppose those institutional relations, gives both those institutions and deliberative process too much legitimacy. It coopts the energy of citizens committed to justice, leaving little time for mobilizing people to bash the institutional constraints and decision-making process from the outside. Thus the responsible citizen ought to withdraw from implicit acceptance of structural and institutional constraints by refusing to deliberate about policies within them. Let me give some examples.

A local anti-poverty advocacy group engaged in many forms of agitation and protest in the years leading up to passage of the Personal Responsibility and Work Opportunity Reconciliation Act by the US Congress in the spring of 1996. This legislation fundamentally changed the terms of welfare policy in the United States. It abolished entitlements to public assistance for the first time in 60 years, allowing states to deny benefits when funds have run out. It requires recipients of Temporary Assistance to Needy Families to work at jobs after a certain period, and allows states to vary significantly in their programs. Since passage of the legislation, the anti-poverty advocacy group has organized recipients and others who care about welfare justice to protest and lobby the state house to increase welfare funding, and to count serving as a welfare rights advocate in local welfare offices as a "work activity."

In its desire to do its best by welfare clients, the county welfare department proposes to establish an advisory council with significant influence over the implementation and administration of welfare programs in the county. They have been persuaded by advocates of deliberative democracy that proceedings of this council should be publicly accountable, and organized so as to facilitate serious discussion and criticism of alternative proposals. They believe that democratic justice calls for making this council broadly inclusive of county citizens, and they think legitimate deliberations will be served particularly if they include recipients and their advocates on the council. So they invite the anti-poverty advocacy group to send representatives to the council and ask them to name recipient representatives from among the welfare rights organization with which they work.

After deliberating among themselves for some weeks, the welfare activists decline to join the council. The constraints that federal and state law set on welfare policy, they assert, make it impossible to administer a humane welfare policy. Such a council will deliberate about whether it would be more just to place local welfare offices here or there, but will have no power to expand the number of offices. They will decide how best to administer child care assistance, but they will have no power to decide who is eligible for that assistance, or the total funds to support the program. The deliberations of a county welfare implementation council face numerous other constraints that will make its outcomes inevitably unjust, according to the activist group. All citizens of the county who agree that the policy framework is unjust, and especially the welfare activists themselves, have a responsibility to stay outside such deliberations and instead pressure the state legislature to expand welfare options, by, for example, staging sit-ins at the state department of social services.

The deliberative democrat finds such refusal and protest action uncooperative and counterproductive. Surely it is better to work out the most just form of implementation of legislation than to distract lawmakers and obstruct the routines of overworked case workers. The activist replies that it is wrong to cooperate with policies and processes that presume unjust institutional constraints. The problem is not that policy-makers and citizen deliberations fail to make arguments, but that their starting premises are unacceptable.

It seems to me that advocates of deliberative democracy who believe that deliberative processes are the best way to conduct policies even under the conditions of structural inequality that characterize democracies today have no satisfactory response to this criticism. Many advocates of deliberative procedures seem to find no problem with structures and institutional constraints that limit policy alternatives in actual democracies, advocating reflective political reasoning within them to counter irrational tendencies to reduce issues to soundbites and decisions to aggregate preferences. In their detailed discussion of the terms of welfare reform in *Democracy and Disagreement*, for example, Amy Gutmann and Dennis Thompson appear to accept as given that policy action to respond to the needs of poor people must come in the form of poor support rather than changes in tax policy, the relation of private and public investment, public works employment, and other more structural ways of undermining deprivation and income inequality.[10] James Fishkin's innovative citizens' forum deliberating national issues in connection with the 1996 political campaign, to take another example, seemed to presume as given all the fiscal, power, and institutional constraints on policy alternatives that the US Congress and mainstream press assumed. To the extent that such constraints assume existing patterns of class inequality, residential segregation and gender division of labor as given, the activist's claim is plausible that there is little difference among the alternatives debated, and he suggests that the responsible citizen should not consent to these assumptions, but instead agitate for deeper criticism and change.

The ongoing business of legislation and policy implementation will assume existing institutions and their priorities as given unless massive concerted action works to shift priorities and goals. Most of the time, then, politics will operate under the constrained alternatives that are produced by and support structural inequalities. If the deliberative democrat tries to insert practices of deliberation into existing public policy discussions, she is forced to accept the range of alternatives that existing structural constraints allow. While two decades ago in the United States there were few opportunities for theorists of deliberative democracy to try to influence the design and process of public discussion, today things have changed. Some public officials and private foundations have become persuaded that inclusive, reasoned extensive deliberation is good for democracy, and wish to implement ideals in the policy formation process. To the extent that such implementation must presuppose constrained alternatives that cannot question existing institutional priorities and social structures, deliberation is as likely to reinforce injustice as to undermine it.

I think that the deliberative democrat has no adequate response to this challenge other than to accept the activist's suspicion of implementing deliberative processes within institutions that seriously constrain policy alternatives in ways that, for example, make it nearly impossible for the structurally disadvantaged to propose solutions to social problems that might alter the structural positions in which they stand. Only if the theory and practice of deliberative democracy are willing to withdraw from the immediacy of the already given policy trajectory can they respond to this activist challenge. The deliberative democrat should help create an inclusive deliberative setting in which basic social and economic structures can be examined; such settings for the most part must be outside ongoing settings of official policy discussion.

VI. Hegemonic Discourse

The deliberative democrat responds to this activist challenge, then, by proposing to create deliberative fora removed from the immediacy of the given economic imperatives and power structures, where representatives of diverse social sectors might critically discuss those imperatives and structures with an eye to reforming the institutional context. Even at this point, however, the activist remains suspicious of deliberative practices, for still another reason traceable to structural inequality. He worries that the majority of participants in such a reflective deliberative setting will be influenced by a common discourse which itself is a complex product of structural inequality. By a "discourse" I mean a system of stories and expert knowledge diffused through the society, which convey the widely accepted generalizations about how the society operates that are theorized in these terms, as well as the social norms and cultural values to which most of the people appeal when discussing their social and political problems and proposed solutions. In a society with longstanding and multiple structural inequalities, some such discourses are, in the terms derived from Gramsci, "hegemonic:" most of the people in the society think about their social relations in these terms, whatever their location in the structural inequalities. When such discursive systems frame a deliberative process, people may come to an agreement that is nevertheless at least partly conditioned by unjust power relations, and for that reason should not be considered a genuinely free consent. In some of his earlier work Habermas theorized such false consensus as "systematically distorted communication."[11] When such hegemonic discourse operates, parties to deliberation may agree on premises, they may accept a theory of their situation and give reasons for proposals that the others accept, but yet the premises and terms of the account mask the reproduction of power and injustice.

Deliberative democrats focus on the need for agreement to give policies legitimacy, and they theorize the conditions for achieving such agreement, but the idea of false or distorted agreement seems outside the theory. In opening the possibility that some consensus is false and some communication systematically distorted by power, I am not referring to consensus arrived at by excluding some affected people or which is extorted by means of threat and coercion. The phenomenon of hegemony or systematically distorted communication is more subtle than this. It refers to how the conceptual and normative framework of the members of a society is deeply influenced by premises and terms of discourse that make it difficult to think critically about aspects of their social relations or alternative possibilities of institutionalization and action. The theory and practice of deliberative democracy has no tools for raising the possibility that deliberations may be closed and distorted in this way. It lacks a theory of, shall we call it, ideology, as well as an account of the genealogy of discourses and their manner of helping to constitute the way individuals see themselves and their social world. For most deliberative democrats, discourse seems to be more "innocent."

James Bohman's deliberative theory is an important exception to this claim. Central to Bohman's account of the norms of public deliberation is a concern to identify ways that structural inequalities operate effectively to block the political influence of some while magnifying that of others, even when formal guarantees of political equality hold. Without distinguishing them in the way I have above, Bohman analyzes how the forms of exclusion and agenda domination I have discussed so far inhibit public deliberation in which all interests and perspectives are properly considered. An important test of the deliberative legitimacy of a political process, he argues, is the degree to which groups may not only gain a hearing for their opinions about issues and proposals already under discussion, but are also able to *initiate* discussion of problems and proposals.

In analyzing how actual public discussions may fall short of the normative requirements of legitimate democratic discussion, Bohman invokes a notion of distorted communication or ideology. This level of the influence of structural inequality over public discussion is the most insidious because the least apparent to all participants. It concerns the conceptual and imagistic frame for discussion, which often contains falsifications, biases, misunderstandings, and even contradictions which go unnoticed and uncriticized largely because they coincide with hegemonic interests or reflect existing social realities as though they are unalterable. For example, a discourse may distort communication, for example, by means of a rhetoric that presents as universal a perspective on experience or society derived from a specific social position.[12]

Let me offer a couple of examples of hegemonic discourses that may produce false consensus. The first comes from discourses about poverty and ways of addressing poverty through policy. Despite wide and vigorous debates about the causes and cures of poverty, both in the United States and increasingly in other parts of the world, there is a significant new consensus on many terms of the debate. There seems to be wide agreement that poverty should be conceptualized as a function of the failure of individuals to develop various skills and capacities necessary for inclusion in modern labor markets. Disagreement rages about the degree to which responsibility for such failure should be laid on those individuals and their families, or instead should be located in social institutions of education, social service, or economic development. That anti-poverty policy must ultimately transform individuals to fit better into the contemporary structures of wage employment, however, almost goes without saying. There is almost no other way to think about poverty policy than as a labor market policy.

International debates about greenhouse gas emissions, to take another example, contain fierce disagreement about whether and how such emissions should be reduced, and how the burdens of reductions should be distributed across the globe. Should richer, more advanced industrial states be required to reduce emissions in greater proportion to less developed countries? Are markets in pollution rights useful policy tools? Should governments subsidize development of "green" technologies for industrial production and private transportation? These debates take place within terms of discussion that only marginalized environmentalists question. The discussions assume that the economies of any developed society must rely heavily on the burning of fossil fuels, and that a high standard of living involves airconditioned buildings and lots of consumer goods, including a private automobile for every household. The social imaginations of both "developed" and "less developed" countries have few ideas for alternative forms of living that would not produce large carbon emissions.

Certain activists concerned with specific areas of social life claim to identify such ideologies and hegemonic discourses. Their doing so is necessarily partial with respect to social problems and policy issues, because ideology critique of this nature requires considerable thought and study, even for one set of issues. Democratic theory that emphasizes discussion as a criterion of legitimacy requires a more developed theory of the kinds and mechanisms of ideology, and methods for performing critique of specific political discussion. Such ideology critique needs not only to be able to analyze specific exchanges and speech, but to theorize how media contribute to naturalizing assumptions and making it difficult for participants in a discussion to speak outside of a certain set of concepts and images.[13] Because he suspects some agreements of masking unjust power relations, the activist believes it is important to continue to challenge these discourses and the deliberative processes that rely on them, and often he must do so by non-discursive means – pictures, song, poetic imagery, expressions of mockery and longing performed in rowdy and even playful ways aimed not at commanding assent but disturbing complacency. One of the activist's goal is to make us *wonder* about what we are doing, to rupture a stream of thought, rather than to weave an argument.

I have presented the deliberative democrat and the activist as two distinct characters with different recommendations for the best forms of political engagement. Such exclusive opposition between the stances is artificial, of course. Many people and organizations move between the stances in their political lives, depending on the issues at stake, who they are interacting with or confronting, and what they see as possibilities for action and achievement. I have put the stances in dialogue with one another precisely because I think they both are important for democratic theory and practice.

I have separated the stances into two opposing characters, however, in order to highlight the activist stance more than most recent democratic theory has done, and to cast a critical eye on some tendencies in deliberative democratic theory and practice. The activist's charges are serious, and they raise some issues not thematized in recent deliberative theory. From this dialogue I draw two conclusions about where democratic theory should go.

First, democratic theory should keep a distance from democratic practices in existing structural circumstances. While theorists ought to learn from ongoing processes of discussion and decision-making, and as citizens should participate in them in whatever ways seem most just and effective, we should resist the temptation to consider that ideals of deliberative democracy are put into practice when public officials or foundations construct procedures influenced by these ideas. Democratic theory, including the theory of deliberative democracy, should understand itself primarily as a *critical* theory, which exposes the exclusions and constraints in supposed fair processes of actual decision-making, which make the legitimacy of their conclusions suspect.

Second, we can deny that deliberative democracy recommends that citizens be willing always to engage discursively with all interests and social segments, reasonably expressing opinions and criticizing others. We can conceive the exchange of ideas and processes of communication taking place in a vibrant democracy as far more rowdy, disorderly and decentered, to use Habermas' term.[14] In this alternative conceptualization, processes of engaged and responsible democratic communication include street demonstrations and sit-ins, musical works and cartoons, as much as parliamentary speeches and letters to the editor. Normatively emblematic democratic communication here shifts from simply a willingness to give reasons for one's claims and listen to others, to a broader understanding of the generation and influence of public opinion. In this broader understanding participants articulate reasonable appeals to justice and also expose the sources and consequences of structural inequalities in law, the hegemonic terms of discourse, and the environment of everyday practice.

Even if we follow these recommendations, however, the dissonance between the stance of the deliberative democrat and the activist does not dissolve. Individuals and organizations seeking to undermine injustice and promote justice need *both* to engage in discussion with others to persuade them that there are injustices which ought to be remedied, and to protest and engage in direct action. The two kinds of activities cannot usually occur together, however, and for this reason one of them is liable to eclipse the other. The best democratic theory and practice will affirm them both while recognizing the tension between them.

Notes

1   There are some exceptions. Andrew Arato and Jean Cohen theorize the place of social movements and civil disobedience in the context of civil society; see *Civil Society and Political Theory* (Cambridge, MA: MIT Press, 1992). John Dryzek's arguments about the importance of oppositional movements of civil society that stand outside the state also refer to demonstration and protest activity. See *Deliberative Democracy and Beyond: Liberals, Critics, Contestations* (Oxford: Oxford University Press, 2000), especially ch. 4; see also *Demcracy in Capitalist Times: Ideals, Limits and Struggles* (Oxford: Oxford University Press, 1996). The distinction between the norms of deliberation and the norms of activism that this essay explores, however, should not be mapped onto a distinction between state and civil society. Civil society is certainly a site for deliberative politics, as many by now have pointed out, including Dryzek, though it is also usually the site for activism as well.
2   I am grateful to David Alexander, Nick Burbules, Natasha Levinson, Emily Robertson, Stephen White, and an anonymous reviewer for *Political Theory* for helpful comments on an earlier version of this essay.
3   In the effort to give the characters an embodied feel, I have endowed each with gender pronouns, rather than repeatedly using "he or she" for each. This decision

reveals a disturbing dilemma: Shall they both be male, both female, or one each male and female? Deciding that one shall be male and the other female only magnifies the dilemma: which should be which? As I try each one out I discover that my assignment evokes undesirable stereotypes whichever way it goes. If the deliberative democrat is male, then that position appears to carry added weight of rationality and calm, and the corresponding female activist seems to appear flighty and moved by passion primarily. Despite its own stereotyping dangers of making the activist appear aggressive, I have decided to cast the deliberative democrat as female and the activist as male, because at least this assignment more associates the female with power.

4   Michael Walzer offers a useful list of political activities additional to deliberation, some of which characterize the activist. See "Deliberation, and what Else?" *Deliberative Politics: Essays on Democracy and Disagreement*, ed. Stephen Macedo (Oxford: Oxford University Press, 1999).

5   See I. M. Young, *Inclusion and Democracy* (Oxford: Oxford University Press, 2000), ch. 2.

6   Amy Gutmann and Dennis Thompson insist on criteria of publicity and accountability in their book, *Democracy and Disagreement* (Cambridge, MA: Harvard University Press, 1996). Although they certainly agree that inclusion is a criterion, they do not make this a separate principle. For reasons to do so, see I. M. Young, "Justice, Inclusion and Deliberative Democracy," *Deliberative Politics* ed. Stephen Macedo.

7   Fishkin, *The Voice of the People* (New Haven: Yale University Press, 1995).

8   This is the position I argue for in early chapters of *Inclusion and Democracy* (Oxford: Oxford University Press, 2000).

9   This is one of Ian Shapiro's main responses to ideas of deliberative democracy in his essay, "Enough of Deliberation: Politics is about Interests and Power," *Deliberative Politics*, ed. Stephen Macedo, pp. 28–38.

10 Gutmann and Thompson, ch. 8; they are representative here of policy discussion on these issues in the United States, as well as of American public opinion.

11 See Jürgen Habermas, "On Systematically Distorted Communication," *Inquiry*, vol. 13, 1970, pp. 205–18. In light of the fact that Habermas has had much to contribute to contemporary theories of ideology or distorted communication, it is surprising and disappointing that his own theory of deliberative democracy as expressed in *Between Facts and Norms* gives almost no space to theorizing distorted communication and its effects on the legitimacy of political outcomes.

12 See James Bohman, *Public Deliberation* (Cambridge: MIT Press, 1996), especially ch. 3. See also Bohman, "Distorted Communication: Formal Pragmatics as a Critical Theory," *Perspectives on Habermas*, ed. L. Hahn (Indianapolis: Open Court, 2000).

13 John Thompson offers a contemporary theory of ideology that includes consideration of media. See *Ideology and Modern Culture* (Stanford: Stanford University Press, 1990). John Dryzek has a useful discussion of ideology in *Democracy in Capitalist Times: Ideals, Limits and Struggles* (Oxford: Oxford University Press, 1996), ch. 6.

14 Jürgen Habermas, *Between Facts and Norms* (Cambridge, MA: MIT Press, 1996), ch. 7.

6

Optimal Deliberation?

Ian Shapiro

People advocate deliberation for different reasons. Some think it inherently worthwhile. More commonly deliberation is valued for instrumental reasons: achieving consensus, discovering the truth, and consciousness-raising are among the usual suspects. Some of the time, at least, deliberation promotes these and related values. But it also has costs. Wasted time, procrastination and indecision, stalling in the face of needed change, and unfair control of agendas are among its frequent casualties. Sometimes by design, sometimes not, deliberation can amount to collective fiddling while Rome burns.

The question arises, therefore: how much is too much deliberation? And, related to it, what sorts of deliberation are best? Such open-ended questions do not lend themselves to illuminating answers. By way of narrowing the focus, let me hone them to a more specific one that should concern political theorists: What deliberation should government foster, encourage, and perhaps even in some circumstances try to require of people in the course of their collective endeavors? There are, no doubt, many sorts of deliberation that would be good, or wise, for people to engage in that we should nonetheless not want to force on them. Government should, perhaps, even encourage some of these. But the bedrock concern is with what government should try to promote; that is my concern here.

One possible view is that government should seek to maximize the forms of deliberation that enhance the rest of our lives, while minimizing those that do not. Call this the positive sum deliberative thesis. Reasonable as this might sound, it is a view I mean to reject as too demanding in some respects and as insufficiently demanding in others. The reasons it is too demanding have to do with the cognitive demands it places on would-be institutional designers, and its assumptions about the requirements of citizenship. Following some attention to definitional matters in part I, these are spelled out in parts II through IV. The positive sum deliberative thesis is insufficiently demanding, I maintain, because government should sometimes try to promote deliberation even when it detracts from other activities. This claim is explained and defended in parts V and VI.

I. Preliminaries

Think of political deliberation as involving the solicitous search for right solutions in circumstances of conflict. Let me start by explaining the elements of, and motivation for, this characterization.

By deploying the term *solicitous*, I intend to denote a cooperative enterprise – but something more than that. Deliberation is not an isolated activity. Rather it is an interactive one involving two or more people. We can be individually *reflective* but not individually *deliberative*. True, individual acts can be said to be more or less deliber*ate*, but that purposive idea fails to capture what commentators on politics generally have in mind when they refer to deliberation. (Notice that Rawls speaks of *reflective equilibrium*, not *deliberative equilibrium*, to describe the solipsistic exercise of moving back and forth between one's settled convictions and one's speculations about what individuals behind the veil of ignorance would choose. Deliberation differs from this type of activity just because it is conducted with others.)[1]

As well as being interactive, deliberation is a cooperative activity in the sense of being a common enterprise. Some commentators try to capture this aspect of deliberation by reference to reason-giving, as when courts are said to be more deliberative institutions than legislatures on the grounds that they supply published reasons for their decisions.[2] But significant though reason-giving is to legitimacy (particularly in the unelected institutions in a democracy), it does not capture the essence of deliberation. In this connection note that judges are called upon in the first instance to *judge*, not to deliberate (except in bench trials when they are supposed to role-play as jurors). In this they are no different from judges in sporting events or beauty contests. Even in appellate courts, the authors of different court opinions do not engage in deliberative exchange with their readers. Often they do not even engage in deliberative exchange with the authors of other opinions in the same case. Rather they try to show that they have the most cogently reasoned view, the best argument. This is a competitive justificatory enterprise, not a cooperative one. Argument is about winning, which is what lawyers are trained to do. Deliberation is about getting the right answer.

Nor is it the public character of reason-giving that is characteristic of deliberation. This is not to deny publicity's importance. A legitimate demand in democracies is that power-wielders be held publicly accountable.[3] This is one reason opposition politics matters: oppositions demand public justifications. Such demands for public accounting constrain power-wielders over and above the discipline of the ballot box.[4] But publicity is not the same thing as deliberation, as the example of political opposition reveals. Oppositions argue with, pillory, embarrass, and expose governments by holding them to public account; they do not engage in deliberation with them. Indeed, the principled cooperation and search for common ground characteristic of authentic deliberation is often said for these reasons to be undermined by publicity. Thus jury deliberations are held in secret, and motions for change of venue are granted when potential jury pools are said to be contaminated by pretrial publicity. Publicity has advantages for politics, though not unmitigated ones. It can promote grandstanding, and often it rewards those with the resources to shout loudest and longest. However, we need not concern ourselves with the balance of its advantages over its limitations here. Whatever the advantages, they are not those of deliberation.

Deliberation's distinctive focus is less on giving reasons for one's own views, and more on soliciting reasons from others for theirs. Why? One reason is that it can legitimate collective action. Anyone who has ever tried to get anything done among peers will know the importance of consulting them and getting their fingerprints on the result. Hence the epithet "Own the process, own the result," and the efficacy of the (sometimes cynical) "I feel your pain" approach to political campaigning. When people believe that their reasons have been taken into account, that they have been listened *to*, they can sometimes accept results that otherwise they would not, even when no preferences are changed by the deliberation. This will not always be successful, but, when it is, the reason-seeking dimension of deliberation contributes to the success.

This claim should not be confused with more expansive and less plausible claims that are sometimes made for the transformative effects of deliberation on preferences, and in particular the claim that deliberation is a worthwhile engine for generating social consensus.[5] Typically the motivating thought here is that people do not always have unalterable, or even well-formed, desires, so that understanding what others want, and why, can lead to adaptation of preferences in mutually compatible ways. The assumption is that if people talk for long enough in the right circumstances they will eventually be brought to agree, and that this is a good thing.

Both propositions are dubious. Deliberation can bring differences to the surface, widening divisions rather than narrowing them.[6] This is what Marxists hoped would result from "consciousness-raising": it would lead workers to discover their interests to be irreconcilably at odds with those of employers, assisting in the transformation of the proletariat from a class-in-itself to a revolutionary class-for-itself. In the event, these hopes proved naïve. The general point remains, however, that there is no particular reason to think deliberation will bring people together, even if they hope it will and want it to. A couple with a distant but not collapsing marriage might begin therapy with a mutual commitment to settling some longstanding differences and learning to accommodate one another better on matters that cannot be resolved. Once honest exchange gets under way, however, they might unearth new irreconcilable differences, with the effect that the relationship worsens and perhaps even falls apart in acrimony. Deliberation can reasonably be expected to shed light on human interaction, but this may reveal hidden differences as well as hidden possibilities for convergence. It all depends on what the underlying interests at stake actually are.

Even when agreement is achievable through deliberation, it is not always desirable. The advantages of opposition politics already mentioned in connection with publicity depend on argument and the ongoing clash of opinions. This stands in contrast to a consensus model of politics, as those who would move us "beyond adversary democracy" have emphasized.[7] People may not, in any case, want to settle all their disagreements. They may perceive consensus as oppressive, and they may take pleasure in differentiating themselves from one another. Mill and Tocqueville worried about the corrosive effects of the former;[8] modern theorists who celebrate difference see the latter as a solution to this problem.[9] We need not evaluate their arguments here. Suffice it to conclude that deliberation need not lead to agreement, and when it does this may not be advantageous.

A different dimension of deliberation is captured by the emphasis on the *search* for right solutions. It rests on the supposition that there may sometimes be solutions to conflicts which no party is likely to figure out on her own, but might emanate from collective brainstorming in a context where reason-seeking sets a backdrop of cooperative expectations. Two heads are better than one, three better than two, and so on. Up to a point. This line of argument can lead to a too many cooks in the kitchen syndrome, but before that (concededly elusive – see below) point is reached, deliberation can be the mother of institutional invention. Regardless of possible transformative or cathartic effects on preferences, deliberation may throw up ways of dealing with conflicts that otherwise might not come to the fore.

The emphasis on *right* solutions is meant, here, to connote something more than the economist's emphasis on mutually beneficial ones. Deliberation might reveal superior possibilities to those recognized by the parties *ex ante,* as already noted, but arguments for deliberation can be motivated by the thought that there are right solutions in an even stronger sense than this. We might think of them as involving selection among options on the Pareto possibility frontier, or perhaps even options that involve costs to some parties. Another way to put this is that arguments in support of deliberation often proceed on the assumption that there are right answers on which solicitous discussion will converge at least some of the time, particularly if the parties are committed to finding them. In many circumstances there will not be such solutions, in which case deliberation will, from this point of view, have been a waste of time. But, because of human fallibility, if for no other reason, it can often seem desirable for people to commit themselves to the idea that the truth and the right should operate as regulative ideals in working out their conflicts. This is perhaps why jury deliberations are frequently cited as a model in discussions of deliberative democracy: jurors are supposed to get to a right answer, not merely accommodate themselves to one another's preferences.[10]

The types of *solutions* called for by deliberation generally involve choosing among alternative courses of action. That is, deliberation is typically called for when something has to be done, not simply a conclusion reached. People deliberate about whether to convict or acquit a criminal defendant, about which of several policy options to select, or about whether to promote a junior colleague to tenure, but not about what the right answer is to a math problem. People might *argue* about that until someone gets it right, but it is not an appropriate subject for deliberation because there is no choice that has to be made about what to do.

The reference to *circumstances of conflict* is intended to limit our subject to political deliberation. This is not to deny that people can deliberate about many subjects that do not involve conflict, often – though by no means always – to good effect. But, as I elaborate below, these should be differentiated from those dimensions of human interaction involving conflict and hence the possibility of domination. Politics is born of conflict and its endemic possibility in human affairs, and political deliberation should be seen as one type of response to this reality.

II. Cognitive Demands

Bearing in mind this understanding of political deliberation as involving the solicitous search for right solutions in circumstances of conflict, we can now turn to the positive sum deliberative thesis. This is the idea, to recap, that government should seek to maximize the forms of deliberation that enhance our other activities, while minimizing those that detract from them.

Deliberation's benefits are not unequivocal, as we have seen. They depend on many contingencies of circumstance, and sometimes deliberation creates costs without attendant benefits. This reality leads to difficulties for would-be third-party institutional designers: often they do not know how much and what sorts of deliberation will enhance other activities. For instance, even if increasing certain types of deliberation within firms would make them more efficient, why suppose that a government planner will know what these are? It seems better to suppose that those involved in operating firms will know this, or have an incentive to find it out. Should they fail, while their competitors succeed, they will succumb to market discipline. Likewise with sports teams. If certain kinds of deliberation enhance performance, teams that engage in them will win and those that fail will pay the price. These examples suggest the wisdom of opting for a presumption in favor of insiders' wisdom: we should assume that those skilled in a particular activity are more likely than anyone else to know how to do it well, and, *a fortiori*, to know how much and what sorts of deliberation are most likely to enhance it. Insiders' wisdom is pertinent, we may say, to the pursuit of superordinate goods: the purposes for which people strive, from which they derive meaning and value.[11]

A presumption in favor of insiders' wisdom is not a presumption against insisting that the pursuit of collective activities be accompanied by deliberative institutions. It requires only that the purpose, and hence the justification, for such insistence is not enhanced pursuit of the activity in question. There are other reasons for requiring deliberation, linked to the reality that we exercise power over one another in the course pursuing superordinate goods. Managing the power dimensions of our activities well requires a distinctive kind of insiders' wisdom about what I describe as the subordinate good of democratic control. Government should aspire to be knowledgeable about this and deliberation is sometimes pertinent to it; or so I maintain in part V. But that claim differs from my thesis here: that the superordinate goods people pursue are to some degree distinguishable from the power relations in which they are enmeshed, and that, to the extent that this is so, they should be immune from government's reach.

Now it might be objected that my discussion so far depends on the misleading examples of economic efficiency and winning at sports. They have comparatively uncontroversial bottom lines by which success and failure can be judged: the firm makes, or fails to make, profits; the team wins or loses. But the purposes of many collective activities are more contentious and at any rate less clear. Evaluating scholarship in the context of tenure promotions at universities is notorious in this regard, at least in the social sciences and the humanities. One person's brilliant insight is the next person's banal truism, and the bottom line – such as it is – is measured by slippery reputational rankings that come loaded with performative freight: the best people are the best people because those reputed to be the best people declare that they are, and sometimes for no reason other than that. Apparently objective criteria, such as citation indexes, are easily manipulated by cliques of insiders, controlling the definitions of their own success. An external bottom line might at some point substantiate or undermine their judgments, but this can take decades or even generations to eventuate, and in some instances it will not be forthcoming at all.

This is a serious concern, not least because many collective human activities may have more in common with academic evaluation than with winning at sports or making firms profitable. But it cuts no ice with respect to my present argument. There are no more good reasons to believe government officials capable of second-guessing evaluations of Elizabethan poetry or different kinds of social science, however difficult this might be, than there are reasons to believe them capable of knowing how best to run firms or sports teams. Again, government may have a legitimate role to play in ensuring that these evaluations do not masquerade as something other than they are; that topic is for later. Contentious as it might be for insiders to agree on what makes for the best literature or social science, this is scarcely a reason to suppose that someone lacking insider's wisdom will do a better job. Textualists and contextualists disagree on how to read books; postmodernists and statisticians disagree on how to conduct social research. Serious as these disagreements might be, they will not be diminished by supposing that Jesse Helms can know which side, if either, is right.

Another possible objection to my argument thus far takes off from the observation that even when those who control firms generally agree on how they should be run, they could be wrong. Arguments to the effect that economy-wide investment decisions are destructively geared to the short term, that managers systematically undermine the interests of shareholders, and that buyers loot and destroy profitable firms in certain types of corporate buyouts all rest on convictions that this can be the case. Such possibilities should not be discounted. It is important, however, to distinguish arguments for intervention designed to protect the interests of vulnerable employees from arguments that assume outsiders know how to run firms most efficiently – let alone that they know when increased deliberation within the firm contributes to this goal. Too little deliberation might lead to inefficiencies, but so might too much deliberation. Asking the question whether deliberation is a good thing is a bit like asking the question whether a saw is a good tool. If you are making shelving it is, but not if you are trying to repair a watch.

III. Inherent Benefits

Government should take a similar hands-off approach to claims for enhanced deliberation on the grounds that it is inherently, rather than instrumentally, valuable. It may well be good for people to deliberate more rather than less, up to some point, depending on what else they want to do with their time. We should expect this to vary from person to person. The argument that more deliberation is always good calls to mind a group of political junkies sitting in a meeting discussing the dynamics of their last meeting, or the therapist who declares that in the best of all possible worlds everyone would always be in therapy.

Those who argue for deliberation's inherent benefits take a neo-Hegelian philosophical psychology for granted, according to which a kind of inter-subjective recognition is the highest stage of being.[12] We only become truly human, on this view, in justifying ourselves to one another. Deliberation is then seen as constituting that process, rather than to be evaluated by reference to whether it contributes to, or detracts from, other activities. This is one possible view of the human condition, but there are others, and it is difficult to see why it should be privileged over those other views. Skeptics might not want to embrace the robust demands on citizenship it suggests, and there is no reason that they should be compelled to do so. This is not to prevent true believers from deliberating with like-minded others for whom this is an important, perhaps even the most important, superordinate good.

Deliberation that is defended for its inherent benefits is best seen by government, then, as a consumption good; people should be free – but not forced – to engage in it. This is not to say that government should have no interest in it. People with intense preferences for deliberation might be able to exert disproportionate influence on outcomes by monopolizing control of agendas, or simply by virtue of the comparatively large amount of time they devote to politics.[13] When such thresholds are crossed we have too much deliberation, but how can we tell when this occurs? That issue is taken up in part VI.

IV. Locating Politics

First I must respond to a different challenge: that valid as my argument thus far might be, it does not deal with the political arena itself. There the superordinate good involved is government and, at least in a democracy, the presumption is against deferring to insiders' wisdom as far as government is concerned. The people are supposed to govern themselves in a democracy. Perhaps the government should be severely constrained in requiring deliberation of us, but it does not follow that we should be similarly constrained in requiring deliberation of the government.

The assumptions on which this view rests are implausibly romantic and fetishistic. They are implausibly romantic in hearkening back to the Ancient Greek comprehension of democracy as ruling and being ruled in turn. The doctrine of representative government developed as a response to the impracticality of that notion in a world of large nation–states, populations in the tens and hundreds of millions, and an advanced division of labor. It also reflects a partial concession to the idea that governing is an activity within the division of labor that involves distinctive competencies. The modern term *democratic control* suggests an independent activity that is subjected to democratic constraint. In this respect, democratic control of the government is not qualitatively distinct from democratic control of the firm: there are insiders, often but not always career professionals, who are expected both to have expert competence yet also to be constrained by democracy. Outsiders are no more thought competent to insist that Supreme Court justices should deliberate before voting to grant or deny certiorari than to insist that managers should deliberate before investing in a new line of products. Likewise with the jealously guarded House and Senate rules, the frequency or duration of cabinet meetings, or the arcane practices surrounding the Senate filibuster. Such practices may be reformed from time to time in ways that make them more or less deliberative, but this is scarcely in response to outside pressure for more deliberation. Rules for conducting government business are widely seen as part of the superordinate good about which the participants have the relevant insiders' wisdom. The demand that they do things in certain ways rather than others becomes relevant as their actions involve wielding power; in this government is not special.

The idea that politics is distinctive is fetishistic in that it tries to abstract the political dimension from the rest of our lives and then contain it in a distinct arena. Doing this requires specifying the arena's boundaries, but the two leading strategies to achieve this have been notable failures. The first is one of negation; its proponents try to nail down what politics is by establishing what it is not. Their central question is: which domains of human life are beyond politics? Despite an impressive variety of attempts by first-class theoretical minds, at least since John Stuart Mill wrote *On Liberty*, to draw a line on the basis of which an answer to this question can be constructed, no such attempt has won the philosophical high ground. The going answers turn out, on inspection, to rest on appeals to idealized pictures of private life, of traditional communities, or of communitarian utopias yet to be created. Decades of feminist scholarship have now rendered it uncontroversial that even in the family, once held up as the paradigm of the private community, power relations play indispensable roles.[14]

Appeals to apolitical communities of the past or the future run into analogous difficulties. Sociologists and historical anthropologists have been waging war on the idealization of "traditional society" for decades; it is now beyond controversy that the search for historical communities that were devoid of political conflict is vain.[15] No more promising are arguments about the possibility of creating such communities in the future, as in the Marxist claim that under genuine communism politics will be displaced by administration.[16] What many think of as the limits of politics are really limits to the politicization of social life. By declaring a sphere of action to be beyond politics, part of the private sphere, we render it immune from political criticism. Yet the accepted boundaries of politics are constantly shifting as the result of political struggles. When the law changes from denying the possibility of marital rape by conclusive presumption to creating such a crime by statute, a significant movement of this kind has occurred.[17] The public/private dichotomy in this and other prevalent formulations misses such poignant complexities. The general rule (to which there are, doubtless, exceptions) is that the dominated try to politicize to delegitimize, whereas the dominators try to depoliticize to legitimize.

Many who sense the conceptual vulnerabilities of strategies for bounding the political are nonetheless left uncomfortable by the thought that politics are everywhere. Some aspects of life seem at most trivially political, others momentously so; the suggestion that everything is politics threatens to obscure such distinctions in the name of a conceptual clarity that verges on the self-defeating. Partly for this reason, some have pursued an alternative course of trying to specify a domain of human interaction that is basic to politics, in which fundamental conflicts are fought out and social possibilities determined. Religious theorists have sometimes thought in such terms about spiritual life, Marxists about work, feminists about family relations, liberals and fascists – from different standpoints – about the state. Once the genuinely basic domain has been adequately characterized and understood, everything else can be thought about derivatively, as epiphenomenal. Such reductive strategies hold out the joint possibility of focusing our energies on what really matters – spiritual life, material life, family life, civic life – and of placing limits on the demands that might be made of us in a world in which everything is politicized.

Yet no decisive case has ever been made for reductive views of this kind, and the paucity of their explanatory power as well as their unpredictable programmatic consequences routinely belie their pretensions. The troubled twentieth-century history of Marxism is a vivid confirmation of this state of affairs, but in this respect it is scarcely unique. Hobbesian, Freudian, sociobiological, and other reductionisms have all been consigned to similar fates; by the start of the twenty-first century there are good grounds for skepticism toward every reductive and essentialist venture of this kind. Rather than join a vain search for the true essence or site of politics, the account developed here rests on the view that politics are both nowhere and everywhere. They are nowhere in that there is no specifiable political realm; not buildings in Washington, not modes of production, not religious practices, not gender relations, not any bounded domain of social life. Politics are everywhere, however, because no realm of social life is immune from relations of conflict and power.

The significance of this truth varies, to be sure, with time and circumstance, and even from person to person. Yet the appropriate constitution of any activity is always open to dispute; people benefit and are harmed in different ways by prevailing practices, and there is the ever-present possibility that an activity might be ordered differently than presently it is. Politics infuses everything we do, but it is never the totality of what we do. Government is not special, however. What goes on in the diverse array of institutions we describe as governmental involves the pursuit of a heterogeneous class of superordinate goods. Solving collective action problems, regulating monopolies, defending against foreign enemies, adjudicating disputes, representing interests, writing coherent legislation, and enforcing laws through administrative agencies are among the more obvious. These activities all involve insiders' wisdom. For reasons discussed in part II, outsiders are not well equipped to know whether and to what degree they would be enhanced by increased deliberation.

V. Subordinate Deliberation and Exit Costs

Decisions about how to pursue superordinate goods are best left to those with the relevant insiders' wisdom, but their freedom to do this should not always be unfettered. The warrant for this claim is that just noted: superordinate goods are bound up with power relations. This suggests an additional role for government in regulating the pursuit of superordinate goods. It is a conditioning role, however, not sought after for its own sake. Rather, it is pursued via the subordinate good of democratic control.

Democracy functions best when it shapes the terms of our interactions without thereby setting their course. Most superordinate goods can be pursued in a variety of ways, and the challenge is to get people to pursue them – even to *want* to pursue them – in more, rather than less, democratic ways. Democracy should be thought of as potentially omnipresent in that it appropriately shapes the pursuit of all goals in which power relations are implicated, but not as omnipotent. Doing things democratically is important, but it should rarely, if ever, be the point of the exercise. People should be induced to pursue their goals democratically, but not to sacrifice those goals *to* democracy. The task is to get them to rise to the creative challenge this involves.

A helpful way to think about the appropriate place of deliberation in power relations is Hirschmanesque: as the costs of exit increase so does the importance of voice.[18] From this perspective we might say that the right to deliberative participation should vary with the degree to which people are trapped. If a stockholder is adversely affected by what a firm's management does she can sell her shares, buying stock in a firm she finds more congenial. An adversely affected employee seldom has the same freedom of action; hence his stronger claim to deliberative participation. Even when the affected party cannot participate in decision-making, there are circumstances in which it is wise to try to insist on significant deliberation. Hence the unanimity requirement for juries in criminal cases, which is intended to encourage exceedingly thorough deliberation before someone can be convicted of a criminal offense. Decisions to terminate life support of the terminally ill belong in an analogous category: insisting that they be preceded by a deliberative process, perhaps one involving judicial oversight, is justifiable to protect the important interests of someone who cannot escape the effects of the decision.

When exit costs are low for everyone there is no reason to require deliberation; by definition the interests at stake are not hostage to the decision. The same conclusion holds when exit costs are high for all and the interests at stake are the same. If everyone is equally affected by decisions, then it is reasonable to defer to insiders' wisdom concerning what decision-rules to employ and how much deliberation, if any, is required. So long as everyone has equally strong interests at stake (as in an *ex ante* veil-of-ignorance decision by a healthy population about how to ration future organ transplants), then no one has power over anyone else by virtue of the decision-making procedure and there is no reason for outsiders to second-guess it.

When exit costs vary, the interests at stake become significant. The story of apartheid in American public schools is eloquent testimony to what happens when this goes unrecognized. Urban public schools are starved of resources by white middle-class voters who either opt out fiscally, to private schools, or physically, to suburban schools.[19] (It should be added that the latter may live in towns that are paragons of deliberative democracy. In 1995, for instance, a statewide Connecticut plan to reduce school segregation was duly deliberated upon at great length in repeated New England town meetings in which the inner city residents of Hartford and New Haven had virtually no effective voice at all. As a result, their interests were simply ignored and the plan was easily defeated.)[20]

In reflecting on when it is appropriate to try to require deliberation, we should attend to the kind of interest at stake, not merely differences in exit costs. This becomes apparent by considering the limitations of a rule that would link the right to insist on deliberation to the latter exclusively, perhaps by entitling those bearing the greatest costs to rights of delay, appeal, and even veto if the difference in exit costs was sufficiently large. To fix intuitions, think of South Africa's white minority before the democratic transition. They stood to lose vastly more than non-whites (who in fact stood to gain) from the planned transition, because they had vastly more resources, status, and power than non-whites. For the whites the costs of leaving were in this sense greater, but it does not follow that they should have been entitled to rights of delay, appeal, or veto in virtue of that fact. Part of the reason for this is perhaps that their gains were ill-gotten during apartheid, but that is not dispositive. After all, most gains are ill-gotten if we go back far enough. My suggestion is that it is when basic interests are at stake that such protections should be activated.

VI. Basic Interests, Deliberation, and Bargaining

People have basic interests in developing and sustaining what is needed to survive as independent agents in the world as it is likely to exist for their lifetimes, and to protect those interests by participating in decision-making that affects them. This conception belongs in the family of resourcist conceptions of justice. It could be spelled out more or less robustly, and its content varies partly with context. Giving a full account of it is beyond my present concern,[21] which is restricted to the power relations surrounding basic interests. For this purpose it suffices to think of basic interests in terms of obvious essentials, leaving the task of adducing exhaustive lists for another occasion.

Anyone in a position to threaten a person's basic interests evidently has great power over them. An employer who can fire an employee in a world where there is no unemployment compensation has power of this kind. The employer may have vast interests at stake in the governance of a particular business, so that his exit costs might be greater in dollar terms should both decide (or be forced) to leave. But the employee has basic interests at stake in this example whereas the employer does not; this is the justification for strengthening the employee's voice. It was embodied in the National Labor Relations Act of 1935, which rested on explicit recognition of "the inequality of bargaining power between employees who do not possess full freedom of association or actual liberty of contract, and employers who are organized in the corporate or other forms of ownership." The act responded to this situation by "encouraging the practice and procedure of collective bargaining and by protecting the exercise by work- ers of full freedom of association, self-organization, and designation of repre- sentatives of their own choosing, for negotiating the terms and conditions of their employment." It also contained affirmative duties on employers to bargain with elected union representatives, protections of closed shops and other collec- tive rights.[22]

Notice that it was not merely the bargaining power disparity but the fact that employees were found to lack "full freedom of association" and "actual liberty of contract" that was decisive in the decision to enhance employee voice in this way. Employees were found to face what Marxists refer to as structural coer- cion. In my terms, their basic interests are at stake. If we consider other areas where the law limits contractual freedom, similar considerations apply. Courts will not enforce antenuptial agreements that leave spouses destitute (though they will often enforce unequal agreements that do not have this effect). Nor will they enforce rental leases that void certain statutory protections for tenants, agree- ments to sell one's body organs, or to sell oneself into indentured servitude or slavery.

How much "voice" such regulation creates varies. Some agreements (such as selling oneself into slavery) so obviously compromise basic interests that they are treated as void *ab initio,* regardless of the views of the parties. Others, such as certain types of leases, may be suspect and for that reason be challenged in court. This creates the possibility of obligatory deliberation, should the tenant feel ag- grieved. Still others, such as the NLRA, try to mandate deliberation through an affirmative duty to bargain. Generally, we can think of institutional devices that seek to force deliberation as an intermediate form of regulation between pro- scriptive intervention and full deference to insiders' wisdom. As a normative matter we can say that the more one's basic interests are threatened, the stronger is one's claim to insist on deliberation, but that beyond some threat threshold voice is not sufficient.

Saying just where that threat threshold lies is more difficult, and often de- pends on contextual factors. Cases like slavery are conceptually easy, because it so obviously violates basic interests that proscription is warranted. Most of the time, however, the tensions between protecting peoples' basic interests and the pursuing superordinate goods are more nebulous. Indeed, even when basic in- terests are threatened it is not self-evident that governments are best placed to do much about it. This is one reason to press for deliberative solutions where they can be successful. The considerations adduced in my earlier discussion of cognitive limitations will often extend, in practice, from the pursuit of superordinate goods to the protection of basic interests. In many situations, those with the relevant insiders' wisdom might well be better placed than external regulators to discover how best to accommodate tensions between the two. The difficulty arises when there are conflicts of interest about this matter and those with the power lack the incentive to engage in deliberation to facilitate the relevant accommodation. By strengthening the hand of those whose basic interests are threatened, government can shift the balance of incentives indirectly without itself proposing solutions.

In this spirit we might replace proscription of voucher schemes in education with a solution in which parents of those who do not opt out of the public schools are given delay, appeal, or perhaps even veto rights, enabling them to insist on guarantees that promised benefits for their children's education do in fact eventuate. Those proposing voucher schemes would then have to engage in deliberation with them, take account of their concerns, and persuade them that these concerns can be dealt with. How strong their deliberative rights should be would still require an independent judgment as to how seriously threatened the children's basic interests in fact were, but not an exogenous adjudication of the merits of voucher schemes.[23] The goal would be to strengthen the hand of those whose children remained in the public schools sufficiently (but only sufficiently – that is the institutional design challenge) to ensure that they could extract the relevant guarantees, or compensation, from those advocating the change, while interfering as little as possible with its benefits for others. This, in turn, would supply those who wanted the change with the incentive to design it in ways that would work to the benefit of all, to provide fail-safe guarantees in case it did not, and to persuade those whose basic interests are at stake that they have done this. Achieving that would be a triumph for subordinate deliberation.

This approach recognizes the cognitive limitations of governments without denying their responsibility to regulate the power-dimensions of social life in democratic ways. Rather than have government try to evaluate the merits of innovative funding schemes, in this example, it would use its power to make those who advocate them persuade those whose basic interests are most plausibly at stake. Structuring things to induce this kind of deliberation is useful because it gives those with the relevant insiders' wisdom the incentive to turn their creative energy to pursuing superordinate goods in ways that do not involve domination of others when these are available. When they are unavailable, it constrains the sacrifice of vulnerable interests to the efficacious pursuit of superordinate goods. This reflects the sense in which the positive sum deliberative thesis can be insufficiently demanding. Strengthening the hand of the vulnerable in this way is intended to encourage the search for cooperative solutions when interests conflict, while maximizing the odds that these solutions do not come at the price of coerced agreement. In that sense it is optimal deliberation.

It will be objected that the means proposed here are less than adequate for the end sought. I began this essay by delimiting my subject to the types of deliberation that government should seek to require. This deliberation was defined as involving the solicitous search for right solutions in circumstances of conflict. The answer proposed here, to strengthen the hand of weaker parties whose basic interests are threatened in certain circumstances, is sufficient to guarantee more equal bargaining, perhaps, but not deliberation. This is true, but two points should be noted in response. It is doubtful, first, that government can ever really insist that people deliberate. Government can try to structure things so as to make deliberation more or less likely, but ultimately deliberation depends on individual commitment. By its terms, deliberation requires solicitous goodwill, creative ingenuity, and a desire to get to the right answer. These cannot be mandated. Even juries sometimes choose to bargain rather than to deliberate when they want to go home, and, when they do, there is little anyone can do about it. Second, my suggestion is that by strengthening the hand of the weaker party in the types of circumstances discussed, government can increase the likelihood that insiders will deploy their wisdom to search for the deliberative solutions that may be waiting to be discovered. This may often fail in particular cases, so that increasing the voice of weaker parties will be no more than increasing their bargaining power. When this is so, we can take consolation from the fact that it will not be those whose basic interests are at stake who must internalize all the costs of the failure. Bargaining may sometimes be inferior to deliberation, but domination is always inferior to both.

Notes

1   John Rawls, *A Theory of Justice* (Cambridge, MA: Belknap Press, 1971) pp. 48–51, and Rawls, *Political Liberalism* (New York: Columbia University Press, 1993) pp. 8, 28.
2   See John Ferejohn and Pasquale Pasquino, "Deliberative Institutions," December 1999 paper at the Institute of Governmental Studies at U.C. Berkeley, http://www.igs.berkeley.edu:8880/research_programs/ppt_papers/deliberative_institutions.pdf.
3   See Amy Gutmann and Dennis Thompson, *Democracy and Disagreement* (Cambridge, MA: Belknap Press, 1996), pp. 105–27.
4   Ian Shapiro, *Democracy's Place* (Ithaca: Cornell University Press, 1996), pp. 175–261.
5   See Jürgen Habermas, *Between Facts and Norms* (Cambridge: Polity, 1996), pp. 287–328; Michael Neblo, "Deliberate Actions: Identifying Communicative Rationality Empirically" (1998), http://www.spc.uchicago.edu/politicaltheory/neblo98.pdf, and Neblo, "Counting Voices in an Echo Chamber: Cognition, Complexity, and the

Prospects for Deliberative Democracy" (2000), http://www.spc.uchicago.edu/politicaltheory/neblo00.pdf at the University of Chicago Political Theory Workshop Paper Archive; James Fishkin *Democracy and Deliberation: New Directions for Democratic Reform* (New Haven: Yale University Press, 1991).

6 See Adam Simon, "Assessing deliberation in small groups," paper presented at the Midwest Political Science Association Annual Meeting, Chicago, April, 2000. See also Cass Sunstein, "The law of group polarization," pp. 80–101 of this volume, for discussion of empirical conditions under which deliberation leads to divergence rather than convergence of opinion.

7 See Jane J. Mansbridge, *Beyond Adversary Democracy* (New York: Basic Books, 1980).

8 See John Stuart Mill, *On Liberty* (Indianapolis: Hackett, 1978 [1859]), pp. 4, 38–9, 70, and Alexis de Tocqueville, *Democracy in America* (New York: Anchor Doubleday, 1966 [1835]), pp. 250–76. For Mill, as for Tocqueville, the fact that a policy is widely accepted is scarcely grounds for pursuing it. Indeed, Mill is perhaps best known for endorsing Tocqueville's claim that the tyranny of the majority is "among the evils against which society requires to be on its guard." He insists, with Tocqueville, that oppression by received opinion is one of the more insidious forms that majority tyranny can take.

9 See Iris M. Young, *Justice and the Politics of Difference* (Princeton, NJ: Princeton University Press, 1990); Chantal Mouffe, *Dimensions of Radical Democracy* (New York: Verso, 1992); Martha Minow, *Making All the Difference* (Ithaca: Cornell University Press, 1990).

10 See Ned Crosby, Janet Kelly, and Paul Schzefer, "Citizen Panels: A New Approach to Citizen Participation," *Public Administration Review*, vol. 46, No. 2 (March/April 1986), pp. 170–8; Crosby, "Citizen Juries: One Solution for Difficult Environmental Questions," *Fairness and Competence in Citizen Participation: Evaluating Models for Environmental Discourse,* ed. Ortwin Renn, Thomas Webler and Peter Wiedemann (Boston: Kluwer Academic Publishers, 1995).

11 For elaboration, see Ian Shapiro, *Democratic Justice* (New Haven: Yale University Press, 1999) pp. 12, 80–1, 92, 116, 132.

12 G. W. F. Hegel, *The Phenomenology of Mind* 2nd edition revised (London: G. Allen & Unwin, 1949 [1807]), pp. 229, 645, 650, 660.

13 See Carmen Sirianni, *Civic Innovation in America* (Berkeley: University of California Press, 2001) and Sirianni, "Learning Pluralism: Democracy and Diversity in Feminist Organizations," *Democratic Community: NOMOS XXXV,* ed. Ian Shapiro and John Chapman (New York: New York University Press, 1993), pp. 283–312.

14 See Susan Moller Okin, *Justice, Gender, and the Family* (New York: Basic Books, 1989) and Carole Pateman, *The Sexual Contract* (Cambridge: Polity, 1988).

15 See Ian Shapiro, *Political Criticism* (Berkeley, CA: University of California Press, 1990) pp. 91–165, for a critical analysis of the theories of Allan Bloom and Alasdair MacIntyre.

16 Hence Engels' famous comment to the effect that under genuine socialism "the government of persons is replaced by the administration of things." See Frederick Engels, *Anti-Dühring* (Moscow: Foreign Language Publishing House, 1959 [1878]), p. 387.

17 Shapiro, *Democratic Justice*, pp. 57, 113, 116.
18 See Albert O. Hirschman, *Exit, Voice, and Loyalty* (Cambridge, MA: Harvard University Press, 1970).
19 See Jennifer Hochschild, *The New American Dilemma: Liberal Democracy and School Desegregation* (New Haven: Yale University Press, 1984).
20 See Kathryn McDermott, *Controlling Public Education: Localism versus Equity* (University Press of Kansas, 1999), pp. 31–53.
21 See Shapiro, *Democratic Justice*, pp. 85–90 for elaboration.
22 Quotations from the Wagner Act taken from the *Legislative History of the National Labor Relations Act, 1935*, vol. 2 (Washington, DC: National Labor Relations Board, 1959), §§. 1, 7, 8 arts. 1–5, pp. 3270–4.
23 I also assume, for present purposes, that there are not significant conflicts of interest between parents and their children about this matter. The possibility of such conflict is explored in *Democratic Justice*, pp. 64–109.

7

Deliberative Democracy, the Discursive Dilemma, and Republican Theory

Philip Pettit

The ideal of deliberative democracy argues that voters should vote in a way that reflects their deliberatively informed judgments on matters relevant to the common good but it says nothing on how those votes should be aggregated into collective judgments. This makes for a problem, since there are two ways in which the aggregation of judgments might go, as the discursive dilemma shows. One would ensure that collective judgments are maximally responsive to individual judgments but risk the rationality of the judgments collectively maintained. The other would ensure the rationality of collective judgments but reduce the responsiveness of those judgments to individual views. One would preserve the democratic aspect of the ideal and compromise the deliberative; the other would preserve the deliberative and compromise the democratic.

Which way should the ideal be extended to cope with this hard choice? I argue that the republican defense of deliberative democracy suggests that the ideal ought to be extended so that collective rationality is prized over responsiveness to individual views: the deliberative aspect should be given priority over the democratic.

There are five sections to the paper. In the first, I give a brief account of the ideal of deliberative democracy. In the second, I introduce the discursive dilemma, and then in the third section I show why the issue that it raises is of relevance to the deliberative–democratic ideal. How should deliberative democrats resolve that issue? I maintain in the fourth section that the role in which republican theory casts deliberative democracy argues for resolving it so that collective rationality is given more importance than responsiveness to individual views. And then in the final section I argue for the consistency of that position with the main sorts of argument put forward by others in defense of the ideal.

1. The Ideal of Deliberative Democracy

There are three issues on which deliberative democrats divide among themselves. First, the question of how many contexts – electoral, parliamentary, bureaucratic, industrial, educational, and so on – ought to be democratised. Second, the question of how many issues in any democratised context ought to be under democratic control: just the choice of office-holders, or also the choice of general programs, or perhaps the choice of detailed policies. And third, the question of how far a democratic character serves to justify or legitimate a regime and pattern of decision-making, or at least to give them a presumptive authority: to place the onus of argument on the shoulders of those who would not comply.

But no matter what their differences on such questions, deliberative democrats show a remarkable degree of consensus on how democracy should be organized when it is established at a given site. They agree that any democratic way of doing things should be inclusive, judgmental and dialogical in character. These three constraints, then, articulate the deliberative–democratic ideal that they share.[1]

- *The inclusive constraint*: all members should be equally entitled to vote on how to resolve relevant collective issues, or bundles of issues, with something less than a unanimous vote being sufficient to determine the outcome.
- *The judgmental constraint*: before voting, members should deliberate on the basis of presumptively common concerns about which resolution is to be preferred.
- *The dialogical constraint*: members should conduct this deliberation in open and unforced dialogue with one another, whether in a centralized forum or in various decentralized contexts.

The inclusive constraint means that deliberative democracy is to be contrasted with elitist or authoritarian schemes, even ones in which deliberation and dialogue have an important place. It will be satisfied in any context by having a representative democracy, if democratic control only runs to the choice of office-holders, but the general assumption is that, other things being equal, direct participation by all members will be preferred to indirect representation. The constraint includes the stipulation that unanimity is not required for the determination of an outcome, since a combination of inclusiveness and unanimity would lead to a group's being unable to reach a common view on most significant issues; unanimity is probably achievable, at best, only on very abstract constitutional matters.

The judgmental constraint has got two sides to it. First, it requires voters to deliberate or reason about how they should vote, not just vote in an unreflective or spontaneous or reflex manner. And second, it requires voters to deliberate about how they should vote on the basis of considerations as to what is best for the society or group as a whole: what is likely to advance those common interests that members are capable of recognising as common interests. This constraint need not itself specify any particular conception of such common, avowable interests: that may itself be matter for the sort of deliberation recommended. What it counsels against is any pattern of voting in which each individual voter takes account only of what is good for his or her particular corner or circle. The model of voting recommended under this constraint can be described as judgment-voting rather than preference-voting. The idea is that each voter should make up his or her own mind as to what is for the good of the group in question and should vote on the basis of that judgment, not on the basis of brute preference or bargained compromise.

The third, dialogical constraint in the ideal of deliberative democracy marks a further, important level of differentiation. It rules out the sort of plebiscitarian dispensation in which each participant privately forms his or her judgment about common avowable interests, rather than doing so in dialogue with others, and then votes on the basis of that judgment. It is sometimes thought, on the basis of his remarks about the danger of faction, that Rousseau embraced this plebiscitarian ideal. According to Rousseau, so it is said, 'each voter is polled about his independently reached choice, without any group deliberation'.[2] But this interpretation is almost certainly mistaken, if only because it makes no sense of Rousseau's requiring that the people come together in an assembly. What he was anxious to guard against was not dialogue and debate, with the formation of individual judgment that this fosters, but rather the threat of some individuals' being so intimidated or impressed by others – so deferential towards them – that they vote according to the judgments of those others, not according to their own.[3]

The third constraint requires that the dialogue envisaged be open and unforced, while allowing that it may be centralized or decentralized. It must be open in the sense that each can get a hearing and it must be unforced in the sense that no one need fear to speak their mind; it must approximate the conditions for ideal speech that Jürgen Habermas emphasizes.[4] Some will insist that dialogue must be centralized in a single forum, if talk of deliberative democracy is to be justified. But I think that it is better to leave that question open and to take the centralized or collective picture of deliberative democracy as a more specific version of a broader ideal.

2. The Discursive Dilemma

The doctrinal paradox

So much for the different elements in the ideal of deliberative democracy. Now for the discursive dilemma. The dilemma represents the generalisation of a problem that scholars of jurisprudence have recently called the doctrinal paradox.[5] This is a paradox that arises when a multimember court has to make a decision about some matter on the basis of received doctrine as to the considerations that ought to be taken into account.

Consider the case of a three-member court casting votes as to whether someone is liable in tort for something they did that affected another. Legal doctrine requires the judges to make judgments, not just on liability, but also on the related issues of whether there was harm done and whether there was a duty of care. And, more specifically, legal doctrine requires them to let the resolution of those other issues determine the resolution of the liability question. Imagine, then, that the members of the court vote on the pattern in the following matrix about the issues facing it.

	Matrix 1		
	Was harm done?	Was there a duty of care?	Liable?
Judge A	Yes	No	No
Judge B	No	Yes	No
Judge C	Yes	Yes	Yes

The judges represented in this example are each individually consistent in the way they cast their votes. And furthermore they are consistent, so we may assume, out of compliance with legal doctrine. That is to say, they first decide on the issue of harm and on the issue of care and then they each let their vote on liability be driven – driven in consistency – by their votes on those issues. If we look at the majority vote on each issue , however, we see that collectively the court is inconsistent. It supports affirmative judgments on the first two issues – there are two Yes's on each question – and a negative judgment on the third: there are two No's in the final column. Hence the court as a collective body breaches legal doctrine, because it does not draw the conclusion on liability that its positions on the other issues require.

The doctrinal paradox consists in the fact that although each of the judges in a case like this complies with legal doctrine, they still come up with a collective set of judgments that is in breach of consistency and in conflict therefore with legal doctrine. The paradox will arise wherever a majority in the group supports each of the premises, different majorities support different premises, and the intersection or overlap of those majorities is not itself a majority in the group. The fact that those in that overlap are not themselves a majority – in the case considered there is only one judge, C, in the intersection – explains why there is only a minority in favor of the conclusion.[6]

The doctrinal paradox is not confined to cases where a court has to make a decision by reference to a conjunction of premises. It can also arise in cases where the court has to make its decision by reference to a disjunction of considerations; that is, in cases where the support required for a positive conclusion is only that one or more of the premises be endorsed. This is unsurprising, of course, given that a disjunction of premises, p or q, is equivalent to the negation of a conjunction: not-(not-p and not-q). Still, it may be worth illustrating the possibility.

Imagine that three judges have to make a decision on whether or not some-one should be given a retrial; that a retrial is required either in the event of inadmissible evidence having been used previously or in the event of the appel-lant's having been forced to confess; and that the voting goes as in the following matrix among the judges.

Matrix 2

	Inadmissible evidence?	Forced confession?	Retrial?
Judge A	Yes	No	Yes
Judge B	No	Yes	Yes
Judge C	No	No	No

This case also illustrates a doctrinal paradox, since the normal procedure of look-ing at the majority in the last column will lead to giving the defendant a retrial but that collective judgment is out of kilter with the majority-supported judg-ments on the first two issues.

The doctrinal paradox raises a serious question for collegiate courts. Should things be organized, as they are in most jurisdictions, so that judgment on the issue under adjudication – the conclusion – is determined by whether a majority support it? Or should they be organized so that judgment on that issue is deter-mined by the judgments that majorities support on the doctrinally prior issues: if you like, the doctrinal premises?

It should be clear that the doctrinal paradox will generalize in a number of dimensions, representing a possibility that may materialize with any number of decision-makers greater than two and with any number of premises greater than one, whether those premises be conjunctively or disjunctively organized. But there are other, perhaps less obvious ways in which it can be generalized also and I now look at three of these. I describe them respectively as the social generali-zation, the diachronic generalization, and the *modus tollens* generalization.[7]

The social generalization

A paradox of the sort illustrated does not require the presence of a legal doctrine which dictates that certain issues are prior to another – an issue on which a conclusion has to be reached – so that judgments on those prior issues ought in consistency to dictate the judgment on the conclusion. It will also arise when a group of people discourse together with a view to forming an opinion on a certain matter and when they agree that the matter should be determined by the resolution of other, prior issues.

Consider an issue that might arise in a workplace, among the employees of a company: for simplicity, as we may assume, a company owned by the employees. The issue is whether to forgo a pay-rise in order to spend the money thereby saved on introducing a set of workplace safety measures: say, measures to guard against electrocution. Let us suppose for convenience that the employees are to make the decision – perhaps because of prior resolution – on the basis of considering three separable issues: first, how serious the danger is; second, how effective the safety measure that a pay-sacrifice would buy is likely to be; and third, whether the pay-sacrifice is bearable for members individually. If an employee thinks that the danger is sufficiently serious, the safety measure sufficiently effective, and the pay-sacrifice sufficiently bearable, he or she will vote for the sacrifice; otherwise they will vote against. And so each will have to consider those three epistemically prior issues – those premises – and then look to what should be concluded about the pay-sacrifice.

Imagine now that after appropriate dialogue and deliberation the employees are disposed to vote on the relevant premises and conclusion in the pattern illustrated by the following matrix for a group of three workers. The letters A, B and C represent the three employees and the 'Yes' or 'No' on any row represents the disposition of the relevant employee to admit or reject the corresponding premise or conclusion.

Matrix 3

	Serious danger?	Effective measure?	Bearable loss?	Pay-sacrifice?
A.	Yes	No	Yes	No
B.	No	Yes	Yes	No
C.	Yes	Yes	No	No

If this is the pattern in which the employees vote, then a different decision will be made, depending on whether the group judgment is driven by how members judge on the premises or by how they judge on the conclusion. Looking at the matrix, we can see that though everyone individually rejects the pay-sacrifice, a majority supports each of the premises. If we think that the views of the employees on the conclusion should determine the group-decision, then we will say that the group-conclusion should be to reject the pay-sacrifice: there are only 'No's in the final column. But if we think that the views of the employees on the premises should determine the group-decision, then we will say that the group-conclusion should be to accept the pay-sacrifice: there are more 'Yes's than 'No's in each of the premise columns.

There are familiar practices of group deliberation and decision-making corresponding to these two options. Thus the group would go one way if members entered into deliberation and dialogue and then each cast their personal vote on whether to endorse the pay-sacrifice or not; in that case the decision would be against the pay-sacrifice. The group would go the other if there was a chairperson who took a vote on each of the premises – say, a show of hands – and then let logic decide the outcome; in this case the decision would be in favour of the pay-sacrifice.

This example is stylized but should serve to indicate that the paradox is not confined to the domain in which legal doctrine dictates that certain judgments are to be made by reference to certain considerations. There are many social groups that have to make judgments on various issues and that routinely do so by reference to considerations that are epistemically privileged within the group. Any groups that are charged by an external authority with making certain decisions on the basis of designated considerations will have to do this. And so will any groups that aspire to identifying such considerations for themselves, constitutionalizing the relations between members around a recognition of shared, decision-driving commitments.

The diachronic generalization

For all that has been said in this first stage of generalization, the paradox may seem unlikely to figure much in social and political life. The reason is that whereas the judges in a courtroom routinely have to make their judgments by reference to shared considerations, people in other social groups will often reach collective decisions on an incompletely theorised basis.[8] There will be a majority, perhaps even a consensus, in favour of a certain line on some issue but there will be no agreement among the parties to that majority or consensus on the reasons that support the line. The parties will each vote that line for reasons of their own – reasons related to their own interests or their own judgments of the common interest – and there will only be a partial overlap between the different considerations they each take into account. Thus there will be no possibility of their resorting to common premises to determine the line that they ought to take.

But sound though this consideration is, social groups will still have to deal routinely with a problem akin to the doctrinal paradox. In the examples given from judicial life, and in the social parallel suggested, the issues involved – the premise-issues and the conclusion-issue – are up for determination at one and the same time, both by the individuals and by the group. But the problem involved can arise across time as well as at a time; it can have a diachronic as well as a synchronic character. And the fact that it can arise in this way means that incompletely theorized judgments are also vulnerable to it.

Suppose that over a period of time a group makes a judgment on each of a set of issues, deciding them all by majority vote and on incompletely theorised grounds: different members of the group are moved by different considerations.

Sooner or later such a group is bound to face an issue such that how it should judge on that issue is determined by the judgments it previously endorsed on other issues. And in such an event the group will face the familiar problem that majority voting on the new issue may generate a collective pattern of voting that is inconsistent in character – inconsistent, in this case, across time.

The courts will often face this diachronic version of the problem as well as the synchronic version that we considered; this will happen when previous judg-ments of the court dictate the judgment that it ought to make on an issue cur-rently before it. But, more important for our purposes, even social groups that differ from the courts in routinely securing only incompletely theorized agree-ments will have to confront the diachronic version of the problem. They may escape the synchronic problem through not being capable of agreeing on com-mon considerations by which different issues are to be judged. But that is no guarantee that they will be able to escape the problem as it arises in diachronic form.

The diachronic problem is going to affect a wide range of groups. Suppose, to take an illustrative example, that a political party announces in March, say on the basis of majority voting among its members, that it will not increase taxes if it gets into government. Suppose that it announces in June, again on the basis of majority vote, that it will increase defense spending. And now imagine that it faces the issue in September as to whether it will increase government spending in other areas of policy or organization. Should it allow a majority vote on that issue too?

If the party does allow a majority vote, then we know that even in the event of individual members being perfectly consistent across time, the vote may favor increasing government spending in other areas. The members may vote in the pattern of members A to C in the following matrix.

Matrix 4

	Increase taxes?	Increase defense spending?	Increase other spending?
A.	No	Yes	No (reduce)
B.	No	No (reduce)	Yes
C.	Yes	Yes	Yes

Thus the party will face the hard choice between being responsive to the views of its individual members and ensuring the collective rationality of the views it endorses.

The *modus tollens* generalization

In the legal case it is taken to be important, not just that judges be consistent, but that their judgments on the doctrinally prior issues dictate in consistency how they vote on the matter to be adjudicated. Similarly in the shop floor example, it is taken to be important, not just that the workers be consistent, but that their judgments on the epistemically prior issues of danger, effectiveness and bearability of cost determine how they vote on the pay-sacrifice. But the assumption that there are any issues which stand out as doctrinally or epistemically prior is unnecessary. The sort of problem involved will arise just on the assumption that whatever judgments are made on all the issues, they have to be consistent with one another. When we see this, we see a third and still more important way in which the doctrinal paradox generalizes. For reasons that will be clear shortly, I describe it as the *modus tollens* generalization.

When an individual or group relies on an assumption of doctrinal or epistemic priority and argues from the way earlier issues in one of our matrices are resolved to how the last issue is resolved, then they practise what we might loosely describe in the old scholastic term as *modus ponens*: they move from the assertion of certain views on the earlier issues to an assertion of the view that has to be taken on the last. But if no assumption of priority is made among the issues, then it is possible to achieve consistency, either by complying with *modus ponens* or by complying with the traditionally described alternative, *modus tollens*. Under this alternative, the individual or group would stick with the view to which they are independently attracted on the last issue and then argue for the need to withdraw one of the commitments made on the earlier issues.

Consider how the group in the worker example might try to achieve consistency, if the assumption of epistemic priority is lifted. It might still ignore the majority vote on the pay-rise issue, as *modus ponens* would require, and let the majority votes on the other issues dictate the collective view on that conclusion. But another equally salient possibility would be to ignore the majority vote on one of those earlier issues, letting the majority votes on the other earlier issues together with the majority vote on the conclusion dictate the collective view to be taken on that particular issue. Or consider the case of the political party. The members of the party might allow the earlier commitments to determine the commitment on the later issue, thereby achieving consistency. Or they might decide to stick with the majority view on that later issue and then look to withdrawing one of the earlier commitments.

It should now be clear why I speak of a discursive dilemma rather than a doctrinal paradox. The doctrinal paradox arises when certain judicial issues that are up for resolution have to be resolved at one and the same time; and are prioritised among themselves under legal doctrine. The discursive dilemma can arise outside the judicial domain; it can arise even when the issues involved come up over time, not simultaneously; and it can arise just in virtue of the requirement of consistency, not on the basis of any assumed priority among the issues. In these respects it is a problem that is general to discourse, not just a problem associated with legal doctrine.

The problem posed represents a hard choice or dilemma, not anything that strictly deserves to be called a paradox. The hard choice that a group in this dilemma faces is whether to let the views of the collectivity on any issue be fully responsive to the individual views of members – the views they form prior to feedback on the collective pattern – thereby running the risk of collective inconsistency; or whether to ensure that the views of the group are collectively consistent, even where that means compromising responsiveness to the initial views of individual members on one or another issue. You can have individual responsiveness or collective rationality but you cannot have both – or at least you cannot be sure of being able to have both.

3. The Relevance of the Dilemma for Deliberative Democracy

The participatory and regulatory questions raised

Under the regime of deliberative democracy, it is required that with any logically connected propositions in the domain of discussion – they may or may not be cast in the role of premises and conclusion – people make up their minds about the propositions in such a way that reason is satisfied. They do not endorse inconsistent or otherwise incoherent sets of propositions; they do not fail to derive conclusions that are supported, even saliently supported, by what they already endorse; and they do not follow a procedure – say, one of unanimitarian voting – that gives them nothing to say on most issues. This means that they therefore face the prospect of a discursive dilemma; indeed there is a general impossibility theorem that can be invoked to establish the point.[9]

There are two broad questions that will be raised for deliberative democracy by the discursive dilemma. The first is the question of how a group should be organized if majority voting on certain issues is liable, no matter how deliberative, to generate collective inconsistency and there is nothing that members can do in response to feedback about that inconsistency: nothing that they can do to put it right. This, in effect, is the old participatory question as to whether such a group should be allowed to address issues that can give rise to inconsistency or whether the domain of its decision-making should be restricted to the choice of representatives. If the domain of decision-making is restricted in this way, so that members of the group have a say only on the personnel who will represent them and on the platforms that they prefer such personnel to advance, then the spectre of collective inconsistency will disappear.

The second question raised for deliberative democracy by the discursive dilemma arises when the group in question does have a feasible choice between following a procedure that ensures responsiveness to individual views, while risking collective rationality, and following a procedure that ensures collective rationality but compromises responsiveness to initial, individual views. The first procedure will obviously involve having members vote, on a majoritarian or at least non-unanimitarian basis, about each of the issues before the group, and then letting that vote determine the collective view. But what will the second procedure involve? Consistently with behaving in a deliberative democratic manner, the group might let the presumptive set of collective views be determined by having members vote on each issue and only consider moderating those views – amending one or other of them – in the event of feedback to the effect that collective views are irrational in some way. The amendment chosen might involve letting the views with the presumptive status of premise-judgments – if that can be agreed – determine the view on the conclusion. Or it might involve holding on to that conclusion and revising the collectively endorsed view on one of the other issues. It might involve practising *modus ponens* or *modus tollens*.

I describe the question that the dilemma raises for this second sort of group as regulatory rather than participatory in character, since it bears on how the group should regulate its decision-making. The group that confronts this question faces the hard choice that is characteristic of the discursive dilemma. If the procedure adopted favors responsiveness and risks rationality, then it will reduce the deliberative component in the ideal of deliberative democracy. If it favors rationality and compromises responsiveness, then it will reduce the democratic component in that ideal.

The participatory and regulatory questions come up for the ideal of deliberative democracy in different fora and we should look briefly at where in particular they get a grip. We already know that the regulatory question comes up in the judicial context, since that is what the doctrinal paradox establishes. But we should also say a little about three other contexts that are particularly salient in the working of a state: the electoral, the administrative, and the parliamentary.

The electoral context

The members of the electorate in any society, however large-scale, will be individually capable of making judgments in a deliberative and dialogical way and of casting votes that reflect those judgments. But if an electorate proves to support an inconsistent set of positions, say in a series of referendums, there is little or nothing that it may be able to do about that inconsistency. The group will be too loosely jointed and unorganized in any large-scale society to have the capacity to register the inconsistency at group level, to debate the different ways – those associated with *modus ponens* or *modus tollens* – in which consistency might be restored, and to organize a vote on which approach to adopt. Almost any procedure we can imagine whereby the electorate could regulate itself with a view to ensuring collective consistency would be impossibly cumbersome or would involve giving over power to representatives.

This means that if the electorate as a whole is allowed to judge on policy issues, then that will jeopardize consistency in such judgments; the discursive dilemma shows that inconsistency will represent a permanent possibility. Even if the members of the electorate are individually rational and consistent in the judgments they make, still the electorate as a group may give support to inconsistent and irrational collective judgments. The only way for the electorate as a whole to be assured of avoiding such inconsistency will be for the domain of its judgments to be limited to selecting representatives and to identifying preferred programs of policy-making.

The question raised by the discursive dilemma for the case of the large-scale electorate, then, is the old, participatory issue of whether large-scale electoral democracy should extend to policy questions: whether, despite the scale involved, it should be direct rather than representative. Let the electorate serve solely in the selection of representatives – and indirectly in the identification of preferred programs – and inconsistency can be avoided. Let it serve in the selection of policies and inconsistency is likely to prove inevitable.

The administrative context

What of the relevance of the discursive dilemma to the smaller bodies that are of such importance in the administration of any democracy: the committees, agencies and commissions in which so many public decisions are made? What is the relevance of the dilemma, in particular, given the assumption that they are to be organized democratically?

Some of these bodies will be governed by assumptions that identify certain of the issues they confront as prior to others; the bodies will have terms of reference enjoining them to judge on the posterior issues – these may be matters of adjudication or advice or interpretation – by reference to the matters that are designated as prior. In such cases the discursive dilemma will clearly raise the question as to whether the bodies in question should police themselves to ensure collective consistency or whether they should go with the votes on each issue before them, even if this gives rise to collective inconsistency. The question that arises will be almost identical to the question raised in the judicial context by the original doctrinal paradox. Should the bodies envisaged regulate themselves with a view to displaying collective rationality or should they be content to recognise that they are just aggregates of individuals and to support sets of judgments, even inconsistent sets of judgments, that faithfully reflect the views of their members?

What of the administrative bodies in public life where members also vote on rationally connected issues but are free to vote on the basis of their own individual reasons? What, in other words, of the bodies whose members share no predetermined view as to the relative importance of the issues that they face? Does the discursive dilemma raise the same regulatory question here?

Yes, it does. Each of the bodies envisaged will have purposes such that members have to be willing to promote them. And each of the bodies in question will have to make judgments on issues related to those purposes – say, issues of opportunity, issues of cost or issues of means-end connection – as they come up for resolution over time. It is inevitable that sooner or later an issue will arise that is rationally connected with issues on which the group has already judged. And when that happens the group will face the regulatory question raised by the discursive dilemma. Is it to make a collective judgment about the new issue on a majoritarian basis, thereby risking collective inconsistency over time? Or is it to address any inconsistency that majority voting may generate and have recourse to a procedure whereby the inconsistency may be remedied? The problem is well illustrated by the challenge facing the political party in the example given in Matrix 4.

The parliamentary context

We have identified a participatory question that the discursive dilemma raises for deliberative democracy in a large-scale electorate and a regulatory question that it raises for administrative committees, agencies and commissions that are also expected to operate in a deliberative democratic way. What of the houses of parliament or congress, however? What question, if any, does the dilemma raise here?

The houses of parliament may operate, roughly, on a Westminster or a Washington pattern. Under the Westminster system parliament works in the manner of the electorate in a large-scale, wholly representative democracy. It serves to select the members of the government on the basis of which party or alliance of parties commands majority support, and it provides a forum to which the governing party or alliance, its decisions already made, comes to be interrogated for the consistency of its policies and for their more general merits. And that is all that it does. Or at least that is all that it does in the main. Private members' bills make the situation more complex, as does the fact that the decisions of the governing party or alliance have to be ratified by a parliamentary vote, so that they may occasionally be modified or even – a rare event indeed – reversed.

Under the Washington system, parliament has a different role, even though it divides along party lines on many issues. While its decisions may be overturned by the President, they are precisely that: decisions. If the Westminster houses of parliament resemble the electorate in a representative democracy, the Washington houses of congress resemble the electorate in a democracy where referendums – advisory referendums, to be sure – are the order of the day. And as referendums may generate inconsistency across time, so may the votes that the houses of congress support. In the case of congress, of course, members are few enough to be able to register the prospect of inconsistency and try to do something about it; and should they fail to do this, they may rely on the Supreme Court to provide an interpretation of their decisions that restores consistency to them.

Given the availability of these two systems, the discursive dilemma raises the same participatory question on the parliamentary front as it does on the electoral. The question is whether to give parliament the sort of role associated with the electorate in a representative democracy or whether to give it the richer, participatory role of an electorate that rules by referendum: whether to organize it, roughly, on a Westminster or a Washington model. And if a decision is made in favor of giving parliament as such a participatory role in governmental decision-making – parliament as distinct from the governing party or alliance of parties – then the dilemma raises the further, regulatory question as to whether parliament ought to impose the discipline of reason on itself at the collective or at the individual level.

The upshot, then, is this. The discursive dilemma is of relevance for large-scale electoral and parliamentary democracy so far as it raises the participatory question as to whether the group as a whole should be allowed to determine policy matters, as well as matters of personnel and program. And the dilemma is of relevance to administrative bodies in public life – as it is relevant to judicial bodies and perhaps also to parliament – so far as it raises the regulatory question as to whether a body should strive for the consistency of a unified collective presence or allow its judgments, even perhaps at the cost of inconsistency, to reflect the views of its members. In each case of that kind there will be a question as to whether the members of the body should impose the discipline of reason on themselves at the collective or at the individual level.

4. The Resolution in Republican Theory

The republican argument for deliberative democracy

Republican theory, as I have argued elsewhere, puts a premium on people's enjoying freedom as non-domination: that is, on people's having a status such that ideally no one else is able to interfere arbitrarily in their lives.[10] If any other person or agency is able to interfere in their lives, then they must be forced to track people's avowed or readily avowable interests in the interference they practise; they must not have a power of arbitrary interference. My aim in this section is, first, to characterize the case made in republican theory for deliberative democracy and, second, to show that that case argues for a distinctive resolution of the issues raised for deliberative democracy by the discursive dilemma.

The republican image of freedom raises the question of how the state can be blocked from enjoying a power of arbitrary interference in the lives of citizens. The state is a necessary institution and it necessarily has a power of interfering with people: it cannot operate without being able to tax, legislate and penalize the governed. So how is its power of interference to be made non-arbitrary? How is the coercive state to be forced to track people's common avowed or avowable interests? Republican constitutional theory is built around that question and has consistently sought to describe various devices whereby non-arbitrariness may be furthered. These include familiar mechanisms such as democratic election, rule of law, separation of powers, limitation of tenure, rotation of office, and so on.

One important strand in this republican tradition of constitutional discussion has been the idea that if the state's power of interference is to be rendered non-arbitrary, then whatever other devices are in place, people must be able to contest the decisions made by various arms of government. They must have access to the reasons supporting those decisions and they must be able to contest the soundness of those reasons or the degree of support they offer to the decisions made. Moreover they must be in a position, ideally, to expect that such contestations will be heard, will be impartially adjudicated and, if necessary, will be implemented against those in government. The general message is that so far as a government is effectively contestable, to that extent it is less likely to enjoy arbitrary power.

The effective promotion of contestability in the political sphere requires a variety of institutions, especially if it is to guard against unwieldy levels of complaint.[11] From our point of view, however, only two observations are relevant. The first is that putting in place a regime of electoral democracy is essential in guarding against certain possibilities of non-contestability and domination: the colonial, the authoritarian, and so on. And the second is that any such regime still leaves striking possibilities of non-contestability and domination in place: possibilities associated with the tyranny of the democratic majority, in particular, and the tyranny of what we might describe as the democratic elite: those in the corridors of power – for example, in the bureaucracy, the cabinet, the courts, the prisons, or the police force – who can impose their own will in how they interpret and implement democratic policy.

How are people to be empowered in relation to democratic majorities and democratic elites? How are they to be given a power of contestation against them? Whatever else is necessary, it seems clear that they must be able to ask after the reasons that support the decisions, they must be able to question the relevance of the reasons and they must be in a position to expect a fair hearing. And all of that is going to be possible, of course, only so far as the democratic bodies in question operate in a deliberative mode. There must be a dispensation of deliberation in place in the community as a whole, and in the microcosm of parliament, which establishes a currency of considerations that are admitted on all sides to connect with common avowable interests and to be relevant to the doings of government. There must be a commitment in the different arms of government to justifying whatever decisions are taken by reference to the considerations that are relevant, by common consent, in their case. And it must be possible for private individuals, or perhaps for designated representatives, to challenge such decisions on the grounds that the reasons quoted are not sound or do not offer the requisite support for the decisions taken. It is only in the event of democracy having this deliberative cast that contestability, and ultimately nonarbitrariness, can be furthered.

This republican argument for deliberative democracy applies also, of course, to fora beyond those of government. Take the workplace community or the community organization, or indeed the family. Even if decisions are taken democratically in such a body, there will be little protection against arbitrariness – short of exit – unless the democracy in question operates in deliberative mode, giving individuals a chance to contest the decisions made. If decisions are made on the basis of interest-group politics, or bargaining from different levels of power, then there will be no grounds on which any contestation can be made. Brute force or naked preference will rule.

Cass Sunstein probably has the republican case for deliberative–democratic procedure in mind when he describes deliberative democracy as a 'republic of reasons'.[12] Just as people are in a position to know where they stand in relation to a judge only so far as the judge has to provide statements of reasons for his or her decisions, so more generally people can know where they stand in relation to public decisions only if they know what the grounds adduced in support of those decisions are. They will not be able to take a stand in relation to public decisions, if those decisions are the outcome of interest-group bargaining or of voting on the basis of naked, unargued preference. Such non-deliberatively generated decisions would have the profile of dictats or fiats from on high, where the products of deliberative–democratic procedure would present themselves as reasoned – well-reasoned or badly reasoned – judgments that people are in a position to examine, assess and, if necessary, challenge.

The contestability argument for deliberative democracy ought to have persuasive force, quite apart from its connection with republican theory. It is of particular interest here because – unusually among such arguments, as we shall see in the next section – it provides a firm ground, at least in most contexts, for taking a position on the participatory and regulatory questions raised by the discursive dilemma.

The implications for the participatory question

The republican, contestability argument does not offer a quick resolution of the question as to whether parliaments ought to conform to the Washington model, having effective control of legislative decisions, or ought to play the restricted, Westminster role; there are too many issues of detail involved for this to be readily tractable. But the argument does support a firm line on the question as to whether large-scale electorates – large-scale electorates as distinct, for example, from town meetings – should be given control of policy issues or restricted to issues of personnel and platform. It supports a restriction of electoral control to the selection of representatives.

The reason is palpable in light of the discursive dilemma. For that dilemma shows that no matter how deliberative an electorate is, it is liable to give rise to a collectively inconsistent position on related policy issues. And no group that supports such a position is forced to track considerations of common avowable interest, as political powers are required to do under the republican ideal. The inconsistency of the judgments maintained means that the group tracks no single set of considerations or reasons, and no considerations therefore that bear on matters of common avowable interest. If the electorate as a whole is given direct control of policy issues, therefore, then it is liable to be the most arbitrary of powers. It will relate to individuals and smaller groups in the role of an arbitrary despot.

A political power is non-arbitrary, under the republican account, to the extent that it is forced to track the common avowable interest of members of the society. The electorate or populace that is given the participatory role envisaged would fail to be non-arbitrary in the most dramatic of ways. It would fail to achieve this desired profile, not through tracking considerations that are more special than they ought to be – not through serving just the interests of a majority or an elite – but rather through failing to track considerations of any sort. It would represent, not a corrupt form of government, but an utterly capricious one.

Not only would the people as a whole represent an arbitrary, capricious government of this kind, were they allowed the sort of participatory role described. Unlike most capricious governments that we might envisage – say, the rule of a Caligula – they would represent a capricious government that could hope to be morally as well as legally unchallengeable. The ethos of democracy gives any decision that can be described as representing the people's voice a certain morally special status, so that empowering the people in referendums could introduce the worst of all imaginable despotisms: a regime under which the most capricious of powers remains morally as well as legally uncontestable.

This is not to deny, of course, that consistently with republican theory it might be useful in certain predicaments for government to resort to referendum or even for government to allow citizen-initiated referendums on whether to repeal existing legislation.[13] And it is certainly not to downplay the importance of electoral democracy, let alone the importance of civic culture and involvement. Under the representative regime that republicanism would support, it is going to be of the first importance that there is widespread public debate related to the choice of personnel and the identification of preferred platforms. For only debate of that kind can establish the currency of considerations in terms of which it is appropriate to interrogate government. And it is only in the light of the part they play in such debate that representatives can be held to later account. The message is not that electoral apathy is desirable – far from it – but rather that electoral democracy should not have the sort of participatory cast associated with rule by referendum.

There is also a further thought to add. In arguing for the importance of contestability – that is, of effective access to contestation – the republican approach gives support to the idea that people should have discursive standing in relation to government: they should relate to government as parties that can only be interfered with when it is claimed – and the claim can be put to the test – that interference is justified by common avowed or readily avowable interests. The enjoyment of such discursive status is of the first importance in people's personal and political life.[14] While it falls short of the active, discursive participation prized by many deliberative democrats, it offers an attractive substitute for the participatory ideal and may even represent the deeper, motivating value.

The implications for the regulatory question

But what of the administrative and perhaps parliamentary bodies that are given carriage of policy issues and that do have the capacity, like a collegiate court, to regulate themselves for the achievement of collective rationality? Should bodies of this kind work at ensuring such collective rationality? Or should they allow themselves to adopt positions which, at the cost of collective rationality, represent the views of their members faithfully?

Here it should be clear that short of the bodies being so small that contestability can be achieved in relation to the separate individuals involved, it is vital from a republican point of view that the groups work at ensuring collective rationality. The reason, as in the other case, is that a group which does not ensure the consistency of the overall position it takes on issues within its control will be an arbitrary, capricious power in the lives of those whom it affects. People may try to contest its individual decisions but since the potential inconsistency of its views means that it is not subject to any rule of reasons, there are no reasons with which they can hope to confront and confound it.

The uncontestability and arbitrariness of such a group appears in the fact that it will be essentially unconversable. It will be a body with which it is inherently impossible to enter discussion, reasoning with it as to what it ought to do or ought to have done in a given case. Consider the workforce in our earlier example. We might discover that the majority view among its members is that electrocution is a serious danger, that a pay-sacrifice would solve the problem, and that the loss involved is bearable – and that those premises imply that a pay-sacrifice would be desirable; and yet it should be no surprise to find that the group comes down against a pay-sacrifice. There is no talking to a group that operates like this. It will represent a completely capricious center of decision-making.

Might the demands of contestability be satisfied to the extent that the individuals in the group, though not the group itself, are conversable and contestable agents? Might they be satisfied in the way in which they might be thought to be satisfied by the ordinary collegiate court?

I am prepared to concede that where numbers are very small, as in the judicial case, contestability can be achieved in significant measure at the individual level. The court may not represent a capricious power, so far as it is seen as a collection of individually contestable judges. This contestability will be reinforced by the fact that while the court operates as a set of individual judges in dealing with the different issues that come up in a particular case, those judges do look to the consistency of the collective court over time. They recognise the force of precedent and only ignore it when they think that there are good reasons why the court as a whole should set a precedent aside.

I am loathe to think, however, that contestability is best achieved at the individual level, even when numbers are small. It is not clear how satisfactory a model the judicial bench offers, given evidence that members switch votes in order to avoid problems and given recent critiques of the system.[15] And in any case the group, being an entity that continues through changes of membership, is the salient agency that we should want to have in a contestable and conversable role. With many groups, the court included, it will be important that contestability in relation to judgments at different times is ensured, not just contestability in relation to judgments at one and the same time. Since it is only the group that is guaranteed to survive over time – the individual members will come and go – it has to be the group as such that is required to be contestable.[16]

5. This Resolution and Other Arguments for the Ideal

There are many different arguments in support of deliberative democracy to be found in the recent literature and we have been looking only at the implications of one. The question that we must consider, finally, is whether the position taken here on republican grounds runs seriously counter to any of those other arguments. I devote this last section to trying to show that it does not. No devotees of deliberative democracy, whatever the basis of their devotion, are blocked from embracing the position defended in the last section; in particular none are blocked from insisting on the importance of ensuring that collective decision-making bodies regulate themselves for consistency in their judgments and actions.

Arguments for making democracy deliberative

Most of the arguments for deliberative democracy focus on the virtue of making democracy deliberative: that is, on the benefit to a democratic process or society of having deliberation of an inclusive, dialogical kind. Some assert that making democracy deliberative should help to ensure that people's preferences are reflective and informed, not just the brute product of their adaptation to circumstance; or that it should enable people to do better in reaching beyond the chasms of difference that separate the members of certain groups, even if it does not bring them into consensus; or that it should stretch people's imagination and empathy as they are forced to take a general point of view. Without alleging any such psychological transformation, other arguments maintain that making democracy deliberative should at least have the effect of screening out self-regarding concerns in favour of more public-spirited considerations, thereby approximating or advancing an ideal of public reasoning among free and equal participants. And yet a further range of arguments urge that making democracy deliberative would promote such effects as legitimising whatever decisions are reached, making them more likely to take account of the relatively powerless, increasing transparency among members of the group, or promoting just outcomes.

There is no likelihood that any arguments of this kind can be invoked against the view that where this is possible, deliberative democracy ought to require collective rationality; and that where this is not possible, it ought to allow for a purely representative regime. We do not eliminate deliberation by shaping deliberative democracy in this way, and benefits of the kind invoked in these arguments all look to be consistent with doing so.

We do not eliminate deliberation from the electorate, as already mentioned, by restricting electoral democracy to a representative profile. And neither do we eliminate deliberation by requiring other groups to impose reason at the collective level. Consider the workforce deliberating on whether to take a pay-sacrifice and use the money to introduce a safety measure. Even if they agree to reach a decision on the basis of certain premises, they will first be required under the deliberative–democratic ideal to discuss the matter in public. And the benefits that come of making democracy deliberative, according to the arguments under consideration, would all seem to be available under this way of doing things; in particular, they would seem to be available as readily and as richly as under the alternative.

Arguments for making deliberation democratic

A second sort of argument for the ideal of deliberative democracy makes a case, not for having deliberation present in democratic process, but rather for having democracy present in deliberative process; it argues for making deliberation democratic, not for making democracy deliberative. The claim is that if there are matters of truth involved in political deliberation – as in the question, most abstractly, of whether this or that is in the common interest – then the chance of reaching the truth, or of reaching the truth according to received views of reliability, is increased by having in place a regime of democratic decision-making. The argument may be recast for goals other than that of maximizing the chance of reaching the truth or minimizing the chance of falsehood. It applies just as readily to a more specific goal like that of minimizing the chance of a false negative, for example: say, minimizing the chance of finding an innocent defendant guilty. But I shall restrict myself here to the original truth-centered case.

The most famous version of this argument derives from the Marquis de Condorcet's work in defense of his so-called jury theorem.[17] The theorem presupposes that the voters are independent of one another: while they may certainly form their opinions on the basis of dialogue, none of them votes in a way that is blindly deferential to others. It shows that if voters each have the same, greater than evens chance of being right on some yes-no issue then, first, their collective resolution of the issue, under majority rule, will have a yet greater chance of being right and, second, it will have a progressively greater chance of being right as the size of the group increases. Indeed the latter element is assured, even if some voters have a less than evens chance of being right; it will hold so long as the average chance of voters being individually right is greater than evens.[18]

Does the jury theorem provide any reason for resisting a mode of democratic judgment-making that imposes reason at the collective level? Does it run counter to the line taken under the republican approach?[19]

If the group does not enforce reason at the collective level – if it does not try to ensure the rationality of its collective judgments – then it will almost certainly be led to adopt inconsistent judgments, as the discursive dilemma shows. But inconsistent judgments cannot all be true at once and so in this respect at least the procedure would lead the group into despairing of the ideal of truth. The other procedure, by contrast, would ensure that no inconsistency was maintained and would keep open the possibility that the group can hold by a set of judgments that are all true.

This consideration is not conclusive, since it is possible to have more true judgments incorporated in an inconsistent set than there are true judgments in a counterpart, consistent collection. But it is hard to see why anyone would expect a group to do better in truth terms by not enforcing consistency than by enforcing it; there are no special considerations that would explain why this is so. And that being the case, the observation made would seem to suggest that those who are moved by Condorcetian or related claims should be inclined to go along with the line supported by the republican argument, not to challenge it.

I conclude, to return to the general theme, that the various arguments in the literature for deliberative democracy are consistent with the republican way of resolving the questions that the discursive dilemma raises for the ideal. The republican commitment to contestability makes a powerful case for wanting democratic procedure to support collective rationality, where that is achievable, and for restricting the scope of decision-making to the selection of representatives where it is not. And the other considerations that are invoked to support deliberative democracy do nothing to undermine the case made.[20]

Notes

This is a thoroughly revised version of Pettit, P. (2001). 'Deliberative Democracy and the Discursive Dilemma', *Philosophical Issues (supp to Nous)* 11: 268–99. While it maintains the main thesis of that paper, it defends the thesis on the basis of a somewhat different presentation of the discursive dilemma: one which stresses more sharply the contrast between the dilemma and the doctrinal paradox in which it takes its origin, as explained in the second section. More detailed references to background material are provided in the earlier paper.

1   See the readings in Bohman, J. and W. Rehg, eds, *Deliberative Democracy: Essays on Reason and Politics* (Cambridge, Mass.: MIT Press, 1997); Elster, J., ed.,*Deliberative Democracy* (Cambridge: Cambridge University Press, 1998).
2   Grofman, B. N. and S. Feld (1988). 'Rousseau's General Will: A Condorcetian Perspective'. *American Political Science Review*, 82 (1988), 567–76.
3   Estlund, D. and J. Waldron, 'Democratic Theory and the Public Interest: Condorcet and Rousseau Revisited', *American Political Science Review*, 83 (1989), 1317–28.
4   Habermas, J. (1984, 1989). *A Theory of Communicative Action, vols 1 and 2*. Cambridge: Polity Press.
5   Chapman, B., 'Law, Incommensurability, and Conceptually Sequenced Argument', *University of Pennsylvania Law Review*, 146 (1998), 1487–1582; Chapman, B., 'More Easily Done than Said: Rules, Reason and Rational Social Choice'. *Oxford Journal of Legal Studies*, 18 (1998), 293–329; Kornhauser, L. A., 'Modelling Collegial Courts. I. Path-Dependence'. *International Review of Law and Economics*, 12 (1992), 169–85; Kornhauser, L. A., 'Modelling Collegial Courts. II. Legal Doctrine', *Journal of Law, Economics and Organization*, 8 (1992), 441–70; Kornhauser, L. A. and L. G. Sager, 'Unpacking the Court' *Yale Law Journal*, 82 (1986); Kornhauser, L. A. and L. G. Sager, 'The One and the Many: Adjudication in Collegial Courts', *California Law Review*, 81 (1993), 1–59.
6   The structure involved is this:
  a.   there is a conclusion to be decided among the judges by reference to a conjunction of independent or separable premises – the conclusion will be endorsed if relevant premises are endorsed, and otherwise it will be rejected;
  b.   each judge forms a judgment on each of the premises and a corresponding

judgment on the conclusion;

c. each of the premises is supported by a majority of judges but those majorities do not coincide with one another;

d. the intersection of those majorities will support the conclusion, and the others reject it, in view of a; and

e. the intersection of the majorities is not itself a majority; in our example only one judge out of the three is in that intersection.

7   The discussion that follows is based on Pettit, P., *A Theory of Freedom: From the Psychology to the Politics of Agency* (Cambridge and New York: Polity and Oxford University Press, 2001), ch. 5; Pettit, P., 'Groups with Minds of their Own', *Socializing Metaphysics*, ed. F. Schmitt. (New York: Rowan and Littlefield, 2002).

8   Sunstein, C., *One Case At A Time* (Cambridge, Mass.: Harvard University Press, 1999).

9   See List, C. and P. Pettit, 'Aggregating Sets of Judgments: Two Impossibility Results Compared' *Synthese* (forthcoming); List, C. and P. Pettit, 'The Aggregation of Sets of Judgments: An Impossibility Result', *Economics and Philosophy* 18 (2002), 89–110. Let the views of certain individuals on a rationally connected set of issues be rationally satisfactory in the sense of being consistent, complete and deductively closed. The impossibility theorem shows that any procedure whereby an equally satisfactory set of views may be derived from the individual views must fail in one of the following regards. It must be incapable of working with some profiles of individual views. Or it must fail to treat some individual or some issue even-handedly. That is to say, it must let some individual or individuals be treated as less important than another – at the limit, the other may be given the status of a dictator; or it must downgrade some issue in the sense of letting the collective view on that issue be determined, not by majority vote, by the collective views on other issues.

10   Pettit, P., *Republicanism: A Theory of Freedom and Government.* (Oxford: Oxford University Press, 1997); Skinner, Q., *Liberty Before Liberalism.* (Cambridge: Cambridge University Press, 1997).

11   For a review of some of these see Pettit, P., 'Democracy, Electoral and Contestatory', *Nomos,* 42 (2000), 105–44.

12   Sunstein, C. R., *The Partial Constitution* (Cambridge, Mass.: Harvard University Press, 1993).

13   Cf. Michelman, F. I., 'Protecting the People from Themselves', or 'How Direct Can Democracy Be?' *UCLA Law Review* 45 (1998), 1717–3 at p. 1734.

14   See Pettit, P., *A Theory of Freedom: From the Psychology to the Politics of Agency.* (Cambridge and New York: Polity and Oxford University Press, 2001).

15   Kornhauser, L. A. and L. G. Sager, 'The One and the Many: Adjudication in Collegial Courts', *California Law Review,* 81 (1993), 1–59; Stearns, M. L., *Constitutional Process: A Social Choice Analysis of Supreme Court Decision Making.* (Ann Arbor: Michigan University Press, 2000).

16   Imagine that a court has to make a decision on whether or not someone should be given a retrial, as in the case presented in Matrix 2. And suppose that the individual judges vote in the pattern described in that matrix (which is drawn from Kornhauser and Sager 1993, 40).

	Inadmissible evidence?	Forced confession?	Retrial?
A.	Yes	No	Yes
B.	No	Yes	Yes
C.	No	No	No

It is plausible in such a case that the person ought to be given a retrial, despite the fact that a majority rejects each of the relevant grounds. Does this suggest that there is a general problem of plausibility attached to the procedure of requiring collective rationality and group-level contestability?

While it is certainly implausible in such a case that the defendant should be denied a retrial, that implausibility can easily be registered in the approach of a group that seeks to ensure group-level contestability. The implausibility can be taken by the group to indicate that the majority vote in favour of a retrial is more compelling than either of the other votes and that one or more of those votes should be revised. Or the group may think that there is only one proposition which they each have to make a judgment on: viz., the disjunctive claim that there was inadmissible evidence or a forced confession. Or the implausibility may prompt members of the group to argue that while the representation in the matrix is fine, what collective deliberation should be designed to secure in such a case is primarily the avoidance of a false negative – denying a retrial to a deserving appellant – and that only a unanimously rejected ground of appeal should be dismissed by the group. Under any of these interpretations, the procedure that requires collective rationality would enable the group to grant a retrial.

Kornhauser and Sager suggest that while the straightforward premise-driven procedure is generally more satisfactory – more satisfactory from the point of view, roughly, of contestability – the court should resort to a higher-level procedure in any case, like the one illustrated, where there is any doubt about this. It should take a majority meta-vote on which procedure to employ at the lower level, undertaking 'to justify its decision' (31; cf. 33–6): that is, presumably, undertaking to find agreed premises such that the meta-vote can be represented as itself driven by majority endorsement of those considerations in a premise-driven way. Thus the higher-level considerations might be, first, that going along with the lower-level premise-driven decision in this instance would generate a certain result and, second, that the court ought to avoid such a result. Such considerations, if endorsed by a majority, might provide a higher-level, premise-driven case for going along with a different result from that which was supported by a lower-level, premise-driven procedure.

17 See Black, D., *The Theory of Committees and Elections* (Cambridge: Cambridge University Press, 1958); Condorcet, M. d., *Condorcet: Selected Writings* (Indianapolis: Bobbs-Merrill, 1976). The most forceful defender of this sort of approach in the contemporary literature is David Estlund. See Estlund, D., 'Making Truth Safe for Democracy', *The Idea of Democracy* ed. D. Copp, J. Hampton and J. E. Roemer (Cambridge: Cambridge University Press, 1993), pp. 71–100; Estlund, D., 'Who's Afraid of Deliberative Democracy?' *Texas Law Review,* 71 (1993), 1437–77; Estlund, D., 'Opinion Leaders, Independence, and Condorcet's Jury Theorem', *Theory and Decision,* 36 (1994), 131–62; Estlund, D., 'Beyond Fairness and Deliberation: The Epistemic Dimension of Democratic Authority', *Deliberative Democracy: Essays on Reason and Politics,* ed. J. Bohman and W. Rehg (Cambridge, Mass.: MIT Press, 1997).

18   Owen, G., B. Grofman, et al., 'Proving a distribution-free generalization of the Condorcet jury theorem', *Mathematical Social Sciences*, 17 (1989), 1–16.

19   Wlodek Rabinowicz and I explored this question elsewhere in a special context; see the appendix to Pettit, P., 'Deliberative Democracy and the Discursive Dilemma', *Philosophical Issues (supp to Nous)*, 11 (2001), 268–99, and for a later, more comprehensive treatment see Luc Bovens amd Wlodek Rabinowicz 'The Condorcet Jury Theorem and Complex Social Decisions', ms, Dept of Philosophy, Lund University, 2001. We took a case where a group agrees on the premises by which a certain conclusion is to be determined and asked how the prospect of their making a true judgment on the conclusion is best promoted: whether by having the members each vote on the premises, letting the premise-votes determine the conclusion, or by having them each draw the conclusion in their own case, allowing the conclusion-votes to determine the conclusion. But the question considered here is more general. It is the question of how the group may best hope to promote the prospect of its being right on the issues in general: how it may hope to maximize expected true-belief on no matter what issues.

20   I am indebted to Geoffrey Brennan, who first made me aware of the doctrinal paradox. See Brennan, G., 'Collective Coherence?', *International Review of Law and Economics*, 21 (2001). I was helped by comments received when versions of the paper were presented at a number of venues, in particular at the conference on 'Deliberating about Deliberative Democracy', University of Texas, Austin, Feb. 2000. I owe a particular debt to Wlodek Rabinowitz for his helpful comments and I was also greatly aided by exchanges with a number of other people: David Estlund, John Ferejohn, Christian List, Frank Michelman, Victoria McGeer and Fred Schick. Bruce Chapman and Lewis Kornhauser sent me useful written comments on an early version.

8

Street-level Epistemology and Democratic Participation

Russell Hardin

In postwar public choice theory there have been at least three devastating theo-retical claims against the coherence of any democratic theory that is conceived as even minimally participatory, collectively consistent, and well informed. The first of these was Kenneth Arrow's impossibility theorem, which concludes that there is no general, acceptable way to aggregate from individual-level to collec-tive-level preferences.[1] One might have supposed that democracy does not re-quire this kind of aggregation anyway, because it requires only majority rule, not collective rule. But an implication of Arrow's theorem is that with simple ma-jority rule we may have cycles and no genuine majority. Suppose we face three independent policy issues. One majority can carry allocation A across these is-sues over allocation B; another majority can carry B over C, and yet a third can carry C over A. Hence, at least in principle, majoritarianism cannot solve our problem.

In his economic theory of democracy, Anthony Downs presented two addi-tional theoretical claims against participatory democracy, which are quite differ-ent from each other but related.[2] First, he supposed that voters actually have little incentive to vote, because they cannot expect to have any impact on the outcome of any given election. Indeed, they have so little impact that any costs of voting, such as suffering through long queues or foul weather, trump any direct benefit from voting. This claim is a specific instance of the logic of collec-tive action, as generalized later by Mancur Olson.[3]

The second major theoretical claim of Downs is that individual citizens have no incentive even to learn enough to be able to vote their interests intelligently. This immediately follows from the second claim if we suppose that gaining relevant knowledge entails some costs.

Additionally, Downs gave us a model of how candidates must locate them-selves in order to maximize their chances of being elected. This is the median voter model, which says that a candidate must take a position at the median of a normal distribution of voters. A candidate who does not do this can be out-flanked by another candidate who takes a position between the first candidate and the median voter. This model assumes away Arrow's problem by supposing that all policy issues aggregately reduce to a single left–right dimension. Hence, preferences over candidates cannot take all possible orderings, such as my preferring the candidate on the far left to that on the far right to that in the middle. Arrow's result, including the minimal result of cyclic collective preferences, is blocked by Downs's simple left–right distribution of voter preferences. Note that the median voter model seems to run against the second of Downs's theses, which seems to entail that candidates should attempt to influence voters' knowledge.

I wish to push the three challenges to democracy by relating them and, in particular, by subjecting them to an economic theory of knowledge. Knowledge is *prima facie* central to the Arrow problem, the median voter model, and the issue of voters' incentive to learn enough to vote intelligently in their own interests if they do vote. One can also argue that Downs's thesis that the individual has no incentive to vote poses a problem of knowledge of a somewhat different kind. The general argument of the logic of collective action and Downs's narrower version of that argument are both relatively recent discoveries that are not well understood by many people. In general, the individual-level knowledge demands of these issues are no different in kind from the individual-level knowledge demands for ordinary pragmatic choice in daily life and in planning future actions, when the costs of information and the costs of mastering relevant quasi-theoretical understandings can be higher than the seeming pay-off that will come from them.

I will generally focus on issues of voters' interests and will not attempt to take on normative concerns, such as moral commitments to foreign aid, opposing abortion, punishing victimless crimes, or retributive views on punishment. These other issues often override concern with interests for particular citizens. A full account of democratic theory would have to deal with them as well as with interests. Unfortunately, knowledge issues around mere interests already call such theory into question.

After first briefly outlining an economic theory of knowledge, or a street-level epistemology, I will discuss knowledge issues in political participation in the following order. First, I will briefly discuss the widely held view that voters do not know enough to vote intelligently. Second, I will discuss candidates' efforts to place themselves at the median voter's position. Third, I will discuss the problem of knowledge of the logic of collective action, or at least of its specific application to voting. Fourth, I will discuss the newly multidimensional issues of contemporary politics as themselves in part a problem of knowledge that can confound voters' choices and as a reinvocation of Arrow's problem in a somewhat new guise. Finally, I will conclude with some remarks on the implications of these arguments for liberties, which are a peculiar class of collective goods, and on the relation of liberties to democracy.

Street-level Epistemology

The theory of knowledge that I propose to apply to these issues is a street-level epistemology, a theory of the knowledge of the ordinary person. It differs substantially from standard philosophical epistemology. The latter is a theory of how to justify truth claims. It has been developed especially in the context of attempting to understand physics and other sciences. The tenets of such an epistemology are about what criteria make a claim true. The focus is on the matter that is supposedly known, not on the knower. For example, it is about whether Einstein's theory of relativity is true. We could think of it as a theory of the knowledge of a super-knower or of the distributed knowledge of a society.

An economic theory of knowledge is a theory of why the typical individual, or even a particular individual, comes to know various things. In an economic theory, it makes sense to say that you know one thing and I know a contrary thing in some context. I might eventually come to realize that my knowledge is mistaken and therefore correct it, especially after hearing your defense of your contrary knowledge. But there is no role for a super-knower who can judge the truth of our positions. We are our own judges. If we wish to seek better knowledge, it is we who must decide from what agency or source to seek it. Street-level epistemology is not about what counts as knowledge in, say, physics, but rather about what counts as your knowledge, my knowledge, the ordinary person's knowledge.

Most of the knowledge of an ordinary person has a very messy structure and cannot meet standard epistemological criteria for its justification. With characteristic force, David Hume spells out our problem: "Our Thought is fluctuating, uncertain, fleeting, successive, and compounded; and were we to remove these Circumstances, we absolutely annihilate its Essence, and it wou'd, in such a Case, be an abuse of Terms to apply to it the Name of Thought or Reason."[4] Rather than a standard philosophical epistemology, we therefore need a street-level epistemology to make sense of the morass of ordinary knowledge. Street-level epistemology is a subjective account of knowledge, not a public account. I wish here not to elaborate this view but to apply it to the problems of representative democracy. I will briefly lay out the central implications of a street-level epistemology and then bring it to bear on democratic citizenship.

Much of the work on voting behavior and the apparent ignorance of many voters treats the issues as problems of psychological foibles in decision-making.[5] Many − although not all − of these foibles can easily be seen as essentially economic constraints on learning how to judge complex issues, but I will generally not discuss the psychological approach to these problems here. Much work also gives a fairly straightforward account of the problem of the status-based economics of knowledge. For example, Robert Dahl notes that "knowledge, wealth, social position, access to officials, and other resources are unequally distributed" in American politics.[6] I will not take up this issue either but will generally discuss only the general problem of coming to know relevant things for political participation. Bringing unequal positions into such an analysis would be valuable for a complete account of actual participation. Such a move could be fully consistent with street-level epistemology.

In standard philosophical epistemology, it would commonly be incoherent to speak of my mistaken knowledge. Knowledge is, in some epistemologies, "justified true belief." If I am mistaken in my belief, then I most likely lack justification for the belief. Hence, it is not knowledge. And in any case, the category of justified true belief is a category of somehow public knowledge, not personal knowledge. In a street-level epistemology, there may be no ground for claiming in general that my knowledge is philosophically justified in any such sense. There is commonly only a story to be told of how I have come to have my belief. There is therefore little or no point in distinguishing between belief and knowledge, and I will not do so. Typically, at the street level, the term "belief" is commonly used when the substance of the knowledge is a particular kind, such as religious knowledge. There is often no other systematic difference in degree of confidence in knowing those things that are labeled as knowledge and those that are labeled as belief. Indeed, people with strong religious convictions would commonly claim to know the truth of the things they believe religiously far more confidently than the truth of many simple, objective things they might also claim to know. It is true that we sometimes use the term belief to allow for doubt, as when we say, "I believe that's the way it happened, but I might be wrong." But this hedge applies to virtually all our knowledge.

Standard philosophical epistemology is concerned with justification, that is, justification of any claim that some piece of putative knowledge is actually true. Street-level epistemology is economic; it is not generally about justification but about usefulness. It follows John Dewey's "pragmatic rule": In order to discover the meaning of an idea, ask for its consequences.[7] In essence, a street-level epistemology applies this to the idea of knowledge, with consequences broadly defined to include the full costs and benefits of coming to know and using knowledge. Note that the pragmatic or street-level epistemology is essentially an economic theory. But it is not the economic theory that presumes full knowledge, as in rational expectations theory or much of game theory. And it is not merely about the costs of information, as in some economic accounts.

Again, standard philosophical epistemology focuses on the *matter* of belief, for example, on the orbit of a planet. It is about truth and the justification of truth claims. An economic theory of knowledge focuses on the individual believer or *knower*, on the costs and benefits of coming to know, which, of course, vary from person to person and context to context. Perhaps the chief way in which standard epistemologies do not fit much of our ordinary knowledge is that the bulk of our knowledge – perhaps virtually all of it – depends on others in various ways. We take most knowledge on authority from others who presumably are in a position to know it. Indeed, we take it from others who themselves take it from others who themselves take it from others and so forth *all the way down*. There are finally no, or at best vague and weak, foundations for most of an individual's knowledge.

Trudy Govier argues that our knowledge therefore depends on trust.[8] It might be better to say it depends on the trustworthiness of our authoritative sources, although even this is too much. Very little of our knowledge seems likely to depend on anything vaguely like an ordinary trust relationship. I personally know none of the authoritative sources for much of what I would think is my knowledge in many areas. It is not so much that I take that knowledge on trust as that I have little choice but to take it. If I do not take it, I will be virtually catatonic. I am quite confident that much of what I think I know is false, but still I rely on what I know to get me through life because I have to.

Hence, the knowledge that you or I have is from a vast social system, not from anything we actually checked out. Much of it can only be generated by a social system. We depend on knowledge by authority because it is efficient and because, without division of labor in generating our knowledge, we would have no time for putting much of it to use. Since what we mainly want is to use it, we settle for taking it on authority rather than seeking to justify it. We have to rely on others or massively restrict our lives. As Ludwig Wittgenstein says, "My life consists in my being content to accept many things."[9] Henry Sidgwick similarly noted that to live at all is prior to living well and if we are to live at all we must accept many things that do not have reason as their source.[10]

Knowledge of How To Vote

The central epistemological concern in representative democracy is what the typical citizen knows about the actions of public officials. If, in general, we make the effort to know something in large part *because it serves our interest to know it*, then we cannot expect people to know very much about what their representatives do. In the argument of the economic theory of democracy, a citizen typically does not have very much interest in voting. One vote has a miniscule chance of making a difference, so miniscule that, even when it is multiplied by the value of making a difference and getting one's preferred candidate or policy, the expected value of the vote is miniscule (see further below, "Understanding Whether To Vote"). Hence, if there is any real cost involved in casting a vote, that cost swamps the expected benefit to the voter of voting. Hence, by the pragmatic rule, there is little point in knowing enough actually to vote well.

The conclusion that we have no incentive to learn enough to vote well was part of Downs's argument, and it had been even more central to the earlier argument of Joseph Schumpeter. As Schumpeter wrote, implicitly invoking his own pragmatic rule, "without the initiative that comes from immediate responsibility, ignorance will persist in the face of masses of information however complete and correct."[11] I may have reason to acquire knowledge because it gives me pleasure, but not because it will be useful in my causing good public effects through my role as citizen and voter.

Most of the subsequent research and debate on voting has focused primarily on the incentive to vote rather than the incentive to know enough to vote intelligently. The latter is at least logically derivative from the former, because it is the lack of incentive to vote that makes knowledge how to vote well virtually useless, so that mastering that knowledge violates the pragmatic rule. Just because my vote has miniscule causal effect on democratically determined outcomes, there is no compelling reason for me to determine how to vote by assessing the causal effect of my vote on such outcomes. Or, to put this the other way around, the fact that I would benefit from policy X does not give me reason or incentive to know about or to understand the implications of policy X unless, by the pragmatic rule, I can somehow affect whether policy X is to be adopted.

If the citizen has no interest in voting, then the citizen has no interest in making the effort to learn enough to vote well. Something that is not worth doing at all is surely not worth doing well. If the problem of knowing enough to judge government officials is already hard, the lack of incentive to correct that problem is devastating. Indeed, the costs of knowing enough about government to be able to vote intelligently in one's own interest surely swamp the modest costs, for most people in the United States, of actually casting a vote, at least on commonplace issues of public policy outside moments of great crisis. The economic theory of knowledge or street-level epistemology therefore weighs against knowing enough to vote well because the incentives heavily cut against investing in the relevant knowledge. The typical voter will not be able to put the relevant knowledge to beneficial use.

In what follows, I will simply take for granted that typical citizens do not master the facts they would need to know if they were to vote their interests intelligently. There is extensive evidence on this claim, although there is, of course, also great difference of opinion on its significance for electoral choices. For example, Popkin canvasses problems of voter ignorance in American presidential elections but he then refers to "low-information rationality," which is rationality despite abysmal factual ignorance.[12] He also argues for a Gresham's law of political information: bad facts drive out good facts. This law is that "a small amount of personal information [on a candidate] can dominate a large amount of historical information about a past record." The personal information might be some minor thing that comes up during a campaign. The trouble with the large amount of historical information that is, at least in principle, available is that voters do not typically know much of it because it would be silly for them to invest the time needed to learn such information.

As evidence of how little voters even seek better information before voting, consider the difficulty candidates have in getting their message across to voters. Richard Fenno elegantly displays the burden that candidates for the US House of Representatives face in merely finding people to talk to.[13]

Even professional political scientists, who have a strong interest in knowing more about politics than their mere interest in the outcomes of elections would suggest, find it hard to keep up with much of what happens. Weekly tallies of votes in the US House of Representatives and Senate, for example, are reported in some newspapers, but with such brevity that their meaning is often opaque to anyone who has not followed the relevant issues very closely, more closely than many of those newspapers do.

Results of referendum votes on even relatively simple issues suggest astonishing misunderstanding by voters.[14] California voters displayed cavalier irresponsibility in a recent referendum on a so-called three-strikes sentencing law that mandates harsh minimum prison terms for repeat offenders.[15] In an early case to which the new law was applied, a one-slice pizza thief was sentenced to a term of 25 years to life, with no possibility of parole before serving at least 20 years, for his "felony petty theft."[16] And voters apparently displayed complete misunderstanding of a referendum (Proposition 3) to undo a prior referendum (Proposition 198) on open primaries. The prior referendum, passed in ignorance of its consequences by the voters, would have disallowed California representation at the national party nominating conventions in the year 2000. After the electorate failed on this issue, administrative devices were used to enable the state to distinguish Democratic and Republican voters in primary elections.[17] In this failure, democracy was a charade and, when it failed from ignorance, a knowledgeable bureaucratic agent intervened against the democratic result.

Median Knowledge

The argument of the median voter model of elections is demoralizing. It implies that a mere census of voters and their positions would define the median voter and therefore the outcome of any election. Then what is the point of the elections? Ostensibly, each candidate uses the electoral process to influence voters by convincing them that their real positions center on the positions of that candidate. To put this in a positive light, we could say that election campaigns are about giving voters the knowledge they need to vote intelligently in their interest. To put it in a negative light, we could say they are about deceiving voters into thinking their interests are other than they are or that a candidate's position is other than it is. Or perhaps there is a middle way and campaigns are about giving voters any insight at all.

Suppose voters are generally quite ignorant of the nature of issues of objective importance to them and of the stances of candidates on those issues. In such an ignorant population, *the median of the distribution of voters is not well defined*. Hence, with ignorant voters the median voter model does not entail that the candidates must place themselves very near each other. Moreover, the ill-defined median can be volatile. Because voters are ignorant, their positions may be relatively unstable and subject to sudden change in response to new information.[18] This means that a candidate's effort to inform voters can be risky. If voters were well informed, however, campaigns would have little effect unless candidates could generate new issues. The very fact of campaigns suggests the general ignorance of voters. The quality of campaigns, perhaps especially in the United States, suggests that candidates believe that voters are abysmally ignorant.

In principle, if a candidate could do a good enough job of convincing voters where they – the voters – stand, that candidate could even overcome the Arrow problem by violating its condition of universal domain. That condition stipulates that all conceivable preference orderings might actually be held in the population. An effective politician might shift enough people into some particular preference ordering as to make that ordering the majority preference. One might suppose, however, that this would typically be a false achievement, because that candidate's success would in part be *de facto* a matter of deceiving voters about the voters' own interests.

Understanding Whether To Vote

When I have taught the logic of collective action, it has often taken a lot of persuasive effort to get the argument across at the general level to many of the students. Even after I have seemingly managed to do that, however, some students have immediately argued against it in particular applications, such as voluntary payment of union dues in order to gain the collective benefits of union protection of workers. This is, in a sense, a surprisingly different result from the intellectual history of understanding the logic. Typically, the logic has been understood in a particular context, such as John Stuart Mill's discussion of the need for legal enforcement of a shorter workday in order to overcome the inherent incentive of individuals to free-ride on a voluntary agreement to work less by getting paid extra for overtime.[19]

Consider the logic in the context of voting in elections in substantial polities. The odds against a voter's ever making a difference are overwhelming. There was a tie vote in a local election in New Jersey in 1994 – this otherwise trivial vote became national news because it was the exceedingly rare case of a tie in which one more vote could have made a difference. There have also been votes that were *de facto* ties in larger elections in which the counting error is too great to know who really has won in a very close count. In the New Hampshire election for the United States Senate in 1974, Louis Wyman and John Durkin were virtually tied at about 111,000 votes each, with relevant state agencies disagreeing over whether the Republican Wyman or the Democrat Durkin had won the vote. Eventually, the US Senate declared the election undecidable and declined to seat either candidate. The vote was then retaken in a special election (Durkin won by a substantial margin). This odd election shows that merely for practical reasons of the impossibility of counting votes accurately, one more vote is unlikely to make a difference in an election even in as small a polity – less than a quarter of a million voters – as New Hampshire, one of the smallest states in the United States. The individual voter essentially does not count. An editorial response to the presidential vote counting in Florida in 2000 was to lecture citizens with the claim that one's vote does count after all. The far more plausible inference from that debacle is that one's vote clearly could not have counted because it was swamped by the margin of error in counting.

This relatively commonsense claim may actually mislead us on just how little a single vote matters. The very best chance of my vote making a difference would come if, *de facto*, all other voters one by one tossed a fair coin and voted for A when heads turned up and for B when tails turned up, while I voted definitively for A. With 100 million voters, my vote would have so little chance of breaking a tie even in this extraordinarily evenly matched election that, even if I valued the election of A at $1,000, my vote would be worth only eight cents.[20]

Despite such numbers and such supposed logic, many voters claim forcefully, and seem to believe, that it is in their interest to vote. Moreover, they demonstrate their commitment to this view by actually voting. The incentive problem is conspicuously overcome for about half the voters in US presidential elections and for even more of the voters in most other contemporary democracies. One might give an account from a theory of knowledge of why people believe their votes matter. If such an account is successful, it then overcomes Downs's logic, and we might understand why there are substantially higher voting turnouts than that logic, if only it were well understood, would allow.

In typical economic choices, it seems to make sense to suppose that people understand their own interests reasonably well. In collective action contexts, however, this may not make sense. A standard quibble with rational choice theories is that they require individuals to do what best serves their objective interests. If individuals act otherwise, then the theory is thought to fail. Unfortunately, this move short-circuits the mental task of weighing one's objective interests in acting one way rather than another. If I conclude that my interest is other than what some objective analysis by a critic says it is, it does not follow *either* that I am right *or* that, if I am wrong, I act irrationally in acting according to what I believe to be my interest. *A fully adequate account of my rationality must account first for my beliefs and then for my action from these beliefs.*

We generally have no difficulty with this two-stage requirement on judging someone's rationality in certain contexts, such as medical decisions. For example, it would be odd to say that George Washington acted irrationally in allowing the best medical people available to him to bleed him, possibly killing him or hastening his death, during his final, perhaps minor illness. He did the best one could do within reason, which is to say within the economic or rational constraints on what he could come to know about medical care. When he died, his doctor may have concluded that he had not bled the great man aggressively enough and might therefore have determined to bleed people who suffered from, say, a cold and fever, more aggressively lest he lose them too. Given his sadly mistaken view of the efficacy of bleeding, that might even have been the right response.

Our task here is to assess the rationality of individuals' beliefs about the rationality of acting for collective benefit in the face of the logic of collective action. Many of those who vote do so for moral reasons of their duties or the fairness of their doing their part. But many seem genuinely to think it in their own interest to vote. They invoke a rational choice version of the generalization principle in ethics.[21] That moral principle is a response to the query: What if everyone did that? For example, what if everyone took a short cut through a lovely lawn or garden as I wish to do in this moment because I am lazy or in a hurry? Well, if everyone did that, there might be an ugly path through the splendor of the lawn or garden. But one could often answer the query by noting that everyone does not, and evidently will not, do that.

Many voters seem to believe in a *pragmatic (non-moral) version of the generalization argument.* They feel responsible if, after they fail to vote, their party loses. And if their party loses after they do vote, they console themselves with the realization that at least they tried. If they had merely a moral commitment to voting, they should feel guilty for not voting independently of whether their party wins or loses. To feel regret because one's party loses makes no sense unless one supposes one might actually have made a difference.

I have tried to explain the logic of collective action as it is played out in voting to many people on many occasions, including many politically active and sophisticated people. I was not trying to dissuade them from voting but only to defend a casual comment on how voting is motivated, if at all, by moral commitments. Or I was trying to give an analysis of why costs of voting dissuade many people. For example, it is much harder to vote in New York City today than it was to vote in Chicago or Philadelphia when I lived in those cities. And the turnouts in New York are much lower than in those cities. I have attempted to explain that this fact of differential costs, and not some cultural claim about diverse New York, made sense of the variance in behavior. Very sophisticated people have simply rejected the entire argument. And they have commonly asserted a pragmatic generalization argument in favor of voting as in their and everyone else's interest. Utterly against the self-evident facts of low turnouts, they often even held that everyone understands their principle and must reject my argument.

For some years, I thought that people would eventually come to understand the nature of this problem. I no longer believe that. I believe it is easier to understand the logic of collective action and to apply it to real problems of choice than it is to understand, say, the theory of relativity, quantum mechanics, or the workings of DNA. But for many people these are all equally incomprehensible – which is to say, not at all comprehensible. A major reason for their failure of understanding is that people typically suffer no grievous consequences from not understanding these things. As a result of their lack of understanding, some people may put a bit more effort into voting than they might under diffi-cult circumstances, such as vile weather during a New Hampshire primary in February. But that is not a great loss. It is, however, a striking fact that, although they seem not to understand their actual incentives in voting, people neverthe-less do respond to those incentives to some extent, as the comparative behaviors of voters in New York City and Chicago shows.

It would be a greater benefit to many people to understand the tax laws better than to understand the logic of collective action better. And they do not even master the tax laws very well. If many of my academic colleagues are indicative, they typically pay far more than they should under the law (and I probably do so as well). Then why should they be bothered with the logic of collective action? It is a professional hobby of rational choice theorists to understand it and maybe that fact makes it easier for them to understand it. Or maybe rational choice theorists are self-selected from people who find it relatively easy to follow such logic and economic reasoning more generally. They are then motivated by the interest they have in getting arguments right in contexts in which getting them wrong leads to public embarrassment. They are not motivated very much by the actual usefulness of putting the logic to work in their lives – although a few have become adamantly determined to live by its conclusions and not to vote.

Suppose we conclude that it is plausibly rational for a person not to master the argument of the logic of collective action and that they therefore vote despite lack of objective interest in doing so. *Then why do they seem to follow the logic in not investing in the knowledge they would need to vote intelligently?* This is arguably the central theory-of-knowledge question in political participation. As a first answer to it, we can note that any kind of sustained action might fail because it gives too little positive feedback to fool people into believing their own action is benefit-ing them. But a relatively simple, single-shot action with a more or less immedi-ate outcome might make understanding the interests at stake in the action much more difficult. The difference between voting and knowing enough to vote one's interests is partly a difference between a single-shot action and a sustained pattern of actions. The sustained pattern of investments in knowing about political candidates may never be related to any sense that it made a difference, whether mistaken or correct.

Another difference between the two investments – in voting and in knowing enough to vote intelligently – is that there is a substantial public discussion of the first but very little of the second. People come to have an active belief about the value of voting, but they may have none of any consequence about the value of knowing enough to vote intelligently. It is easy enough to understand that people learn wrong theories and then even apply them, especially when the consequences of their application are not substantially painful. It is not merely that people have failed to grasp the logic of collective action but that they have been actively proselytized for a contrary belief. Rather than investigate that logic for themselves, they take the view of the authoritative proselytizers.

To change the focus of these observations, we can address the question from the benefits side and from the costs side. There are no significant objective benefits either of voting or of mastering the knowledge to vote intelligently in one's interest. That there are no benefits of mastering the knowledge merely for the purpose of choosing how to vote follows, of course, from the claim that there are no benefits from voting. For many people there seem to be, however, perceived benefits from voting – they evidently stop working through the issue before reaching the Downsian conclusion. This view may be a mistake, but it is not irrational, anymore than it is irrational of me to get the arithmetic wrong in balancing my bank statement. Moreover, that conclusion was apparently not formally reached by anyone until very recently.

If we are being proselytized to believe in the benefits of voting, then the costs of coming to perceive the logic against voting have been raised, perhaps very high for many people. It would be much harder to proselytize people for the view that massive study of current politics and politicians is in their interest, because the real costs of such study would be substantial and readily felt. In conclusion, we can say that there are real differences in both the benefit and the cost functions of voting and of learning enough to vote intelligently. The differences in both of these suggest more reason to expect people to vote than to expect them to be well informed enough to vote intelligently in their interest.

Finally, we may note that people often do understand the logic of collective action, perhaps especially in relatively local contexts in which the cooperative contributions would be costly and readily perceived. The slogan, "Let George do it," is grounded in a recognition of the logic. It may have taken a very substantial level of proselytizing to get people not to see that logic in the case of voting, although the proselytizers may themselves have been led to believe in their own preachment.

Among those who have done best at understanding the logic of collective action have been union leaders and members. This makes sense from the fact that theirs has been a problem of collective action from the beginning. They have long been forced to recognize that voluntarism does not work very well and that coercive laws are necessary to induce contributions of dues and efforts. It was, as noted earlier, in the context of collective action for workers that Mill recognized the logic. Samuel Gompers, an early leader of the American union movement, asserted the logic clearly in 1905.[22] He had learned the logic through extensive, no doubt painful experience at a level most of us will never even vaguely match. Perhaps the first I ever heard of the logic of collective action was from a union neighbor before I was a teenager. I asked him how he had voted on election day. He replied that he had not bothered to vote because his vote would not have mattered and it would have been a lot of trouble because he would have had to knock off work early or miss his pre-dinner beer on the patio. He took a dime from his pocket and said, "My vote is not worth this much." Yet he understood the election very well in the sense that he knew how he should have voted if he had voted. He predicted, rightly, that Dwight David Eisenhower would defeat Adlai Stevenson with ease because, he supposed, people liked Ike and were not smart enough to see that Stevenson would serve the interests of most of them better.

When the costs of voluntaristic collective action are substantial and clear and, perhaps especially, when the significance of joint action is driven home repeatedly in some context, such as union or neighborhood organizing, people can grasp the logic of collective action clearly. Generalizing it, however, is quite another matter. Only with Olson's generalization in 1965 did the logic become generally clear to large numbers of social scientists with a strong professional interest in understanding it. The best and the brightest of them had typically got it wrong before. Downs himself famously seems to slip on his own argument when he discusses the value of voting *per se* as the value of making democracy work and survive, as though a reason for voting is to prevent the collapse of democracy. This bad argument – arguably some orders of magnitude worse than the argument that it is in my interest to vote in order to affect the outcome of the present election – is commonly and perversely cited by critics as a refutation of Downs's central argument.

In sum, many people do vote despite the absence of a personal benefit from doing so. Hence, the Downsian instance of the logic of collective action is *de facto* resolved for a substantial fraction of the electorate. Therefore, the problem of investing in enough knowledge to vote intelligently may well be the more fundamentally serious issue in democratic theory, as Schumpeter seemed to think. To assess whether it is, we would need even more extensive studies of the fit between votes and objective interests than we have had so far.

Multidimensional Issues

Arrow's theorem differs fundamentally from Downs's in its assumptions. In Arrow's preference orderings, there is no reason to suppose that there is a simple left–right dimension along which individuals can order their rankings of states of affairs. There could be as many dimensions as there are issues that might be relevant to defining states of affairs. In some respects, Arrow's vision of the nature of the issues over which a collective is choosing is a much better fit to European and North American national politics today than is Downs's. The left–right model of Downs's normal distribution arguably fit the politics of the 1950s better than it fits today. I therefore wish to discuss the median voter model in the context of an electorate facing issues that are not simply arrayed along a single dimension. Because of this characteristic of contemporary issues, there may be much severer knowledge demands for a voter today than there were in the earlier era, as I will argue below.

In a sense, the era in which the Downs model was a plausible approximation was a golden age of simplicity, an age that may have lasted on and off for a couple of centuries in the Anglo-Saxon world, and for a century or more in other industrial states that became democratic later. But that era has now passed, perhaps only temporarily but perhaps permanently. Its passing may have significant consequences for the form that politics will take in the near future, because simple left–right parties can no longer represent the key issues at stake.

One reason for contemporary multidimensionality is that there are many non-economic issues. I wish to continue to focus, however, on issues that primarily concern interests rather than those that are matters of moral commitment that is not based on interests and that might even run against interests. One might suppose that these issues must therefore really just be matters that can be arrayed on a left–right dimension, just as general economic policy once was thought to fit such a model. But where knowledge and understanding of the impact of various policies – for example, on environmental issues, military expenditures, basic research, health care, and on through the list of most major economic policies of contemporary industrial states – is at issue, we cannot simply put all these issues into an additive function that goes from, say, more to less government expenditure. I want more spent on the environment, you want less on the environment and more on health care, another wants to cut both these if necessary to spend more on defense or education. If these were all marketable goods to be consumed at the individual level, then, subject to our resource constraints, I could buy what I want and you could buy what you want. But they are not, and we typically decide collectively on the levels of provision of these things, and we all get roughly the same levels.

If we could believe that there is something like a basic welfare or utility function that we all share, as George Stigler and Gary Becker have argued, we might be able to array these issues, at least in principle.[23] But even then, the ordinary citizen cannot perform such a trick and there will be remarkably strong disagreement on where to put our public money. Hence, although all these issues might be clearly seen as merely about interests, they define different dimensions because individuals have such different evaluations of them. For private consumption goods in modern economics, this would merely mean that we would have reason to exchange with each other to improve our welfare. I prefer your bit of something to my bit of something else and you have the opposite preferences, so we trade. This is the great simplifying move of modern market economics: We can each trade off bits of some things for bits of others, all to increase our own welfares.

This simplifying move fails for many public allocations. For public provisions of essentially collective goods we have to agree on single allocations of various things for everyone at once, and we cannot then trade with each other to come closer to our own preferred outcomes. We all get the same outcome. If we all started with the same endowments of private consumption goods, we could improve our lots by trading. That is not the position we are in for collective goods once these are provided. I cannot trade part of my share of environmental protection for part of your share of health care coverage. If we start with the same endowments of collective goods, we keep the same endowments. As a result, we each must view the collective allocations as occurring on *de facto* different dimensions, because I do not aggregate them in the same way you do. The aggregate of our collective allocations might seem splendid to you and miserable to me in comparison to plausible alternatives at the same total public cost.

Even though they commonly cannot affect their own welfare through their private actions without interaction effects from the actions of others, people surely have more control in general over their own welfare through the private than through the political sphere. They therefore have much greater incentive to understand their private concerns than to understand public concerns. This is an analogue of the common claim in utilitarianism that we should typically focus our beneficent efforts on those close to us, because we can be surer of acting effectively for the good this way than if we try to act for the general welfare. (This claim is a response to the supposed criticism of utilitarianism that it violates our particularistic moral concern with our own families and requires us instead to care only for the generalized other without special concern for any individual merely on the ground of their closeness to us.) Ideally, we could overcome this problem of unequal incentives to a large extent if we could reduce collective goods to individual goods. This is not possible for collective bads, such as pollution, which are not deliberately produced but are, at best, external effects of desirable activities. And the reduction could not be efficient for many goods that are collectively provided by governments and other agencies.

It may also generally be harder to understand public concerns for such things as environmental protection than it was to understand at least the supposed implications of policies to enhance economic activity. For the short term of the present generation, workers might generally think it in their interest to increase wages even at cost to investment, while owners and the relatively wealthy might think it in their interest to increase investment even at cost to wages. But neither workers nor owners might have a clear sense of whether general environmental protections are in their interest, although they might readily conclude that protections that specifically burden their industry are not in their interest. Even workers exposed to carcinogens, such as benzene and the gases involved in the production of polyvinylchloride film (plastic wrap for food and other things), might think it in their interest to keep their jobs with such exposure rather than to escape the exposure by enclosing various processes and, coincidentally, eliminating workers.

One might read recent elections in the United States, the United Kingdom and Germany as responses to the fading of the traditional economic divide between left and right parties, between concern for wages and concern for profits, as leaders of both left and right parties begin to suppose that relatively free market devices are best for running contemporary economies. The focus in recent years has been on other issues, including the single issue focus of many groups on such issues as abortion and gun control in the United States, and the environment in Germany. Indeed, in Germany there is a specifically Green party, because environmental issues are not the natural concern of either the conservative Christian Democrats or the Socialists. These other issues are generally not conspicuously tied or related to the traditional divide over wages and profits. Hence, neither traditional party is able to capture them for its agenda to help trump the opposing major party. Traditional parties and voters alike now face a world in which multiple issues *de facto* represent multiple dimensions.[24]

The main left–right economic issue defined the two chief parties in the United States and in many other democratic nations for much of this century. Other issues were many and varied, but they commonly did not dominate the central economic issue.

It is the fact that various contemporary issues, which themselves seem like matters of mere interest, are collectively determined or provided that makes them each an independent dimension for collective choice. Hence, so long as these diverse issues are politically important, traditional left–right party alignments may not fit actual political issues very well. Therefore, the more of these issues we can get off the collective agenda, the better for making collective choice coherent. With many of these issues on the collective agenda, we may increasingly witness the break-up of any major party focus and, *de facto*, sharpen the relevance of the problem of Arrow's multiplicity of quasi-orthogonal dimensions of major issues. The response of candidates to such a change cannot be that of Downsian candidates. Instead it is likely to become unspecific and bland, without major policy positions other than those that can gain relatively general support. But of course, policies that gain general support cannot differentiate candidates.

Concluding Remarks on Liberty

We can amplify some of the discussion above through consideration of a particular set of goods that are collectively secured through government: political and personal liberties. The liberties I have are almost entirely in the context of my private life, not in the context of my public or political life. I may have the political liberty to vote and even to run for office. But most citizens do not typically have the liberty actually to make any difference to their own welfare through politics. I may indeed come to have substantially enhanced welfare from my political activities and I may even vote with the majority to achieve benefits for us. But if my vote is worthless, then the liberty to cast it is of little value either. Having the liberty to cast it is roughly as valuable as having the liberty to cast a vote on whether the sun will rise tomorrow.

In general, the ratio of liberty to restraint is greatest for those in a frontier context in which they need not be bound by any cooperative or coordinative arrangements. But that is not a very desirable state of affairs because it is likely to be impoverished, and liberty with poverty does not enable one to do much or to prosper well. To be much better off one must submit to substantial restraints of social order for mutual benefit. The anarchist's liberty comes at a dreadfully high price. This is an instance of Brian Barry's argument that, in democratic politics, it is better to be lucky than powerful.[25] It is better to just happen to be with the majority than to have a little bit of influence over public policy. One does not then cause one's preferred policies to be adopted, but one benefits from their adoption. Most of us who have liberty are merely lucky to have it; we did not bring it upon ourselves.

The liberty we get from democratic politics is, usually, the liberty we get from constitutional government and its protections. When democracy fails in the sense of producing an anti-constitutional regime, as it did in Germany in the 1930s, liberty may fail with it. An anti-constitutional regime can be democratic in the strongest sense of the term in that it can be wildly popular, as such regimes have been in many fascist and other nations historically.

The fact that we can readily recognize the infraction of a personal liberty gives reason to defend liberties through individual actions – that is, of necessity, through courts rather than through majoritarian devices. It is not merely that we need to fear a tyranny of the majority but also that we should doubt the capacity of a majority to act on its own behalf in general defense of liberties. The generalized logic of liberties might seldom impress itself upon citizens. The specific violation of my liberty, however, will immediately impress itself on me. Hence, although we have a genuinely collective interest in various liberties, we should want to have them enforced through individual initiative.

In this respect, liberties can be handled to some extent the way we might want other collective allocations to be handled: individually. That is to say that, ideally, we could reduce collectively provided goods to individually provided goods. This move is not possible for collective bads and it might be inefficient for many collective goods. As long as there is great demand for such goods and for the regulation of such bads, therefore, we can expect politics to be multidimensional and we can expect voters to be rationally ignorant of their own interests and of candidates' positions on all the dimensions they face. Finally, we can also expect that they can no longer simply rely on traditional left–right parties to represent their interests on all these dimensions.

Notes

Presented at the meetings of the European Public Choice Society, Lisbon, 7–10 April 1999; at a seminar at Tel Aviv University in June 1999; at a conference at the University of Texas in February 2000; and at the William H. Riker Memorial conference at the University of Washington, St. Louis, in December 2001. I thank participants at those meetings for their comments. I thank Kenneth Arrow, Bruce Bueno de Mesquita, James Fishkin and Kenneth Shepsle for careful critical readings.

1   Kenneth J. Arrow, *Social Choice and Individual Values* (New Haven, CT: Yale University Press, [1951] 1963), 2nd edition.

2   Anthony Downs, *An Economic Theory of Democracy* (New York: Harper, 1957).

3   Mancur Olson, Jr., *The Logic of Collective Action* (Cambridge, MA: Harvard University Press, 1965).

4   David Hume, "Dialogues Concerning Natural Religion" [1779], in *David Hume on Religion*, ed. John Valdimir Price (Oxford: Oxford University Press: 1976), part 3, p. 180.

5   See, e.g., Samuel L. Popkin, *The Reasoning Voter: Communication and Persuasion in Presidential Campaigns* (Chicago: University of Chicago Press, [1991] 1994), 2nd edition, esp. ch. 4.

6   Robert A. Dahl, *Who Governs?* (New Haven, CT: Yale University Press, 1961), p. 1.

7   John Dewey, *Reconstruction in Philosophy* (Boston: Beacon Press, 1948), p. 163.

8   Trudy Govier, *Social Trust and Human Communities* (Montreal: McGill–Queens University Press, 1997), pp. 51–76.

9   Ludwig Wittgenstein, *On Certainty*, ed. G. E. M. Anscombe and G. H. von Wright (Oxford: Basil Blackwell, 1969), §344.

10 Henry Sidgwick, "The Philosophy of Common Sense," [1895] in Sidgwick, *Lec-

tures on the Philosophy of Kant and Other Philosophical Lectures and Essays, ed. James Ward (London: Macmillan, 1905), 406–30, at p. 427.

11   Joseph A. Schumpeter, *Capitalism, Socialism and Democracy* (New York: Harper [1942], 1950), 3rd edition, p. 262.

12   Popkin, *The Reasoning Voter*, p. 78.

13   Richard F. Fenno, Jr., *Home Style: House Members in Their Districts* (Boston: Little, Brown, 1978).

14   Russell Hardin, "The Public Trust," in *Disaffected Democracies: What's Troubling the Trilateral Democracies*, ed. Susan J. Pharr and Robert D. Putnam (Princeton: Princeton University Press, 2000): 31–51.

15   Susan Estrich, *Getting Away with Murder: How Politics Is Destroying the Criminal Justice System* (Cambridge, MA: Harvard University Press, 1998).

16   "25 Years for a Slice of Pizza," *New York Times*, 5 March 1995: 1.21.

17   Elisabeth R, Gerber, A. Lupia, M. McCubbins, and D. R. Kiewiet, *Stealing the Initiative: How State Government Responds to Direct Democracy* (Upper Saddle River, NJ: Prentice-Hall, 2001) pp. 71–4.

18   Popkin, *The Reasoning Voter*, ch. 4.

19   John Stuart Mill, *Principles of Political Economy*, ed. John M. Robson (Toronto: University of Toronto Press [1848], 1965), p. 958. See further, Russell Hardin, *Morality within the Limits of Reason* (Chicago: University of Chicago Press, 1988), pp. 92–4.

20   Russell Hardin, *Collective Action* (Baltimore: Johns Hopkins University Press for Resources for the Future, 1982) p. 60n.

21   Marcus George Singer, *Generalization in Ethics*. (New York: Knopf, 1961); Hardin, *Morality within the Limits of Reason*, pp. 65–8.

22   Samuel Gompers, "Discussion at Rochester, N. Y., on the Open Shop – 'The Union Shop Is Right' – It Naturally Follows Organization." *American Federationist* 12 (April 1905, no. 4), 221–3.

23   Gary S. Becker, *Accounting for Tastes* (Cambridge, MA: Harvard University Press: 1996) pp. 24–49.

24   Hardin, "*The Public Trust*."

25   Brian Barry, "Is It Better To Be Powerful or Lucky?" *Political Studies*, 28 (June and September 1980) 183–94, 338–52.

9

Deliberative Democracy and Social Choice

David Miller

If we are in the business of thinking about liberal democracy and possible alternatives to it, we must begin by drawing a distinction between institutions and their regulative ideals. Liberal democracy may be taken to refer to the set of institutions – free elections, competing parties, freedom of speech – that make up the political system with which we are familiar in the West; or it may refer to the conception of democracy that underlies and justifies that system. The relationship between institutions and regulative ideals is not necessarily simple or one-to-one. The same institution may be justified from different points of view, although characteristically those who favour contrasting regulative ideals will aim to shape the institution in different ways. Thus, to take a familiar case, the practice of electing representatives to a legislative assembly may be seen as a way of subjecting legislators to popular control; alternatively, it may be seen simply as a means of removing visibly corrupt legislators from office. Which of these views you take will affect your preferences as to the form of the practice (How frequent should elections be? Should the voting system be first-past-the-post or something else? And so forth).

The argument that follows has mainly to do with competing regulative ideals of democracy. In comparing liberal democracy with what I shall call deliberative democracy, my aim is to contrast two basic ways of understanding the democratic process. In favouring deliberative democracy, therefore, I am not recommending wholesale abolition of the present institutions of liberal democracy, but rather a reshaping of those institutions in the light of a different regulative ideal from that which I take to be prevalent now. I shall only address the institutional questions briefly. My main aim is to bring out what is at stake between liberal and deliberative democracy, particularly in the light of social choice theory, which appears to challenge the cogency of anything beyond the most minimal of democratic ideals.

Let me now sketch the contrast between liberal and deliberative democracy as regulative ideals. In the liberal view, the aim of democracy is to aggregate individual preferences into a collective choice in as fair and efficient a way as possible.[1] In a democracy there will be many different views as to what should be done politically, reflecting the many different interests and beliefs present in society. Each person's preferences should be accorded equal weight. Moreover, preferences are sacrosanct because they reflect the individuality of each member of the political community (an exception to this arises only in the case of preferences that violate the canons of liberal democracy itself, such as racist beliefs that deny the equal rights of all citizens). The problem then is to find the institutional structure that best meets the requirements of equality and efficiency. Thus liberal democrats may divide on the question of whether majoritarian decision-making is to be preferred, or whether the ideal is a pluralist system that gives various groups in society different amounts of influence over decisions in proportion to their interest in those decisions. This, however, is a family quarrel in which both sides are guided by the same underlying ideal, namely, how to reach a fair and efficient compromise given the many conflicting preferences expressed in the political community.

The deliberative ideal also starts from the premise that political preferences will conflict and that the purpose of democratic institutions must be to resolve this conflict. But it envisages this occurring through an open and uncoerced discussion of the issue at stake with the aim of arriving at an agreed judgement.[2] The process of reaching a decision will also be a process whereby initial preferences are transformed to take account of the views of others. That is, the need to reach an agreement forces each participant to put forward proposals under the rubric of general principles or policy considerations that others could accept. Thus, even if initially my aim is to support the claims of a particular group to which I belong or which I represent, I cannot in a general discussion simply say 'I claim that group A – farmers, say, or policemen – should get more money'. I have to give reasons for the claim. These might be that the group in question has special needs, or that it is in the common interest to improve the living standards of the group. By giving these reasons, however, I am committing myself to a general principle, which by implication applies to any other similarly placed group. Thus I am forced to take a wider view, and either defend the claim I am making when applied not only to my group but to groups B, C, and D, which are like A in the relevant respects, or else to back down and moderate the claim to something I am prepared to accept in these other cases too. Although finally, when a decision has to be reached, there may still need to be a vote taken between two or more options, what participants are doing at that point is something like rendering a judgement or a verdict on the basis of what they have heard. They are expressing an opinion about which policy best meets the various claims that have been advanced, or represents the fairest compromise between the competing points of view that have been expressed.

The deliberative view clearly rests on a different conception of 'human nature in politics' from the liberal view. Whereas the latter stresses the importance of giving due weight to each individual's distinct preferences, the former relies upon a person's capacity to be swayed by rational arguments and to lay aside particular interests and opinions in deference to overall fairness and the common interest of the collectivity. It supposes people to be to some degree communally oriented in their outlook. It also seems to be more vulnerable to exploitation, in the sense that the practice of deliberative democracy can be abused by people who pay lip-service to the ideal of open discussion but actually attempt to manipulate their colleagues to reach decisions that serve private interests.[3] We shall shortly see, however, that liberal democratic procedures are themselves vulnerable to political manipulation. At this stage, therefore, we must take it as an open question which of the two democratic ideals is more likely to be subverted by manipulative individuals or groups.

In presenting my account of deliberative democracy, I mean to distinguish it not only from liberal democracy but from what has been called 'epistemic' democracy.[4] The epistemic conception of democracy sees the aim of democratic procedures as being to arrive at a correct answer to some question facing the political community. It is assumed here, in other words, that there is some objectively right or valid answer to the question that has been posed, but because there is uncertainty as to what the answer is, a decision-procedure is needed, and democracy, in the form of majority voting, is the procedure most likely to produce the right answer. This was, for instance, the view of Condorcet,[5] and it has also been attributed to Rousseau,[6] although my own belief is that Rousseau's view is ambiguous as between deliberative and epistemic conceptions of democracy.[7]

I believe the epistemic conception sets an unrealistically high standard for political decision-making. Although occasionally a political community may have to decide on some question to which it is plausible to suppose a correct answer exists (say some scientific question in circumstances where there is complete consensus on the ends which the decision should serve), it is much more likely that the issue will concern competing claims which cannot all be met simultaneously in circumstances where no resolution of the competition can be deemed objectively right. In the deliberative conception, the aim is to reach agreement, which might be achieved in different ways. One way is for the participants to agree on a substantive norm, which all concur in thinking is the appropriate norm for the case in hand. Another way is to agree on a procedure, which abstracts from the merits of the arguments advanced by particular claimants. (Thus suppose the question is how an available resource such as a tract of land should be allocated as between several groups that lay claim to it. One possibility would be to agree on a principle, such as that the resource should go to the group which needs it most or which could use it most productively, and then on the basis of the arguments advanced decide which group that was. Alternatively the deliberating body might feel that it was not competent to make such a judgement, and opt instead for a procedural solution, such as sharing the resource out equally between the groups, rotating it between them, or deciding by lot.) In either case, the outcome is a decision that all the parties involved may feel to be reasonable, but this does not entail that it reflects any transcendent standard of justice or rightness. The emphasis in the deliberative conception is on the way in which a process of open discussion in which all points of view can be heard may legitimate the outcome when this is seen to reflect the discussion that has preceded it, not on deliberation as a discovery procedure in search of a correct answer.[8]

My aim in this paper is to see whether deliberative democracy may be less vulnerable than liberal democracy to the problems posed by social choice theory for democracy in general. In arguing in this way, I am apparently reversing a common opinion which is that social choice obliges us to abandon 'populist' models of democracy, in which democratic decisions are represented as expressions of 'the people's choice' or the 'popular will', in favour of 'liberal' models, in which democratic elections are construed merely as a safeguard against the emergence of tyrannical rulers. Democracy on this view is a matter of the voters having the right, at periodic intervals, to remove from office governments that they have come to dislike. Any notion that the voters should in some more positive way determine public policy is misguided. This argument plays some role in the classical defences of liberal democracy by Schumpeter and Dahl[9] and has recently been developed at length and with great intellectual force by William Riker.[10]

From my perspective, however, both liberalism and populism as understood by Riker count as variants on the liberal ideal of democracy. For populism is the view that individuals' preferences should be amalgamated, by voting, to yield a general will which then guides policy. Liberalism in Riker's sense is less ambitious in that it sees the purpose of elections in negative terms as involving the removal of unpopular leaders. Both views see democracy as a matter of aggregating voters' preferences: they differ over the question whether policy can be chosen in this way, or only the personnel of government. The idea that democratic decisions are not a matter of aggregating preferences at all but of reaching agreed judgements is foreign to both.

Let me now remind readers of the challenge which social choice theory poses for these liberal views of democracy. Suppose a voting public has to decide between a number of policy options – suppose, to take a concrete case, that the issue is how Britain should generate its electricity, and the public has to choose between coal-fired, oil-fired, gas-fired and nuclear power stations. The message of social choice theory, and in particular its most celebrated constituent, Arrow's general possibility theorem,[11] is that one cannot devise a mechanism for making such decisions which simultaneously meets a number of quite weak and reasonable-sounding conditions that we might want to impose, such as monotonicity or the requirement that if a voter raises the position of one option in his own personal ranking, this cannot have the effect of lowering it in the social ranking.

This, one might say, is *the* problem posed by social choice for democracy – that is, in general there is no fair and rational way of amalgamating voters' preferences to reach a social decision – but it entails two more specific problems. The first is the arbitrariness of decision rules and the second is the near-unavoidability of strategic voting, or more strictly of opportunities for strategic voting. Decision rules fall broadly speaking into two classes, which following Riker we may call majoritarian and positional methods of selecting a preferred outcome. Majoritarian rules proceed by offering voters a series of binary choices and, depending on which option wins which encounters, identify an overall winner. So, in our example, voters would be asked to choose between coal and oil for generating electricity, between coal and gas, and so forth. There would be a series of majorities on the questions asked, and then some rule for discovering the overall choice. Positional rules ask voters to rank the available options and then compute a winner using all or part of this fuller information. Thus voters might be asked to rank order the energy options from 1 to 4 on their ballot papers, and then a winner found by some rule such as giving an option two points each time it is someone's first choice and one point each time it comes second.

The problem of arbitrariness arises because it is not clear which of the many possible rules best matches our intuitive sense of 'finding the option which the voters most prefer', or to put the point another way, for any given rule it is possible to give examples where using that rule produces an outcome that seems repugnant to our sense of what a democratic decision should be. Among majoritarian rules, a strong contender is the Condorcet rule that any option which beats all the others in a series of binary choices should be the social choice. But there is no guarantee in any particular case that such a Condorcet winner can be found, so the rule is incomplete. Thus gas might beat coal and oil but lose to nuclear power, which in turn was beaten by one of the other options. If the rule is to be complete it has then to be extended to cope with this possibility, but there is no extension that is obviously the right one.[12] Among positional rules, the one most often favoured is the Borda count, which scores each option according to the place it holds in each voter's ranking, so that my top option gets n points, my second option $n-1$ points and so on right the way down. One problem with this is that it may make the decision among quite popular options depend upon the way some voters rank way-out or eccentric options if these are on the ballot paper. Finally, it is an embarrassment that the Condorcet and Borda rules do not necessarily converge; that is, a Condorcet winner may exist, but a different option may be selected by use of the Borda count. This might occur where the Condorcet winner – nuclear power, let us say–was the first choice of a fair number of people but tended to be ranked very low by those who were against it, whereas another option – gas, let us say – was the first preference of just a few, but ranked second by quite a lot. Here it is not at all clear which way we should jump. There is a case for the option with most first preferences, and a case for the compromise proposal which comes reasonably high in most people's rankings.

The second problem is strategic voting, which means misrepresenting your true preferences when you vote with the aim of increasing the chances of your favoured option. Obviously the success of this depends on your having some knowledge of the preferences of other voters. It can be shown that there is virtually no decision rule that is not vulnerable to strategic manipulation if some voters choose to act in this way.[13] Again a couple of examples may help to bring this out. Suppose we are using a majoritarian decision rule. It is possible by strategic voting to block the emergence of a Condorcet winner. Thus suppose in our example nuclear power is the Condorcet winner if everyone votes sincerely. I am not particularly averse to nuclear power, but I am very strongly committed to coal-fired stations. I cannot prevent nuclear power defeating coal in a run-off between these options, but if others think like me we can stop the nuclear power bandwagon by voting insincerely for gas when the choice between gas and nuclear power is posed, thus preventing the emergence of nuclear power as a Condorcet winner and triggering whatever subsidiary rule is being employed in the hope that coal will win. Equally, if a Borda count is being used and I know that gas, say, is the likely winner, then I can boost the chances of coal by insincerely pushing gas down into fourth place. There is of course no guarantee that my strategy will work, since my opponents may behave strategically too. But this only serves to underline the arbitrariness of the eventual decision which in these circumstances would have very little claim to be called anything like a popular will.

So the challenge posed by social choice to democratic theory can be reduced to two basic claims: that there is no rule for aggregating individual preferences that is obviously fair and rational and thus superior to other possible rules; and that virtually every rule is subject to strategic manipulation, so that even if it would produce a plausible outcome for a given set of preferences if everyone voted sincerely, the actual outcome is liable to be distorted by strategic voting.

Working from within the liberal view of democracy, pessimists such as Riker respond to this challenge by reducing the significance of the electoral process to that of providing a safeguard against what Riker calls 'tyranny'. But even this safeguard is quite weak, since if the outcome of elections is to some degree arbitrary (as the social choice analysis shows), it is not apparent why they should pick out for removal unpopular or 'tyrannical' leaders. Coleman and Ferejohn put this point well:

Nonreasoned removal from office is precisely what follows if Riker is correct in interpreting the instability results of social choice theory as demonstrating the meaninglessness of voting. If outcomes are arbitrarily connected to the preferences of the electorate, we cannot infer from his removal from office that an officeholder's conduct was in fact disapproved of by the voters. This is hardly the ideal of officeholders being put at risk by elections that we associate with liberalism.[14]

Social choice theory seems to undermine the liberal view of democracy in a systematic way, regardless of the precise function that is assigned to the act of voting in elections.

Can the problems of social choice be avoided altogether by switching to the deliberative ideal of democracy? Social choice theory postulates voters with given preferences over outcomes, and it is sometimes suggested that, once we allow that voters' preferences may alter in the course of decision-making, its results no longer apply.[15] But this response is too simple-minded. So long as there is a problem of amalgamating the voters' wishes at the point of decision – so long, to be more precise, as three or more policy outcomes are still in play and there is no unanimous preference for one of these outcomes – the social choice results apply. A decision rule must be found, and this is potentially vulnerable to the problems of arbitrariness and strategic manipulation. In my account of deliberative democracy, I indicated that, although full consensus was the ideal guiding discussion, it would be quite unrealistic to suppose that every instance of deliberation would culminate in unanimous agreement. Votes will still have to be taken, and where voting occurs so, potentially, will social choice problems.

Rather than sweeping away social choice theory at a stroke, my aim is the more limited one of showing that deliberative democracy has the resources to attenuate the social choice problems faced by the political community. The case I shall make has two main aspects. The first concerns the way in which deliberation may limit the range of preferences that have to be amalgamated in the final judgement. The second concerns the way in which knowledge of the structure of opinion in the deliberating body may influence the choice of decision rule.

The first part of the argument addresses one of the axioms of Arrow's original theorem, namely the requirement that the social choice procedure should be able to accommodate any possible set of individual rank orderings of outcomes. This axiom may indeed seem self-evident; it appears to pick up the liberal idea that each person is entitled to express whatever preferences he chooses, so that any limits on individual rank orderings would be discriminatory. (As Riker puts the point, 'any rule or command that prohibits a person from choosing some preference order is morally unacceptable (or at least unfair) from the point of view of democracy'.)[16] But rather than some external prohibition of possible ways of ranking alternatives, the possibility I wish to contemplate is that some initial sets of preferences might spontaneously be transformed through the process of deliberation, so that the final set of rankings from which a decision had to be reached was much smaller than the original set. If this were so, we could drop Arrow's unrestricted condition in favour of the weaker requirement that the social decision procedure should be able to cope with all possible sets of *post-deliberation* rankings.

I shall shortly suggest how this might help to resolve the social choice problems we have identified. But first we need to consider why some initial preferences might be eliminated in this way. The most straightforward case is that of preference orders that are irrational because they are based on false empirical beliefs. To use the energy policy example, someone might judge energy sources entirely on the basis of environmental soundness and begin with the rank order coal, gas, oil, nuclear power. However, in the course of debate strong evidence is produced about the atmospheric effects of coal-burning power stations which decisively pushes coal below gas and oil from an environmental point of view. This is not to say that the original rank order is completely untenable because there may be other value stances from which it remains appropriate. But then again it may be that no-one, or virtually no-one, holds these value stances, so the effect of debate is to crystallize the rank orderings into a smaller number of coherent patterns.

A second case is that of preferences that are so repugnant to the moral beliefs of the society within which the decisions are being made that no-one is willing to advance them in a public context. This seems to be roughly the position with racist beliefs in contemporary Britain: a number of people hold them privately, but it is generally recognized that they cannot be articulated in political forums like Parliament. And this does constrain the set of policies that can be supported. You may favour immigration restrictions for racist reasons, but the fact that you cannot present these reasons publicly means that the policies you advocate have to be general in form; that is, they cannot explicitly discriminate between black and white immigrants.

The most important way in which deliberation may alter initial preferences, however, is that outlined in my original description of the deliberative ideal. Preferences that are not so much immoral as narrowly self-regarding will tend to be eliminated by the process of public debate. To be seen to be engaged in political debate we must argue in terms that any other participant could potentially accept, and 'It's good for me' is not such an argument. Or as Bob Goodin has put the point, when we adopt a public role, we must launder our preferences so that only public-oriented ones are expressed.[17] I discount here the possibility of people expressing one set of preferences in debate and voting according to another set at decision time. If voting is public, this could only occur at the cost of immediate loss of future credibility, and this may be a good reason for having an open voting system under conditions that approximate to deliberative democracy, as Brennan and Pettit have recently argued.[18] However, even under a secret ballot, it seems to me quite unlikely that we would witness widespread hypocrisy such as is involved in arguing for one position and then voting for another. This is a claim about human psychology: it says that if you have committed yourself to one position publicly you would find it demeaning to retreat to a more selfish posture at the point of material decision.[19] I do not say this is universally true, but I think it is widely true.

Since this claim about the moralising effect of public discussion is crucial to my argument about deliberative democracy, I would like at this point to illustrate it with some empirical evidence, although not, alas, drawn directly from the field of politics. The first piece of evidence comes from psychological experiments which try to simulate the behaviour of juries.[20] In these experiments, a number of subjects are shown a video recording of a trial in which the evidence for and against the accused is fairly evenly balanced. They are then asked to give their private guilty/not guilty verdict and on the basis of this formed into a number of mock juries divided evenly between the two views. The question is: which verdict will the jury eventually reach? *A priori* one would predict some hung juries, and then equal proportions of guilty and not-guilty verdicts. In fact, however, there is a marked tilt towards the not-guilty side, which the researchers attribute to the presence of a 'leniency norm'. That is, where the presence of conflicting opinions suggests that there is real doubt as to the guilt or innocence of the accused, you should give the accused the benefit of that doubt by returning a not-guilty verdict. Now the leniency norm is always present to some degree, but the point to which I want to draw attention is that allowing the 'jurors' a period of discussion before asking them to give their collective verdict shifted the outcome noticeably in the non-guilty direction. The best explanation seems to be that the effect of discussion was to activate the norm so that some participants who went in thinking 'Yes, he did it' ended up thinking 'We can't agree on this, so I'd better give him the benefit of the doubt'. In other words, the effect of discussion was to shift at least some people from a particular judgement to a general norm that people in liberal societies tend to apply to cases of this sort.

I want, however, to claim not only that discussion can activate norms but also that it can create norms by inducing participants to think of themselves as forming a certain kind of group. Broadly speaking, discussion has the effect of turning a collection of separate individuals into a group who see one another as cooperators. Perhaps I can again illustrate this with some experimental evidence, this time involving groups confronting a classic Prisoner's Dilemma. Each member is given a small sum of money and told that he can either keep it himself, or donate it to a common pool whereupon it will be doubled in value and shared equally among all members of the group. Obviously if everyone donates, everyone doubles their income, but the individually rational thing to do is to hold back the money. In the experiment I am describing, a ten-minute period of discussion more than doubled the rate of cooperation, from 37.5 per cent to 78.6 per cent.[21] Exactly what the normative mechanism at work here is may be open to question, but plainly the effect of debate was to generate a norm of cooperation within the group strong enough in the great majority of cases to override individual self-interest. A group of friends would have no difficulty extricating themselves from a Prisoner's Dilemma – they would trust one another already. Talking to one another appears to be a fairly effective way of simulating friendship in this case.

The upshot of this argument is that we have good reason to expect the deliberative process to transform initial policy preferences (which may be based on private interest, sectional interest, prejudice, and so on) into ethical judgements on the matter in hand; and this will sharply curtail the set of rankings of policy outcomes with which the final decision procedure has to deal. How does this help to eliminate the social choice problems we identified earlier? Take first the indeterminacy problem, and our observation that the Condorcet rule may be defeated by the existence of voting cycles (where, say, majorities favour gas over coal, coal over nuclear power, and nuclear power over gas in two-way comparisons). Here I wish to appeal to the well-known finding that cycles of this kind (and the Arrow problem more generally) can be avoided on condition that voters' rank-orderings are 'single-peaked'.[22] That is to say, the alternatives can be arrayed on a continuum such that if, say, a voter ranks the alternative on the left the highest, he does not rank the alternative on the right above that in the centre.[23] Where preferences are single-peaked in this sense, one option must be the Condorcet winner and it would be possible to find this by repeated binary votes.

What does single-peakedness reveal about voters' preferences? It shows that they understand the choice before them in the same way, even though they adopt different positions on the spectrum. Thus suppose in the example we are using that coal is the cheapest of the three fuels but environmentally the most harmful; that oil is the most expensive but environmentally the best; and that gas stands between coal and oil in both respects. Then we might see the choice facing the voters as essentially that between economic cost and environmental soundness, and they would naturally divide into economisers (who put coal first but prefer gas to oil), greens (who put oil first but prefer gas to coal) and moderates, who favour gas as the best trade-off between the two values. A single dimension of choice underlies the various positions, and this is sufficient to guarantee that the rank orderings will be single-peaked.

In many cases we may expect ethically informed judgements to display this property: the policy options represent a choice between two values, and different groups of voters weight these values differently.[24] However, it is still possible for single-peakedness to fail even where ethical judgements are involved. For an example of this consider the following. Suppose nuclear power replaces oil as the third possible source of energy, and the facts about it are these: it is moderately cheap, it is environmentally sound in general, but it carries with it the risk of a major accident. We might then have three groups of voters: economisers, whose ranking is (1) coal (2) nuclear power and (3) gas; pessimistic greens, whose ranking is (1) gas (2) coal and (3) nuclear power; and a more optimistic group of greenish voters who believe that the risk of a nuclear accident can be borne in the light of the all-round benefits of nuclear power, and whose ranking is therefore (1) nuclear power (2) gas and (3) coal. As a moment's inspection shows, if no group of voters forms a majority we have a voting cycle in which each energy option can defeat one of the others.

How has this come about? There are two dimensions of disagreement underlying the decision in this case. One is the balance to be struck between cost and environmental safety; the other is the relative weighting to be given to predictable pollution as against the risk of a nuclear accident *within* the fold of environmental concern. The economisers think the issue is only about costs; the out-and-out greens think it is only about environmental safety; the third group think it is about both, but they also disagree with the greens about what environmental safety consists in. It is this condition of cross-cutting disagreement that produces rank orders that are not single-peaked and threatens to produce a voting cycle.

Now consider how such a choice might be handled within the context of deliberative democracy. Participants in the debate, aiming to convince others to support the alternative that they favour, must inevitably give grounds for their preference. As the various views are articulated, one thing that will be revealed is whether there is just a single dimension of disagreement underlying the original set of alternatives, or more than one dimension. If there is more than one dimension, then it may be possible to split the original decision into components. I say 'may be' here because it is of course possible that the original alternatives were discrete and irreducible. Consider again the choice between types of power station. It looks as though this might be a case where the alternatives are discrete (a station must *either* be coal- or gas-fired, and so on) whereas many possible dimensions of disagreement underlie the choice: relative costs, levels of employment, issues of environmental safety, and so on. However, I do not think that the choice is really so discrete. For instance, coal-fired stations might in general be favoured on cost grounds, but there could be a separate issue as to whether they should be fitted with filters to reduce emissions of sulphur or carbon dioxide at the cost of some loss of output. If it became clear in the course of debate that the major reason why some speakers were opposing coal-fired stations was their polluting emissions, then the obvious solution would be to have two votes, or series of votes, one concerning the basic technology, another concerning the environment/efficiency trade-off given that technology.

Such a solution is obvious in the sense that it enables a final outcome to emerge that can reasonably be regarded as the majority's choice, even in cases where it is not a Condorcet winner.[25] Here one is taking an Olympian perspective and saying what ought to happen. From the point of view of the participants, some may have an incentive to prevent the issues being disaggregated because they envisage that the alternative they favour will lose when this is done.[26] Indeed they may have an incentive to yoke issues together artificially – I am not a student of Labour Party politics, but I suppose this is the art of compositing as practised at party conferences, that is, running together motions to create artificial majorities encompassing the particular position you are interested in. However, the conditions for this technique to work appear to be that there is a group of people who are in a privileged position to manipulate the agenda in the sense of deciding which decisions will be taken separately and which together; and that this group also has a better sense of the pattern of preferences among ordinary participants than those participants do themselves. In a deliberative democracy the pattern of opinion – the extent to which opinions on one issue correlate or fail to correlate with opinions on others – should become public knowledge as different speakers argue for and against the various composite proposals on the table. It would then be difficult to make a public argument against the disaggregation of decisions where it was clear that the original choice was multidimensional. In cases where it was not so clear, speakers might of course try to bamboozle their fellows into choosing simply between composite proposals in the hope that their favoured composite might win.

Let me try to summarise the point I have just made. I have suggested that the major reason apart from empirical error why preference orders are likely not to be single-peaked is that the issue under discussion amalgamates separate dimensions of choice to which different voters attach different weights. I am claiming that it is a virtue of deliberative democracy (unlike, say, simple opinion-polling) that it will reveal this to be the case. Unless a lot of people are prepared to behave strategically, there should be a general willingness to break the decision down along its several dimensions, on each of which we should expect to find a winning position. Putting the bits together again, we would have an overall result which can fairly be said to represent the will of the majority, since it follows the majority's judgement on each dimension of policy choice.

In the foregoing discussion the Condorcet criterion has been used as the test of a democratic choice. Starting with preference orders that produce cycles, we have looked at ways in which the process of discussion might be expected to change either the preference orders or the decision agenda so that non-cyclical majorities emerge. However, earlier in the paper I observed that majoritarian methods of decision-making competed with positional methods as represented, for example, by the Borda count, and this particular dilemma has still to be addressed.

The Condorcet criterion invites us to look for the policy option that can win a majority vote against any other, if one can be found. The Borda count invites us to look at voters' complete rank-orderings and to choose the alternative with the highest overall score. What is at stake in the choice between these potentially conflicting decision rules? I think the question can best be brought into focus by citing Michael Dummett's case for preferring the Borda count to majoritarian methods of decision-making:

> The question turns on whether it be thought more important to please as many people as possible or to please everyone collectively as much as possible. The latter is surely more reasonable. The rule to do as the majority wishes does not appear to have any better justification than as a rough-and-ready test for what will secure the maximum total satisfaction: to accord it greater importance is to fall victim to the mystique of the majority.[27]

What is noticeable about this is that it treats political decisions as delivering variable amounts of satisfaction to those who vote for them. Now some decisions approximate to this stereotype. If, say, we have to take a vote on what dish is to be served at the annual College feast, then Dummett's argument that it matters much more that overall satisfaction is maximized than that a majority's will prevails seems a good one, and it would be perfectly sensible to use a Borda count to decide this matter. Equally, though, many other decisions are better represented as judgements about what is the right thing to do – say a decision about whether to impose the death penalty for a particular crime – and here it would be very odd to defend the Borda count in the way that Dummett does. Indeed it seems here that the natural procedure would be to use one of the majoritarian methods, since what seems important is that whatever is done is done by the will of the majority – if possible what the majority wills in preference to all other options.[28]

If that intuition is right, then the best and fairest decision procedure to use will depend on the issue at hand. Now one virtue of deliberative democracy here is that the process of deliberation will reveal what sort of issue is at stake, if indeed that is not obvious from the outset. In my presentation of the deliberative model, I focused on its most distinctive aspect, namely, the process whereby individual preferences are transformed into ethically based judgements about matters of common concern. However, in any real democracy there are going to be other issues that come closer to the College feast stereotype in the sense that personal preferences should reasonably play a large role in deciding them. This will be true of many ordinary public goods, for instance. If we have to make a budget allocation as between football pitches and the swimming pool in the local park, the main consideration is likely to be the general direction and strength of preference between these options. So here, once the alternatives are identified, it would be sensible to use a Borda count to find the most satisfactory way of allocating funds, and if no other considerations intervene, the final decision would simply amount to ratifying that result. This is a case where the role of deliberation is to identify a procedure for making a decision rather than to arrive at a substantive agreed judgement.

What we have seen here is that standard social choice theory invites us to pick a mechanism for aggregating preferences regardless of the content of those preferences; whereas deliberative democracy, precisely because the content of people's preferences emerges in the course of deliberation, can in theory select the decision procedure most appropriate to the case in hand. Now, clearly, once we allow that the decision procedure might be flexible in this way, we open the door to manipulation by those who opt for a procedure not on grounds of its appropriateness to the issue, but because they believe it enhances the chances of their preferred policy being adopted. This highlights the point that, for deliberative democracy to work well, people must exercise what we might call democratic self-restraint: they must think it more important that the decision reached should be a genuinely democratic one than that it is the decision that they themselves favour. This depends in turn on the level of trust that exists in the deliberating body: people will tend to behave in a democratic spirit to the extent that they believe that others can be trusted to behave likewise. Here the evidence cited earlier, showing that discussion itself is a good way of building up trust among the participants, is relevant. But this evidence, obtained from research in small group contexts, does also raise the question of the scale on which deliberative democracy can be expected to operate.

It is a mistake to think that the deliberative ideal requires us to treat the citizens of a modern nation–state as a single deliberating body. Although it is a requirement of democracy that every citizen should have the opportunity to participate in collective decision-making in some way, this requirement can be met in a system embodying a high degree of pluralism. Pluralism may work in either or both of two ways: decisions may be parcelled out to the sub-constituencies that are best placed to make them, or most affected by the outcome; or else lower-level deliberating bodies may act as feeders for higher-level ones, with arguments and verdicts being transmitted from one to the other by representatives. Thus one might, for instance, envisage primary assemblies at town or city level making decisions on local matters, and at the same time debating issues of national concern in the presence of their parliamentary representatives: the latter would not be bound by the outcome, since they would themselves be involved in a deliberative process in which new arguments might be presented, but part of their job would be to convey the sense of the local meeting to the national body.[29]

For citizens to be directly involved in deliberation even at local level poses major problems of organization, although recent technological developments can help us see how relatively large bodies of people might be brought together to engage in something we would recognize as common debate.[30] Nor do I want to consider the question whether citizens will be sufficiently motivated to take part in debating assemblies if these are brought into existence. Clearly these are key issues when considering the extent to which the deliberative ideal can be realized in a large society. My focus here has been on what I take to be a key weakness in the liberal conception of democracy – the vulnerability of preference-aggregating procedures to problems of social choice – and the way in which deliberative democracy can overcome that weakness. If we take social choice seriously, as I do, then, rather than retreating to a minimal form of liberalism, we can seek to shift democratic practice towards the deliberative ideal, encouraging people not merely to *express* their political opinions (through opinion polls, referendums, and the like), but to *form* those opinions through debate in public settings.

Notes

I should like to thank Joshua Cohen, David Held, Iain McLean, William Riker and Albert Weale, as well as the participants in the *Political Studies* conference on Alternatives to Liberal Democracy, for their very helpful comments on earlier versions of this chapter.

1   This is how liberal democracy, *qua* regulative ideal, will be understood for the purposes of the chapter. Some liberals may protest at this appropriation of the term. However, although my interpretation only fastens upon one strand of liberalism – the importance it attaches to individual preferences and their expression – I take it to be an important strand. It is also the strand that prevails in contemporary liberal societies, where democracy is predominantly understood as involving the aggregation of independently formed preferences.

2   The ideal of deliberative democracy has recently been advocated and discussed by a number of political theorists. The most incisive presentation is probably J. Cohen, 'Deliberation and Democratic Legitimacy', *The Good Polity* ed. A. Hamlin and P. Pettit (Oxford: Blackwell, 1989). See also B. Manin, 'On Legitimacy and Political Deliberation', *Political Theory*, 15 (1987), 338–68; J. Dryzek, *Discursive Democracy* (Cambridge: Cambridge University Press, 1990); and my own earlier discussion in *Market, State, and Community* (Oxford: Clarendon Press, 1989), ch. 10.

3   This point is well made in J. Elster, *Sour Grapes* (Cambridge: Cambridge University Press, 1983), ch. 1, section 5.

4   See J. Coleman and J. Ferejohn, 'Democracy and Social Choice', *Ethics*, 97 (1986–7), 6–25 for this view.

5   See H. P. Young, 'Condorcet's Theory of Voting', *American Political Science Review*, 82 (1988), 1231–44.

6   See B. Barry, 'The Public Interest', *Political Philosophy* ed. A Quinton (London: Oxford University Press, 1967); B. Grofman and S. L. Feld, 'Rousseau's General Will: A Condorcetian Perspective', *American Political Science Review*, 82 (1988), 567–76.

7   Some of the ambiguities are brought out in the exchange between D. Estlund, J. Waldron, B. Grofman and S. L. Feld, 'Democratic Theory and the Public Interest: Condorcet and Rousseau Revisited', *American Political Science Review*, 83 (1989), 1317–40.

8   This is not to deny that deliberation tends to improve the quality of decisions. It may indeed be part of the process of reaching a decision that alternatives which initially find favour with some people are eliminated because these preferences rest on empirical misapprehensions which discussion exposes (I give an example of this later on.). But it is wrong to suppose that this is the only or in many cases the main purpose of deliberation.

9   J. A. Schumpeter, *Capitalism, Socialism and Democracy*, 5th edn (London: Allen & Unwin, 1976); R. A. Dahl, *A Preface to Democratic Theory* (Chicago: University of Chicago Press, 1956). Schumpeter wrote before Arrow had stated his theorem, but I believe it is informally anticipated in some of Schumpeter's remarks. Dahl refers explicitly to Arrow.

10 W. H. Riker, *Liberalism Against Populism* (San Francisco: W. H. Freeman, 1982).

11 K. J. Arrow, *Social Choice and Individual Values*, 2nd edn (New York: Wiley, 1963).

12 See Riker, *Liberalism Against Populism*, ch. 4.

13 This is the so-called Gibbard–Satterthwaite theorem after A. Gibbard, 'Manipulation of Voting Schemes: a general result', *Econometrica*, 41 (1973), 587–601 and M. Satterthwaite, 'Strategy-proofness and Arrow's conditions', *Journal of Economic Theory*, 10 (1975), 187–217.

14 Coleman and Ferejohn, 'Democracy and Social Choice', p. 22. See also the discussion in J. Cohen, 'An Epistemic Conception of Democracy', *Ethics*, 97 (1986–7), 26–38, esp. pp. 29–31.

15 The literature of social choice theory may give the impression that voters' preferences are taken as immutable, with apparent changes being explained in terms of changes in the choice set. But in fact a social choice theorist can quite readily concede that preferences vary, are subject to social influences, and so forth, so long as for any particular decision or set of decisions they are taken as fixed and identifiable. The shift of approach occurs when we see preferences as altering within the process of decision-making itself, so that individuals end up making judgements that do not necessarily correspond to their initial preferences.

16 Riker, *Liberalism Against Populism*, p. 117. Arrow himself, however, concedes that the condition may be too strong, and indeed in his original proof of the Possibility Theorem used a somewhat weaker version; see *Social Choice and Individual Values*, pp. 24–5 and 96–7.

17 R. Goodin, 'Laundering Preferences', *Foundations of Social Choice Theory* ed. J. Elster and A. Hylland (Cambridge: Cambridge University Press, 1986).

18 G. Brennan and P. Pettit, 'Unveiling the Vote', *British Journal of Political Science*, 20 (1990), 311–33.

19 Jon Elster argues along similar lines in *Sour Grapes*, p. 36.

20 See J. Davis, M. Stasson, K. Ono and S. Zimmerman, 'Effects of Straw Polls on Group Decision-Making: Sequential Voting Pattern, Timing and Local Majorities', *Journal of Personality and Social Psychology*, 55 (1988), 918–26.

21 J. M. Orbell, A. van der Kragt and R. Dawes, 'Explaining Discussion-Induced Co-operation', *Journal of Personality and Social Psychology*, 54 (1988), 811–19.

22 This idea was first introduced and explored in D. Black, *The Theory of Committees and Elections* (Cambridge: Cambridge University Press, 1958).

23 Suppose the alternatives are coal, gas and oil and they are arranged from left to right in that order. For single-peakedness to obtain, each voter must rank them in one of the four following ways: (1) coal, (2) gas, (3) oil; (1) gas, (2) coal, (3) oil; (1) gas, (2) oil, (3) coal; or (1) oil, (2) gas, and (3) coal; conversely, no voter may have (1) coal, (2) oil, (3) gas, or (1) oil, (2) coal, (3) gas. The requirement is not that voters should agree, but that there should be a certain logic to their disagreement.

24 Arrow himself accepts that if decisions are made on impartial, rather than self-interested grounds, voting cycles are less likely to occur. 'If voters acted like Kantian judges, they might still differ, but the chances of coming to an agreement by majority decision would be much greater than if voters consulted egoistic values only.' (K. J. Arrow, 'Tullock and an Existence Theorem' in *Collected Papers of Kenneth J. Arrow*, vol. I (Oxford: Blackwell, 1984), p. 87)

25 The majority position on the two dimensions may still be defeated when run against the minority position on both. Thus suppose the first issue is whether to have coal- or oil-fired stations and the second is whether to fit pollution filters or not. Majorities may judge that coal is preferable to oil and that filters are desirable; yet if we were to take a vote between coal-with-filters and oil-with-no-filters, the latter might still win by attracting the support of enough people strongly committed to oil together with people strongly opposed to filters. In my view we should still regard coal-with-filters as the majority choice in these circumstances.

26 This is so even where their support for that alternative is based on ethical beliefs: convictions as well as interests may give people a motive to manipulate democratic procedures.

27 M. Dummett, *Voting Procedures* (Oxford: Clarendon Press, 1984), p. 142.

28 The assumption here is that we have an issue about which reasonable people may disagree, but on which some collective decision is needed: in such a case the decision with the greatest democratic legitimacy will be that which follows the will of the majority, which points us towards the Condorcet criterion. If, however, we took the epistemic view – i.e. we thought that there was indeed a right answer to the question being posed, and justified democratic decision-making as the most likely means of finding it – then with more than two options on the table the best method will probably be to take a Borda count. See Young, 'Condorcet's Theory of Voting' for this result.

29 This is not the only way in which deliberative institutions might be created, and advocates of deliberative democracy disagree to some extent about the best institutional setting for their ideal. Tocqueville, one of the founders of this tradition, pointed to voluntary associations as well as to town meetings as sites of public debate. Others have emphasized the role of political parties as institutions within which policies are put together in coherent packages, enabling ordinary voters to arrive at more ra-

tional decisions. See Manin, 'On Legitimacy and Political Deliberation' and J. Cohen and J. Rogers, *On Democracy* (New York: Penguin, 1983), ch. 6 for the latter view.

30 For a good discussion, see I. McLean, *Democracy and New Technology* (Cambridge: Polity Press, 1989).

10

Deliberation Between Institutions

Jeffrey K. Tulis

I would like to offer a case for the existence, and for the theoretical significance, of a form of deliberation that has been overlooked in the growing literature on deliberative democracy. Since Joseph Bessette coined the term deliberative democracy in 1980,[1] we have seen a proliferation of fine studies of deliberation within institutions, such as Congress (for example, Muir, Bessette),[2] or constitutional conventions (Elster),[3] as well as discussion of the practice and potential for deliberation in the demos at large, whether through deliberative opinion polling (Fishkin),[4] citizen juries, intermediary groups, organizations, and movements (such as those designated "middle democracy" by Gutmann and Thompson),[5] national plebiscites (Ackerman and Fishkin),[6] the mass media (Page)[7] or "everyday talk" (Mansbridge).[8] The growing literature on democratic discourse includes many studies which do not specify the locus of deliberation (for example, Bohman and Rehg; Benhabib),[9] concentrating instead on the normative structure and significance of democratic reason, but these studies all seem to presuppose a locus either within an institution, or among a "people" or subset of a people.

There is another form of deliberation that occurs *between* constitutionally constructed institutions rather than just within them, and under the auspices of popular opinion, although not conducted by a "people." In the American context, this form of deliberation is characteristic of separation of powers, and indeed may be regarded as part of the very meaning of separation of powers. Deliberation *between* Congress, the president, and the Court is a key attribute of the American separation of powers system and that fact lends considerable support to Cass Sunstein's claim that deliberative democracy is a defining feature of the American Constitution.[10] I think this idea, and this phenomenon, may have been overlooked because deliberation between institutions need not (though it sometimes does) involve a face-to-face encounter of persons. In the place of a face-to-face encounter (or sometimes accompanying one) are texts exchanged by institutions. In the construction and exchange of texts institutions address the merits of public policy and the best of these exchanges manifest the most important attribute of deliberation: reciprocal respect for, and responsiveness to, opposing arguments regarding the issue addressed.

Institutionally induced deliberation is not unique to America, of course. Similar processes can be witnessed in other liberal democracies and also among some non-governmental institutions. It is also true that American institutions and practices were to a large degree modeled on those found in Britain and elsewhere. I focus on the American case not because it is unique or normatively superior to other liberal democracies, but because it furnishes rich illustrative material for points of more general theoretical interest. Much as *The Federalist* serves as a convenient text for many discussions of democratic deliberation, the practices and underlying constitutional theory of separation of powers in America may be viewed as a larger "text" useful for locating lacunae in, and identifying improvements for, theories of deliberative democracy more generally.

Theories of deliberative democracy often assume that, given a properly constructed setting, the demos will be able to deliberate, to consider and properly assess all matters relevant to its decisions. For example, if we assume a setting composed of a demos that is either the entire citizenry or a representative sample of the citizenry, that is furnished with information relevant to all important sides of the issue at hand, and that is given sufficient time to deliberate, it is also assumed that all important and relevant arguments will be aired and considered. But might it also be possible that the structure designed to induce deliberation privileges some arguments over others? Can institutional structures insure that, over time, all considerations relevant to the sustenance of a democracy are given their due? Separation of powers is an example of a theory in which multiple institutions are designed to represent and advance different perspectives and arguments relevant to democratic sustenance. Separation of powers is a theory premised on the idea that no one democratic institution would be sufficient to ensure consideration of all concerns relevant to democratic sustenance.

Theories of democratic deliberation also tend to assume that successful deliberation requires arguments to be advanced sincerely or honestly in order for the deliberative product to be rational or mature. To the extent that we design institutions to encourage deliberation, our burden would include sanctions for pretextual, hypocritical, and other categories of argument in which the merits of the case are not sincerely advanced. Separation of powers theory offers a picture of deliberation in which politicians and citizens may retain their ambitions, interests, and prejudices, yet nevertheless contribute to a deliberative outcome.

The Rhetoric of Reply

To give a more concrete sense of inter-branch deliberation on the model of separation of powers, let me offer a "thick description" of an old set of institutional practices ritualized and performed each year beginning with the first day of George Washington's presidency and ending after Thomas Jefferson's first inaugural.

To satisfy the constitutional duty to "give to the Congress information on the State of the Union and recommend for their Consideration such Measures as he shall judge necessary and expedient," Presidents Washington and Adams opened each session of Congress with an Annual Address, which later came to be known as the State of the Union Address. The President appeared in person and read the address to both the House and the Senate, sitting together in the Senate Chambers.

After the speech, each House reconvened separately in their respective chamber, printed copies of the President's speech were commissioned, and a resolution was offered (and on several occasions debated) outlining the general purposes of a Reply by each legislative body to the President's Address. In each chamber, a committee of three to five legislators was chosen to draft a Reply in the spirit of the resolution adopted. (The chair of the first several House committees for this purpose was James Madison.) The drafting committees spent as little as several hours and as much as a week drafting a Reply.

When the drafting committees completed their work, their legislative body reconvened as a "committee of the whole." In the case of the House, the clerk read the entire draft followed by the Speaker who structured the debate by proceeding through the draft Reply again, paragraph by paragraph. In the case of the Senate, the committee's draft was signed and delivered to the Senate by the Vice-President (though he did not serve on the drafting committee) and he chaired the deliberations of the Senate on its adoption, taking that body through the draft paragraph by paragraph. In both chambers, these Reply paragraphs were, in turn, generally direct responses to the order of points and considerations raised by the President in his original Address. Sometimes the debate was perfunctory and expeditious, but on several occasions the debate was detailed and elaborate, taking up an entire week or more (in one case two weeks) of legislative business. Proposals to amend particular phrases, sentences, and paragraphs or to add paragraphs were decided by majority vote, followed by a final vote on adoption of the entire text of the Reply.

After the Replies to the Address were adopted, the Speaker and Vice-President designated colleagues to ascertain from the President when it would be convenient for him, for the House or the Senate to "wait on" the President and present their Reply. Except for the first occasion when the President returned to the House, times were arranged for the House and Senate to present their Replies at the President's residence. Separately and at different times, each house of Congress transported its entire membership to the President's house where the Speaker, or in the case of the Senate, the Vice-President, read the Reply. Since the debates were well covered in newspapers (there was no official congressional record), the President was already familiar with each Reply presented to him, and immediately following the Reply he read his own Reply to the Reply.

After the formal presentation to the President and his own Reply, the houses returned to Congress and usually reconvened and discussed the President's original Address once again, this time for the purpose of assigning the various paragraphs which contained recommendations to committees charged to study the problem or develop legislative proposals. Often paragraphs were assigned to existing committees, but frequently committees were newly constructed to take up a novel issue raised or measure recommended by the President.

Although the occasion for each intervention in the Congressional deliberations was usually a seemingly minor matter of wording of a sentence or paragraph, the debate induced was often about large issues such as the alleged state of the union, whether prosperity was due to the efforts and policies of the administration, to the Constitution, or to factors beyond political control, state support of manufactures, the merits of a foreign policy of neutrality between England and France, the need for a navy, relations with the Indian nations, the nature of legislative and executive power under the Constitution, or questions of American political identity.

The issue of political identity offers an interesting example of the enlargement of a merely semantic debate into one of political significance. In the draft Reply to President Washington's last Address, the committee proposed the following paragraph:

> The spectacle of a whole nation, the freest and most enlightened in the world, offering by its Representatives the tribute of unfeigned approbation to its first citizen, however novel and interesting it may be, derives all its lustre – a lustre which accident or enthusiasm could not bestow, and which adulation would tarnish – from the transcendent merit of which it is the voluntary testimony.[11]

One would think that this bit of self-congratulation would not be the occasion for more than passing criticism, if any criticism at all. But, in fact, several days were spent debating this paragraph at the end of which the critics prevailed. The basic criticism was that it was unseemly for a nation that is truly great because it is the freest and most enlightened in the world to announce that fact to nations less fortunate. It was, the critics argued, self-refuting that we were the most enlightened nation if we were to so announce that, for that would be an unenlightened thing to do. One critic claimed: "Although I wish to believe that we are the freest people and most enlightened people in the world, it is enough that we think ourselves so; it is not becoming in us to make the declaration to the world; and if we are not so, it is still worse for us to suppose ourselves what we are not."[12]

Defenders of the paragraph urged that it was always enlightened to speak the truth, that other nations routinely claimed various virtues for themselves without incurring the envy or scorn of other nations, and that our citizenry deserved the acknowledgment of their greatness by their representatives. The critics insisted that there was a world of difference between the claim that we are among the freest and most enlightened nations and that were the only truly free or enlightened nation. Some disputed the claim that we were the most enlightened nation, which provoked the defenders of the paragraph to demand a list and accounting of nations more enlightened than us. After several iterations of alternatives, a critic proposed that the first sentence of the paragraph be changed to read: "The spectacle of a free and enlightened nation." This proposal narrowly carried 42 to 37.[13]

Although I have just given a mere hint of the flavor of that debate, it illustrates several features of deliberations on Reply more generally. First, although matters suitable for legislation were discussed, those discussions, like this one, were conducted in a manner that was accessible to ordinary citizens. *The Annals of Congress*, from which I have drawn this account, did not exist at the time. That official record was reconstructed between 1834 and 1850 on the basis of many newspaper accounts of the debates which offered renditions more detailed than twentieth century newsreporting of political debate. Second, although accessible to ordinary citizens, the debates could be conceptually subtle. Third, the debate was structured by, but not confined to, written texts. Fourth, and I shall return to this point at greater length below, although there was undoubtedly a political agenda beneath or beyond the debate (for example, to secure partisan advantage in the upcoming election) or issues of personal ambition that prompted the intervention, the debate was conducted and resolved on the plane of reason – reason as articulated in the debate itself.

Perhaps the most interesting deliberation of Reply occurred in 1797 during the Adams administration. President Adams called the Congress into special session in order to report on and respond to a crisis with France. In his Address, the President summarized a series of encounters with France that began with French seizures of American ships in order to prevent goods from being delivered to their enemy, Britain. The United States was neutral in the dispute between Britain and France and objected to the interference with its commerce and the detention of its citizens. The international law on these kinds of issues was ambiguous and President Adams decided to send a special envoy, a Minister Plenipotentiary, to France to "restore the cordiality which was at once the evidence and pledge of a friendly union." Charles Cotesworth Pinckney was given this assignment but when he arrived in Paris, the French revolutionary five-man Executive, The Directory, refused to receive him or to acknowledge his credentials. The French threatened to arrest Pinckney and he moved to Amsterdam to try to monitor the situation from there. Adams outlined the breakdown in normal diplomatic relations which had the consequence of making it impossible for the United States to listen to or to respond to French concerns or to articulate its own. Among the proposals he pressed in this speech was the need for a powerful American navy.

The debate over the Reply to this speech consumed two weeks of legislative deliberation. The substance of the debate turned on the relative merits of a conciliatory versus an aggressive stance toward France and necessitated competing interpretations of the history and character of American foreign policy beginning with the Jay Treaty. For my purposes here I would like to note several formal, rather than substantive, features of this extensive debate. After presenting his Address, President Adams delivered to Congress 18 documents that provided evidence of the claims he made in the speech. These texts became part of the inter-branch discussion. The Senate deliberations and Reply concluded before the House. The Senate Reply became a text referred to and debated in the House's deliberations. The House also referred back to previous texts of its own Replies. Partisans on all sides repeatedly warned that the text that was to be adopted would itself partly constitute American foreign policy and thus every phrase was treated as having enormous significance. Interestingly, Congressmen felt free in debate to express severe criticisms of France and of President Adams that all agreed were inappropriate for the final official Reply, even though the debate was public and fully reported in the press. The day-to-day concern with textual and inter-textual matters was extraordinary from the point of view of twentieth century practices.

Students of this period of American history might find the debate on the Reply to President Adams somewhat surprising. In the debate there is little evidence of the considerable strategizing for partisan advantage that occurred during this period, little overt expression of personal ambition, little indication of bargains being sought or struck. The arguments are serious, animated, and often quite critical of a sitting President, but they are also civil and constrained by several artifices: the parliamentary rules of the body, the several written texts that frame the debate, and the incipient body of institutional norms of civility. Faced with all the inter-textual references, the respectful attention to arguments advanced, and the movement of rhetoric in response to those arguments, historians and political scientists might be inclined to view this debate as a misleading cover-up of the real play of politics, a web of rationalizations, a kind of collective hypocrisy. Such historians and political scientists would be right, of course. There is a true story of the hard-nosed politics of this period that one would learn little about from this debate.[14] But if hypocrisy is a defect of individual character, it is an institutional virtue intended by the design of the Constitution, and perhaps by the nature of modern liberalism more generally. The debate over Replies to the President's message well illustrates the ability of a separation of powers system to tie the ambitions of office-holders to the duties of the office in such a manner as to produce impressive arguments, however insincere or inauthentic. These arguments take on a life of their own, and far from being *merely* the cover or rationalization for private interest and ambition (of "real" politics), they become the substance and action of politics itself. One can see a movement, a rhetorical movement, in this debate that has real consequences for the conduct of American foreign policy.

The rhetoric of Reply illustrates the logic that lies beneath the claim of *The Federalist* that ambition counteracting ambition can produce a common good.[15] The transformation of interest into good is accomplished by a series of rhetorical translations. Personal ambition is translated into partisan position; partisan position is translated into an institutional point of view; institutional points of view are translated into statements of public good, often in constitutional language. This remarkable achievement of modern liberal constitutionalism so evident in the rhetoric of Reply offers a nice counterpoint to those present-day discussions of democratic discourse that seek to delegitimize arguments that are insincere, pretexts, or are rooted in some less than public-spirited motive. It may be unnecessary for democratic theorists to try to tether good argument to individual virtue. It may be unnecessary because if arguments take on a life of their own, the motives become irrelevant.[16] As indicated in the first number of *The Federalist*, there are often partisans of doubtful virtue and possessed of mixed motives on both sides of important questions. It does not detract from the true merits of an argument that its author's motivation to make it is less than virtuous, nor does it add to the merits of an unsound argument that its author is sincere, honest or virtuous in some other way.

The two vignettes that I just sketched offer a glimpse of an extraordinary democratic practice. The President of the United States and the Congress of the United States were routinely engaged in an exchange of ideas, a deliberation between the branches. Of course, much of what I reported was deliberation *within* a branch of Congress. But it was legislative deliberation induced by and responsive to executive action, publicly reported. Part of my point is to suggest that under separation of powers, Congressional deliberation, Executive deliberation and decision, and public deliberation are all facets of a separation of powers arrangement, mutually dependent and, in the best of cases, mutually fructifying. Indeed, one might reasonably speculate that the decline in the quality of Congressional deliberation today is tied to the withering of robust interbranch practices. As Congress has turned inward, become more specialized in its organization and technical in its approach to public policy, public canvassing of the state of the union or the character of a presidential administration has become rare.

The President's Annual Address and the congressional Replies were modeled on the British King's speech to Parliament. In the British model the competing institutions represented alternative claims to rule in a "mixed regime." According to *The Federalist*, the American innovation was to convert a mixed regime into a separation of powers, in which competing institutions represented aspects

of democracy rather than a mixture of regime types. In appropriating the rhetorical practices of King and Parliament, the American founders attempted to
alter their meaning and effect by making them components of a practice of
democratic deliberation.

Thomas Jefferson abandoned the practice of appearing in person before Congress to deliver an Annual Address and he also abandoned the practice of receiving a Reply and Replying in turn. For Jefferson, the practice of speech and
Reply was insufficiently democratic.[17] When Woodrow Wilson revived the
oral tradition of appearing before Congress for the State of the Union Address
he did not revive the practice of Reply. Jefferson and his followers seized on the
fact that the designation of committees to "wait on" the President was a monarchic
practice. Thus, though the deliberation represented by the ritual was thoroughly
democratic, some of the pomp attendant on the practice descended from and
reminded of monarchic practice. It is ironic that after the practice of Reply was
abandoned as insufficiently democratic for America, it persisted in Great Britain
as a component of that regime's own democratic development.

Nevertheless the debates over Reply in early America were studied by that
country's greatest nineteenth-century Congressmen. John Randolph lamented
the demise of the practice, as did Daniel Webster. Both considered the practice
thoroughly democratic. For example, according to Randolph:

> The answer to an Address, although that answer might finally contain the most
> exceptionable passages, was in fact the greatest opportunity which the opposition
> to the measures of the Administration has of canvassing and sifting its measures
> . . . This opportunity of discussion of the answer to an Address, however excep-
> tionable the answer might be when it had received the last seasoning for the presi-
> dential palate, did afford the best opportunity to take a review of the measures of
> the Administration, to canvass them fully and fairly, without there being any ques-
> tion raised whether the gentleman was in order or not; and I believe the time
> spent in canvassing the answer to a speech was at least as well spent as a great deal
> that we have expended since we discontinued the practice.[18]

Although the practice of Reply was discontinued the deliberative relation it
illustrates between the legislature and executive is present in less visible ways in
the constitutional logic of separation of powers which continued to operate well
into the present century.

Separation of Powers

Just as students of deliberation have overlooked separation of powers, students of
the American separation of powers tend not to talk about deliberation. Legal
academics generally discuss the development of a "separation of powers doc-

trine," designed and elaborated to confine specified constitutional powers to assigned institutions. Political scientists usually understand separation of powers as a form of checks and balances, noting that it is hard to theoretically demarcate legislative and executive power. Attention to the issue of deliberation between institutions allows us to recover an older more capacious understanding of separation of powers. This older understanding, which I will sketch below, may have become unfamiliar because the practice of politics in America has departed from it over time. But elements of this theoretical view of the constitutional order persist despite this attenuation in practice.

Legalists tend to depict separation of powers as a doctrine marking the boundaries of legal powers assigned to the President, Congress and the Court under the Constitution. Political scientists are fond of pointing out just how messy those boundaries are. It is hard to distinguish the "natures" of legislative and executive power and the Constitution itself seems to make such distinctions difficult by involving each institution in traditional prerogatives of the other. For this reason, Richard Neustadt described the American system as one of "separate institutions sharing power" and that locution has caught on and is now reported as established truth in most textbooks on American government.[19] But in stressing that institutions share and compete for a common entity known as "power," political scientists lose the theoretical wherewithal to account for the very real differences that characterize, and ought to characterize, the activities of legislation, execution, and judgment.

Both the legalistic and political views of separation powers are better understood as facets of a larger conception at the core of which is deliberation between the branches. In ordinary political discourse, the term separation of powers is used both to designate an aspect of the American system of governance (such as the legal doctrine discussed by courts) and as a label for the system as a whole. How might it make sense to describe the whole American system of governance as separation of powers?

The President, Congress and the Supreme Court are constituted not just by assigned power but rather by congeries of structures and powers. Plurality or unity of office-holders, extent of the terms of office, modes of selection for office, as well as specified powers and duties combine to create a set of institutions that behave and "think" quite differently from each other. In older "mixed" regimes these differences could be traced to different social orders. A crucial invention of the new American science of politics was to design institutions to represent differing desiderata of democratic governance rather than represent social orders or alternative regimes.

Basic desiderata of all democratic regimes include provision for the expression of popular will in and about public policy; protection of individual rights; and (common to all regimes) provision of security or self-preservation for the regime. These desiderata exist in tension with each other. Separation of powers can be thought of as an attempt to productively resolve those tensions by representing them in and among competing institutions. To some degree Congress, the President, and the Court all concern themselves with all three desiderata of democratic governance – but the priority of their concern varies. Congress, generally, protects the expression of popular will; the Court, generally, is designed to protect individual rights; the President, generally, is designed to have greater concern for security than do the other branches. The structure of each institution, as well as the arrangement of legal powers, can be thought of as an institutional design to make productive the tension between popular will, rights, and security both within and among the major institutions of government.

Abraham Lincoln once remarked that the same political or constitutional issue may arise before the President as before the Court and be resolved differently. If left to any one branch the same issue might be resolved differently because each branch brings to the issue a different perspective, a different set of priorities and considerations. Inter-branch deliberation is a way to insure that competing perspectives, competing arrays of reasons and considerations, are brought to bear on major issues of public policy. If it is true that, by design, Presidents tend to look at political issues differently than Congresses or Courts, separation of powers can be conceived as a way to bring these different perspectives into a deliberative mix. Separation of powers can be conceived as an effort to give institutional voice to different democratically relevant concerns and perspectives.

As with the issue of motives and reasons, here we have another counterpoint to much of the discussion of deliberation among democratic theorists. Considerable effort has been expended to define and describe the range of considerations and the kinds of arguments appropriate for democratic deliberation, but there is little discussion of institutional mechanisms to maximize the likelihood that relevant arguments, or relevant perspectives, will actually be advanced. If it works as intended, separation of powers makes it more likely that relevant perspectives will be advocated because these arguments are so tethered to interest and institutional position. In most major policy debates in this country there are institutionally induced arguments for the "parts" of the country versus the "whole," for short-term considerations versus long-term matters, for the concerns of minorities versus the preferences of majorities.

Of course, separation of powers does not always work as intended. Instead of the rhetoric of Reply, we now have partisan rhetorics of popular appeal. For example, the President's State of the Union Address is constructed as a televised appeal over the heads of Congress to the people at large. Instead of a deliberated Reply, television time is given over to a representative of the party opposite (not necessarily a member of Congress, let alone a Speaker for the Congress) who constructs his or her "reply" before hearing the speech to which it is an answer.

Given the extensive television coverage of the State of the Union, one could say that we have considerably more talk and considerably less deliberation than exhibited in the nineteenth-century practice.

And instead of vigorously defending institutional prerogatives, Congress and the President have in recent years given away power and responsibility to each other, to the Court, or to newly devised institutions or commissions. For all the complaints that our system is inclined to deadlock or gridlock and partisan bickering, there are a remarkable number of instances in which the institutions cede power rather than assert it, defer to others rather than protect turf, and abdicate responsibility rather than manifest the duties of office. These issues are, in fact, the subjects of my current research. I do not mean to suggest that our constitutional order is some sort of deliberative paradise. Here I simply wish to stress that when separation of powers does work as designed, it has at its core the notion of inter-branch deliberation. That, in turn, suggests several important issues whose elaboration can improve democratic theory: 1) the utility of written texts as constraints upon oral deliberation; 2) the mutual dependence of intra-institutional, inter-institutional, and public deliberation; 3) the use of motive and interest as an inducement to reason rather than as a contaminant of reason; and finally, 4) the use of constitutional institutions to generate differing perspectives upon politics as a way of ensuring, over time, that competing considerations are brought to bear on matters of political debate.

Notes

1   Joseph M. Bessette, "Deliberative Democracy: The Majority Principle in Republican Government," *How Democratic is the Constitution?*, ed. Robert A. Goldwin and William A. Schambra (Washington: AEI, 1980).

2   William K. Muir, Jr., *Legislature: California's School for Politics* (Chicago: University of Chicago Press, 1982); Joseph M. Bessette, *The Mild Voice of Reason: Deliberative Democracy and American Government* (Chicago: University of Chicago Press, 1994).

3   Jon Elster, "Deliberation and Constitution Making," *Deliberative Democracy*, ed. Jon Elster (Cambridge: Cambridge University Press, 1998).

4   James S. Fishkin, *Democracy and Deliberation* (New Haven: Yale University Press, 1991).

5   Amy Gutmann and Dennis Thompson, *Democracy and Disagreement* (Cambridge, MA: Harvard Univ. Press, 1996).

6   Bruce Ackerman and James Fishkin, paper for conference on Deliberating about Deliberative Democracy, University of Texas, Austin, 4–6 Feb. 2000.

7   Benjamin I. Page, *Who Deliberates?* (Chicago: University of Chicago Press, 1996).

8   Jane Mansbridge, "Everyday Talk in the Deliberative System," *Deliberative Politics*, ed. Stephen Macedo (New York: Oxford University Press, 1999).

9   James Bohman and William Rehg eds, *Deliberative Democracy: Essays on Reason and*

Politics (Cambridge, MA: MIT Press, 1997); Seyla Benhabib ed., *Democracy and Difference: Contesting the Boundaries of the Political* (Princeton: Princeton University Press, 1996).

10 Cass Sunstein, *The Partial Constitution* (Cambridge, MA: Harvard University Press, 1993). Compare, Bessette, *Mild Voice of Reason*, pp. 232–3.

11 *Annals of Congress*, 1796, p. 1612.

12 Ibid., p. 1614.

13 Ibid., p. 1654.

14 See, for example, Samuel Eliot Morison, Henry Steele Commager, and William E. Leuchtenburg, *The Growth of the American Republic* (New York: Oxford University Press, 1980) vol. 1, pp. 317–23.

15 *The Federalist*, No. 51. "Ambition must be made to counteract ambition. The interests of the man must be connected with the constitutional rights of the place."

16 In *The Federalist* #1, Hamilton puts the point this way: "My motives must remain in the depository of my own breast. My arguments will be open to all and may be judged of by all."

17 Henry Adams, *History of the United States During the Administration of Thomas Jefferson*, 5 vols (New York: Scribner's 1889), 1, pp. 247–8. See also, Noble E. Cunnigham, *The Process of Government under Jefferson* (Princeton: Princeton University Press, 1978) ch. 5.

18 Quoted in Adams, *History*, 248. See also, Daniel Webster, "The Presidential Protest," speech delivered in the Senate on May 7, 1834 (in Daniel Webster, *The Works of Daniel Webster*, 6th edn, 4 vols [Boston: C. C. Little and J. Brown, 1853], 4, p. 374).

19 Richard Neustadt, *Presidential Power* (New York: John Wiley, 1980), p. 26.

11

Environmental Ethics and the Obsolescence of Existing Political Institutions

Peter Laslett

Introduction

It is easy in expounding this subject either to record what is crassly obvious or to be unrealistic and alarmist. In the situation in which we find ourselves there is however some virtue in setting out what is well known and widely agreed. An orderly recension of the information that we have and some suggestions about what we can and ought to do about it could help. But scare tactics and exaggeration, that tendency to linear extrapolation from a few not very well established facts, which has too often disfigured environmental discussion and weakened its effectiveness, will be avoided here as far as possible. We must also try to resist the tendency to excessive abstraction that so readily attaches itself to discussion of time, and environmental justice is inevitably justice over time.

I shall proceed, therefore, by laying down some straightforward propositions. The first is that justice between humans in respect of the environment, and justice also between humans and non-human animals, or between ourselves and inanimate 'nature', however those tricky propositions are resolved, does require effective institutions. Implementation has to take place, and weakness and inappropriateness in the instruments we have for the purpose must concern us.

The second proposition is that such institutions as we have show signs of losing their power to do what is wanted for environmental justice, but signs also of uncertainty of scale. They vary between the colossal and the miniature, between more than a billion in China and tens of thousands in Iceland. They are no firm presence on the global scene.

The third proposition is that existent institutions are not only inadequate to some degree but they are also inappropriate. They were not set up and developed with environmental justice in mind, for that concept is new in political, intellectual and cultural history.

Fourth comes the fact that goes some way to explain the inappropriateness. Issues of environmental justice affect all humans, and all the other entities mentioned above and are not confined to collections of them or collections of collections, that is, nations and the United Nations for the most part. Moreover, the effects are not for now or for the foreseeable future. They are forever. Existent institutions were not designed for eternity and must always be to some degree defeated by environmental challenge.

Proposition one

Although we have resolved to stick to what is obvious, it is already evident that there are complications, and that an enquiry about obsolescence in institutions raises questions about their basic character, their status and the thinking behind them. To my mind this is one of the fascinations of the new intellectual world of environmental discussion: it leads so easily to the posing of fundamental questions. For the first of my straightforward propositions – that we must have authoritative institutions – that which may seem to be quite obviously true can be denied. It has indeed been denied, in a tradition of Western political theory with a long history, that is to say, anarchism.

Quite apart from the narrow autarchy of nationalism which informs every contemporary sovereign state, it is government itself, say the anarchists, that limits freedom. Freedom for humans at large to fashion and maintain ethically correct relations between men and women in respect of the environment is certainly subject to such limitations since it may infringe national sovereignty. Sovereignty in the established view is necessary to governance, which is indispensable in its turn to ordered social life. But governance in the anarchist system can and should be maintained by spontaneous collaboration between individuals. Constituted government such as we are familiar with is therefore otiose.

These two last positions I myself reject and they would, I think, be rejected by most concerned people. Whatever we may think about sovereignty, reliance on spontaneous collaboration offends against the conviction, which surely we all share, that we want control and change in the right direction in environmental matters, such change as we can get in an imperfect world, and we cannot wait for the creation of an ideal world order of the anarchist or any other kind. If the nation-state of which we happened to be citizens is increasingly incompetent in these respects, then it is our duty as citizens to do what we can about it, by personal conviction, by persuasion, and by political action at local, national and international levels.

But it is a sad fact that most environmentally conscious people fail to take such action, to which the relative weakness so far of Green political parties, except perhaps in Germany, bears witness. This laxness in our attitudes and action gives too much room for the ecological fanatics to swell upon their alarmist exaggerations.

We need not go further into the content of anarchism or its place in political thinking, although its principles have an unexpected relevance to the environmental movement, and are not far from those which inform the attitude which I shall end by recommending. This is particularly so of the original English anarchist writers and of the tradition which succeeded until the French, the Germans and other continental peoples took up the strain 150 years ago and bombs began to be thrown. Such actions were and are entirely alien to anarchist thinking and practice, and this disastrous association gets in the way of their being taken seriously. In propounding a radically critical attitude to established political organizations, to parties as well as to governments and nationalisms, we are harking much further back to William Godwin or even to Gerard Winstanley the Leveller.

Proposition two

Let us turn to the second of our self-evident propositions about the obsolescence of established political institutions, that they are increasingly ineffective in carrying out what we expect them to be able to do. Put bluntly in familiar terms, nation-states and the United Nations with its agencies do not and perhaps cannot control the major polluters of the environment, which are the multinational corporations. In an age of worldwide market capitalism, regulative institutions are not only in a weak position to control such activities, but as we all know are liable to be manipulated by the multinationals themselves. Some of these are more powerful than most of the world's nation-states, and collectively the corporations might well be able to frustrate the United Nations, by evasive strategy and clever propaganda perhaps, rather than by outright defiance.

This is very familiar ground, familiar even in the media in every country, always eager to prophesy doom given the opportunity, defying if necessary the capacity of multinationals to dictate what should and should not be published. More interesting, and the proper theme of this present chapter, is why these failures have come about, and especially whether this is because of the character, structure and history of the established institutions, which have made it all inevitable, rather than its being the outcome of particularly unfavourable events and circumstances. But before we get on to this central ground there are a number of significant things to be said.

It is not true of course that all environmental outrages and all assaults on our ethical relationships with 'nature' have been made by supranational corporations. Some of them have been committed by established governments, but it is also untrue that the governments of nation-states have been unwilling to set out to control the activities of those who menace the environment, or that their efforts and those of the agencies of the United Nations have not had beneficial effects. Nor can it accurately be said that those who control mining, forest clearance, manufacture, construction, the laying out of highways, the production of energy, chemical processes, biotechnology including genetic modification, and so on and so on, are themselves necessarily and personally indifferent to the impact of what they are doing to our common environment.

In the case, for example, of the 42 transnationals that came together in 1997 to declare their intention to protect the environmental future, we should take them seriously, and assume their sincerity. We should do this because not only is it unsympathetic and lacking in trust to refuse, but it is also unrealistic to suppose without convincing evidence that they must be insincere, that there are no people of good will and environmental sensibility running these corporations and signing the declaration, well aware as they must be of its potential effect on their corporate interests. If in the last resort we do have to rely, as anarchism supposes, on the good will of the next individual to collaborate with us in our intentions for the world, then we should be prepared initially to trust everyone and believe that they mean what they say. You will note that I say initially.

To do otherwise might look paranoid, a move in the direction which, as I believe, has made environmentalism less effective as a movement than it might have become. It begins to savour of the attitude of authoritarian communist regimes and their propaganda, for which incidentally even the slightest hint of anarchism was and is anathema. It could be suggested that a similar strain comes out in references to global capitalism and the global market, so frequently denounced as the enemies of environmental justice because propelled by persons wholly insensitive to environmental values since limitless acquisitiveness is their one and only motive. The assumption seems to be that capitalism will have to go forthwith, along with the market and even social development, before the field can be cleared for a saner political order. The motor car itself might not escape the righteous holocaust. Reality in the world of politics, society and beliefs has never been as simple as this, and it is not to be wondered at that those who have assumed it was so have become labelled as 'econuts'. The inappropriateness and obsolescence of contemporary political institutions for our purposes have to be met with realistic appraisal, plans and policy, ones which are more in accord with the preferences and common sense of ordinary people.

Proposition three

There are further considerations of this kind, to do with the frequent appeal to a traditional past when humans and 'nature' were in harmony and justice prevailed between generations. No historical sociologist concerned with traditional societies, certainly not one like myself whose interest has been in that which once existed in pre-industrial Western Europe, supposes that such societies had in place a respect for the environment or for 'nature' as we conceive of them, least of all a policy of environmental ethics.

The inhabitants of the European West, before development appeared among them, certainly had futurity in mind in some of the things they did and thought. This comes out in their awareness of the interest of posterity in the physical structures they erected: the cathedrals, the bridges, the layout of the cities and so on. They were confident, moreover, that the social entities which they created had a rationale of endurance, as it might be called, in that their full significance and usefulness would only become apparent over time. But in spite of the fact that they must have recognized that their predecessors had exhausted the deposits of the precious metals that had once existed on their continent, a palpable loss that was remedied by colonial conquest and by commercial exchange with the rest of the world, they do not appear to have had much notion of any final limitation on natural resources. They can be seen to have possessed what their representatives surviving in our time still display, a symbiotic strain in their outlook and behaviour, living as they did and do in a given set of surroundings on which they have compulsorily relied for food, shelter, and the means of living itself.

It is also true that they had a strong sense of their own indebtedness to their predecessors. However, I have found no evidence that they felt obliged to repay the debt or at least refrain from impairing the natural inheritance of their successors.[1] In fact it is very uncertain whether they were aware of the possibilities of damaging the natural world as a whole in any way whatever. Their agricultural practices were decidedly exploitative rather then preservationist. By the eighteenth century in Europe the intellectuals looked upon wilderness with horror and its clearance with satisfaction.

That we can learn from the outlook of persons who live and lived in what we are pleased to call 'undeveloped' or even 'savage' and 'barbarian' societies is no doubt true. That we should most decidedly do nothing to interfere with the natural resources on which such societies continue to rely is granted by everyone responsive to the issues. Putting an end to those activities of the northern, industrial world that go in this direction is one of things that we ourselves expect as a matter of course of contemporary constituted authority, national and international.

The possible effect of the obsolescence of that authority weakening such controls is a capital point in the discussion. But the discourse of environmentalists has not ended here. For it frequently seems to dwell on the imperative of preserving traditional social structures for their own sakes and for maintaining that variety in the social world which the preservation of species represents in the natural world. On this view, we as twenty-first-century Westerners should contemplate whether we ought not to abandon our high industrial condition and live as our predecessors did in the medieval era – attempt in fact to restore what I have called 'the world we have lost'.[2]

To go to any length in these directions is in my view entirely to lose touch with the realities we are faced with, and indeed to essay an impossible task which is not our proper concern. It is such unfortunate tendencies that encourage the harder-headed and better-informed commentators on the ethical problems of environmental justice to publish works with such titles as *Small is Stupid, Blowing the Whistle on the Greens*.[3]

Let it be added that meeting the challenge of a book like this, indeed all discussion which enlightens and informs environmentalists, has crucially important purposes. The convictions of knowledgeable people at large have so far been the major incitement to remedial environmental action and we must not let any doubt we may have concerning the effectiveness of the agencies that have taken that action, and are continuing to take it, interfere with our confidence in the value of the spread of knowledge and of the intensification of our reformist attitude. This is, after all, the world of politics, persuasion, power and even propaganda, but propaganda which has to stop short of unrealistic exaggeration and distortion.

Proposition four

Let us turn at last to what I believe to be the objective reasons for the tendency towards obsolescence in extant political institutions in relation to what is required to establish and maintain a proper environmental ethic. We begin with that supposedly omnicompetent political instrument, the nation-state, its government with its multifarious offices and subordinate local institutions. The inadequacy for environmental purposes of such an entity, or of such a complex of entities, stands out at once because they differ so much in size and in efficiency. What is more, in such matters provision has to be made for persons, indeed all persons, living outside national borders.

There is little point, therefore, in just adding environmental security and control to the list of traditional functions of national and local government, alongside external defence, internal safety and tranquility, welfare, education and so on. Environmental ends can only be assured to a national population or any part of it if its government negotiates and consistently maintains agreements with other governments for the purpose, and we have seen that it is all other governments which have to be in question because environmental damage can be brought about virtually anywhere and environmental liability affects every single citizen of every single state in the world, along with all other humans who do not belong to nation-states at all.

Looked at from the global point of view, and this is the only one open to an environmentalist, it is difficult to imagine a more rickety edifice of authority than this, a worldwide network of agreements between governments – not peoples but their governments – each one of which has as its overriding function the defence of national sovereignty, no matter what infringes it, the environment or anything else. 'Assured' was too strong a word to use in the previous paragraph, for it is evident that the protection either of the citizen or of 'nature' must always be to some extent partial, limited to some degree in space and in efficiency, and to the greatest possible degree, limited in time.

I do not have to dwell for very long on the constitution and the history of the United Nations as an assemblage of nation-states and its agencies along with their performance in relation to the environment to drive this point home. All that is necessary is to point to the agreements made at Rio and at Tokyo with their aftermaths. The situation of populations not organized into nation-states has, however, to be noticed. The universal tendency here is to blandly assume that although such populations are small and undeveloped, it will not be long before they too become nation-states or parts of nation-states. This may be so, though not necessarily, and the really significant thing about such a comment is that the nation-state is so much the medium of all political perception that it is seemingly impossible at present to conceive of political organization in any other way. A worldwide organization and an executive which would take into account the environmental needs of every single extant human looks to be a very long way off indeed.

Sweeping as these statements have to be, they are only the beginning of the shortcomings of nation-states, or any association of them, as instruments of environmental regulation. To their limitations in respect of space has to be added their limitation in respect of duration. As has been said, we have to reckon not in years, decades or centuries, but in thousands or millions of years, or indeed for indefinite time. This is a scale beyond the reach of nation-states even though each one of them presents itself as being very, very old, with a very, very long future ahead of it. Not all that convincing, from our point of view, this familiar claim. Where now is the great Soviet Union as it was between the 1940s and the 1980s? Or the worldwide polity of the British Empire which only 50 years ago boasted that it contained a sixth of the world's peoples? A community of citizens relying on either of these for environmental purposes has now to look elsewhere. And yet both these national political institutions had more political authority than the United Nations, one of whose functions could perhaps be claimed nevertheless as the provision of that permanence which the nation-state cannot guarantee.

In practice, as we have seen, environmental control through the global political process in the contemporary world does not, cannot, rely on the United Nations. It has to be backed up by concerted agreement and subsequent action on the part of governments of nation-states, as when over a hundred national governments were reported in 1977 to have agreed to tighten control over chemicals whose emissions, scientists warn us, threaten the earth's protective ozone layer. But 100 governments is not the whole world; the agreement falls short of a total ban: the most powerful nation-state, the USA, opposed the move because 'the threat does not warrant the cost to business'. Who said so? Whose business? What are the figures? Why were the criticisms of the Friends of the Earth overridden? Opposition by an individual nation-state encourages resistance by others, especially when the objector is strong and influential. This example of itself makes plain the uneasy position of such regulations, agreed between the powers, their susceptibility to national governments pleading sovereignty, and to corporate interests too. It also draws attention to a particular feature of the situation affecting environmental measures taken by both national and international bodies alike.

That feature is the entire dependence of the actors, or would-be or should-be actors, on scientific information, usually of a highly sophisticated kind, difficult to translate into terms understandable by politicians and administrators or by reporters for the media, indeed by more than a highly select few individuals at large. The information concerned frequently changes its content, is subject to revision without notice and is not always agreed by the scientists themselves. This being the case, who would choose to rely on political organizations whose *raison d'être* is competition with each other, that are led by power-conscious individuals singled out for their capacity to concentrate national feeling, always directed towards diplomatic and military success, and dependent upon, swayed by, media people avid for sensation? This is a particularly needling question at a time when politicians are increasingly dismissed as self-serving by ordinary people, and even ineffectual in their attempts to carry out policy. In the USA indeed, and now, it appears, in Australia, there actually exists a fanatical movement directed against all governmental action of any kind. Anarchical perhaps, but certainly not anarchist in the sense that that word is used here.

Framing appropriate policies in relation to scientific discovery, opinion and advice is one more of those formidable, entirely unprecedented problems that the beginnings of the recognition of humanity's place in 'nature' has brought to the fore and which give fascination to our studies.[4] It is not easy to see how effective would be the remedy perpetually urged in such dilemmas as reveal themselves, which is to put the person as a whole in charge, intensifying the democratic process and so eliminating every partial interest, and incidentally rooting out that tendency to corruption so sadly apparent even in the best ordered political systems when the environment arises as a political issue.

A single world government, then, sustained by the familiar democratic apparatus – universal voting, federal provisions, party allegiance and competition – is the picture which seems to come to mind when people reflect on remedying the universal environmental crisis. Highly desirable as this would be, it is decidedly utopian and would require a worldwide programme of outright revolution.

Moreover, the model itself seems a little conventional. Surely the fresh intellectual horizons which are opening out should persuade us to think again about political forms as well as political assumptions. We must examine every possible mode of conducting collective life, by no means omitting those established among peoples living physically closest to 'nature'. No doubt the more academic and idealistic might wish to revive Plato's doctrine in his *Republic* where intensively educated philosophers would do the diagnosis and the ruling, philosophers with maximal capacity for scientific understanding, along with practical insight and personal responsibility.

It must be noticed here that in so many respects the obsolescence of our political institutions consists not so much in their lessened capacity to do what they have always done as in their now evident inability to cope with the absolutely new, a challenge which will recur in perpetuity. A body of supremely intelligent, perfectly informed, entirely technically competent philosopher-rulers might indeed be what is needed, in perpetuity too, as Plato had argued.

To find ourselves exploring for our purposes something as abstract and impractical, some would also say as tendentious, as the Platonic system, after what has been said here about the necessity of being sensible and hard-headed and close to popular sentiment, may perhaps have to be taken as indicating that the problem in hand is in fact insoluble. Further discussion could lead only to despair, should such be the case.

This is not how we shall conclude. But before the finale appears upon the stage we must make an end of the argument as to the obsolescence of nation-states as well as collections of them like the UN and its agencies. These last institutions, along with a miscellany of less official ones, mostly concerned with arbitration, are all that exists in the way of truly global executive and judicial instruments for environmental or any other purpose. All the rest is done by constellations of national governments, some by Big Brother USA acting on its own. So dominated by the nationalist ideology is the sphere of world relationships that no entity other than a sovereign nation-state can plead before the Court of International Justice, the most august of UN agencies, although it appears that commercial corporations can get something of a look-in, especially with the arbitration bodies.[5] World environmental opinion as given voice by organizations such as Greenpeace and Friends of the Earth, therefore, have no direct access to established 'international' justice. Nationalism, crystallized community aggressiveness, dominates all, however modulated it may seem to be.

Once again we find ourselves on the verge of maintaining that nothing effective is possible unless and until everything extant is swept away and a new beginning made by mustering individuals all over the world into a new political association. This is no constructive policy for us as things now are and look likely to be.

There is, however, an emergent feature growing up with the political processes of nation-states which could just conceivably offer an escape route. The opacity of the relationships of self-styled democratic governments with the masses of individuals for whom they are responsible has been vividly illustrated in recent years in the remedial exercises carried out by what are called Citizens' Juries in Britain, and much more rigorously and to our point by the Deliberative Polls undertaken in Britain, the United States and Australia.

These novel departures have demonstrated that it is indeed open to every single one of us to participate by proxy of a particular kind in instructed, responsible, socially oriented deliberation on national public affairs, and if national, why not 'international', global affairs?

Provided that the myriad linguistic and organizational problems were resolved, there could conceivably exist something like a notional world assembly, so to speak, of participating persons, deliberating not as citizens of nation-states in contact with each other, but as members of the whole order of humans. That assemblage, were it ever to come into existence, would be intermittent, lasting no longer on any one occasion than a television programme broadcast and received quite literally worldwide. It would also be virtual, consisting of a random sample of all the world's adult individuals, some hundreds of them in total, assembled in one place with access to all the instruction and information which could be managed, and deliberating together as a face-to-face society. The participants, moreover, could be watched as they talked by any individual with access to a television set, and the number of these is already a high proportion of the population of the world. In the not too distant future it will likely include all humanity who could share the thoughts, adopt or resent the attitudes of the deliberating sample of itself, deliberating on environmental issues whenever occasion arose. This is what happened on a national scale in the Deliberative Polls held during the US presidential election of 1996 and the British general election of 1997.[6] That order of all humans represented by a deliberating world sample would not necessarily be what we define as a secular order, and here the topic of my exposition changes key for a paragraph or two.

Much has recently been made of the growing approximation of speculative thought about the ethics of the environment with religious intellectual systems. In *Environmental Values*, the leading journal in the field, this tendency has come closer and closer to the surface since its foundation early in 1994. Finally, in April 1997, *Environmental Values* gave rise to a new periodical: *World Views, Environment, Culture, Religion*. The first contribution by Mary Evelyn Tucker was headed 'The Emerging Alliance of Religion and Ecology', appearing along with 'The Vedic Heritage for Environmental Stewardship' and 'The Varieties of Ecological Piety'. In early 1999 *World Views* was in the third number of its second volume, the religious or spiritual themes proliferating.

Now, no intellectual or cultural historian can harbour any doubt of the difficulties in the way of the emergence of a religious-type belief system being adopted by concerned individuals over the whole globe, and expecting just and effective environmental actions from it in any direct way. The precedents are not at all encouraging. Religious history has always and everywhere, but perhaps particularly in the West, been marked by fierce ideological prejudices, of racist antipathies, of crusades and conquests, particularly when religion is a constituent of the belligerent ideology of the nation-state. Who knows what would happen if strong religious commitment entirely dominated environmental attitudes? But the religious tendency is present and could become the overwhelming force of belief that its early devotees would like to see: a religion of the environment.

It has to be clearly recognized that if the deliberative arrangement speculated upon here should ever become a practicality, environmental thinking in the religious mode would not require access to the means of mass solidarity and aggressiveness, or to collective power of any kind. It is improbable that such thinking would be revolutionist or scriptural to any great degree. It would be unlikely to have much in common with existent religious cults, but no obvious reason to be hostile to them, and would in no way be inconsistent with rational, secular beliefs and attitudes, which would assuredly persist.

Nevertheless, my personal judgment is that the revelationary phase of the environmental faith is already upon us. It began with me as much as 50 years ago on the day in 1949 when, sitting with Fred Hoyle in a BBC studio, I heard him describe space flight as it would be, and indeed was about to be. Our view of who and what we are, where we are and to what we belong, said Fred, will be transformed for ever once we are able to see the earth from space.[7] And so it has come about. The sight of that infinitely lonely, tiny pale blue globe hovering in limitless space, with a faint scratch and stain or two on its surface, the solitary evidence of the work of man, but bearing the potential of destruction of itself and its minuscule celestial habitat, has indeed been revelatory. A novel spiritual reality has come to press upon us all.

On the political side of the question the simultaneous growth of intense micro-nationalism within ever larger macro-national, overarching bodies has already been mentioned as significant of the obsolescence of established institutions. Neither extreme gets at all close to providing an efficient and effective instrument for our global, everlasting purposes. But a very small polity like Iceland, with a citizen body of not much more than 100,000, begins to resemble a face-to-face society where the interplay of individual opinion really counts. It is an eminent quality of the random sample of persons who come together in a Deliberative Poll that it does form a genuinely face-to-face society, with a psychology different in order from that which informs the political consciousness of the nation-state.

As we have seen, a Deliberative Poll drawing its members from the whole population of the world, if ever such an event or continuing series of events could be brought about, would enable the world as a whole to deliberate by proxy as a face-to-face society on matters which affected every single human. The national governments and the international organizations, the politicians, the administrators, the party bosses, the media people and the propagandists would see every issue of environmental significance in a new light. In an exceedingly notional way the world itself would be speaking to all of them, and to all of us as well.

This may be an extravagant notion or a fantasy but it could bring each and every person in the world up against any given issue that 'nature' presents. Deliberated opinion and policy choices could be elicited from individuals, as individual citizens of the world, without any intervention whatever by the agencies of the nation-state and with no danger of manipulation by corporations, the media, political personages or environmental crackpots. As for the execution of environmental policies elicited in this way, that would still have to be carried out by existent authorities, micro and macro, obsolescence being provided for by all of us doing our duty and making our suggestions as deliberating, democratic citizens. It is in these directions that the environmental faith would make its presence felt.

The consideration of obsolescence in our institutions in relation to 'nature' and the environment has brought us a very long way. But it has not led us to suppose that what has now to be worked for is a revolutionary change towards a new set of political organizations to replace the obsolescent ones. Nor has it taken us into the philosophical problems raised by the subject, which have been left on one side in this introductory essay. It will be noticed that the very word 'nature' is in quotes and the varieties of ecological spiritual experience have gone without mention – 'non-anthropocentric ecology', 'deep ecology' and the rest.

Conclusion

We have come to an end by forecasting a spiritual awakening and by discussing and recommending a technique rather than a programme of political and intellectual change, though both are implied by the statements which have been made. It is a technique which, if it could be implemented, might permit us to think our disillusioned thoughts about extant political organization and its fundamental limitations in respect of our relationship with our earthly habitat, secure in the knowledge that the totality of inhabitants of our planet had at last acquired a voice of its own which the powers-that-be could not ignore. Some might say that this hoped-for solution is no more realistic than global revolution, or even the Platonic utopia, notwithstanding it is so much closer to the interests and outlook of ordinary people.

However this may be, clearly finding any way to take account of the global opinion that environmental matters require will be an exceedingly complex and lengthy undertaking. If trying to find a way to adopt the dual scheme sketched out here makes us into anarchists, anarchists of a peculiarly contemporary kind, so be it.

Notes

1   This would have extended the theory of contract so widely accepted as an explanation of social and political authority in an earlier Europe to questions of intergenerational obligation, called by Laslett the intergenerational tricontract. See Peter Laslett, 'Is there a Generational Contract?' *Philosophy, Politics and Society Vol. 6: Justice Between Age Groups and Generations*, ed. P. Laslett and J. Fishkin (New Haven and London: Yale University Press, 1992).

2   Peter Laslett, *The World We Have Lost: Further Explored*, 3rd Edn (London: Methuen [1965] 1983).

3   W. Berkerman, *Small Is Beautiful: Blowing the Whistle on the Greens* (London: Duckworth 1995). Scathing as this book is as to current discussions of sustainable development, it recognizes and goes far to decide the central issue, securing that justice shall obtain between us as we are now and our successors as inhabitants of the earth.

4   This point should be well appreciated in Britain where in recent years and months the character of scientific opinion and advice has been much to the fore in relation to BSE and genetically modified foods.

5   International law (the only available title of course) is in any case an undeveloped area as compared with other legal systems, with little recent reflection and reform.

6   See James Fishkin, *The Voice of the People: Public Opinion and Democracy* (New Haven and London: Yale University Press, expanded edition 1997).

7   I was the responsible producer of his famous series of broadcast addresses.

Index